WHOLE

A GUIDE TO SELF-REPAIR

WHOLE

How I Learned to Fill the
Fragments of My Life with Forgiveness,
Hope, Strength, and Creativity

MELISSA MOORE
with Michele Matrisciani

RODALE.

RODALE *wellness*

Live happy. Be healthy. Get inspired.

Sign up today to get exclusive access to our authors, exclusive bonuses, and the most authoritative, useful, and cutting-edge information on health, wellness, fitness, and living your life to the fullest.

Visit us online at RodaleWellness.com
Join us at RodaleWellness.com/Join

Rodale books may be purchased for business or promotional use or for special sales. For information, please write to: Special Markets Department, Rodale Inc., 733 Third Avenue, New York, NY 10017

Printed in the United States of America
Rodale Inc. makes every effort to use acid-free ♾, recycled paper ♻.

Grateful acknowledgment is made to Anthony Scioli, PhD, for permission to reprint his exercises from his unpublished manuscript, *New Hope: For Anxiety, Depression, and Mind-Body Healing.*

The names of some individuals have been changed in the true stories written for this book in order to protect their privacy and identity. In some cases, composite stories have been created from various encounters of the authors.

Book design by Carol Angstadt

Library of Congress Cataloging-in-Publication Data is on file with the publisher

ISBN 978–1–62336–744–2

Distributed to the trade by Macmillan

2   4   6   8   10   9   7   5   3   1   hardcover

We inspire health, healing, happiness, and love in the world. Starting with you.

CONTENTS

INTRODUCTION

I am the daughter of a serial killer. For all intents and purposes, the first twenty years of my life were nothing but crappy. My suffering and self-inflicted guilt and shame went beyond my father's name in national news, his creepy smiley faces left on letters to the detectives who were looking for the crazed murderer. They would find out later all of it was unmotivated by money, greed, jealousy, or passion. All murder is senseless, but without any motive, the trail of women's bodies found along wooded paths didn't add up to much of a pattern that could help detectives determine if the murders were linked. My father was eventually caught when the police had the wrong man in custody and my father's ego just couldn't take it. He wrote letters to authorities begging them to notice him. Who knows what would have happened if his pride hadn't given him away; would he still be driving his truck on long hauls, dropping into my house to ruffle the hair of his grandkids and eat at our table, snapping the bread sticks in the very way he casually snapped women's necks?

At some point in my life, as my children grew and my elders aged, I realized that life is but a blink. What was once a forever moment of holding my newborn has turned into a flash of a teenager's life. What was once me being a little girl has turned into my not remembering how to do child's play.

And in those small spaces where time slips away, I have spent so much of it in self-deprecation: filling voids with food, numbing guilt with isolation, sacrificing good sleep to anxiety, seeking solace in random religious practices, and generally believing that this was pretty much it—the way it goes. But then there came a point in my life; call it midlife or simply the pivotal moment when you realize all it really comes down to is a choice. I can choose to hate, chip away at relationships, and continue living a false identity created by labels, other people's opinions, fear, hopelessness, blame, and an irrational need to do penance and pay restitution for other people's sins. Or I can choose something else.

I've been told by therapists and experts alike that "daughter of a notorious serial killer" can no longer be my identity. One of the famed researchers I interviewed for this book called this identity dangerous. These people say I must forge a new path and become Melissa. But my past is what got me to my present. It's what empowers me to interview on television other people who have been victims of horrendous crimes against them or their loved ones, and to act as a type of spokesperson for surviving all kinds of painful experiences. So one doctor thinks this is dangerous, while others who don't know me or my work with survivors and families affected by violence assume I am capitalizing on my father's crimes, using them to become "famous" myself.

But what if I choose joy? What if I choose to wake up every single day and pursue the good in life rather than wallow in the bad? We have so little time on this earth; to really comprehend the shortness of this process we call life is to receive a gift. I simply decided one day to say yes to receiving the message—the one that is alerting me that I am squandering my short time here—and to get with the program.

The question then became, what is the program? There are several practices that, while not etched in stone tablets somewhere, are the tenets of life itself. For a long time, I had turned my back on many of the experiences discussed in the following pages out of pure ignorance of the many parts of what it takes to be fully human. I denied the divine medicine that we have been gifted with in biology, psychology, and spirituality—esoteric and complex aspects of living: hope, fear, awareness; plus the day-to-day things that are so front and center, so "in our faces" that we often cease to see them, things like nature, compassion, forgiveness, and love. Especially love.

When I set out on my journey to say yes to life, I thought it would be about healing and transformation, but it wound up being about becoming one with the deepest version of myself. This meant loving oneself, forgiving oneself, and finding peace within oneself to the point where your highest confidence leads you to follow the path that you think is the right one, and then to have the courage to face the fact that that very road might not be leading you home. And when you have to change course, being aware of yourself gives you the faith and knowledge to make a change without the drama of beating yourself up, sinking into quicksand, or pulling away from others and opportunities.

So what does this all mean? Where does the journey begin? By acknowledging that you have somehow woken up in the vastness of life, in the middle of where you are and where you must go; by accepting that you are not living the life you want to live. It is the facing of fear, the fear that the voices in your head dance to and turn louder while you are holding your ears screaming for it to PLEASE JUST STOP. It's overcoming those gremlins in your head that love nothing more than to watch you try to cross the street and make you question whether you know how to cross the street until you are paralyzed in the middle of the road being mowed down by a bus. It means forgiving yourself when you are guilty as charged, but especially when you did nothing to earn your self-loathing. It means trying to forgive yourself and your trespassers, and living a life that is not driven by the pain that you have experienced.

What I am talking about is saying goodbye to a state of neglect and walking toward light. It's about holding on to hope, dreamy hope, that state we mock because we don't understand it. It's about tapping inner resources that we are born with, whether we have an IQ of 60 or 160. It's about supporting ourselves by getting to know ourselves beyond the identification of the pain experience—beyond what people have told you you couldn't do and, worse, what you have told yourself couldn't be done! It's about being artful and creative and being one with nature.

I know it sounds like a bunch of kumbaya crap, but is that really where we are in this society? To believe that positivity and optimism and self-love is just a load of crap, something those "crazy" people do? That's sad. That's why we're *all so sad*.

After years of fostering shame and horror about my past, I decided that I didn't want to be sad anymore. I didn't want to look into the eyes of my children and not feel complete joy. How could that be? All my life I was told I would know a love no purer and no more powerful than the love of a child, but still something was missing. And now I know what that was. Love. Self-love. Without it, I wasn't whole. And that's what led me on my journey.

From the moment I wrote Dr. Phil and went on his Get Real Retreat in 2008, I believed I wasn't whole because of my father and what he did. I believed I wasn't whole because I was spawned by a malicious, violent, sick predator and murderer and because I wore clothes from Goodwill, had a mouth full of bad teeth, was on the brink of being homeless, and lived under the "guidance" of a hardworking but emotionally unavailable family, along with my physically and emotionally abusive tyrant of a stepfather who threw my mother across the room if one of us kids drank too much juice—the very juice that my father would buy us on one of his random visits just days after raping, strangling, and leaving women for dead in the most beautiful wilderness areas of the Pacific Northwest—God's Country.

I thought I wasn't whole because I didn't have religion, I didn't know God; I wasn't a good Catholic and then wasn't a good Mormon, then a terrible Christian, until I wavered between believing in God at all. These are good reasons to believe one is not whole, in my biased opinion.

Whatever led you to this book, perhaps you totally get how easy it is to lean on horrific things to define you and your worthlessness, whether they were in your control or not. But labels aren't real. Because they aren't me. And they aren't you. And hopefully after you close this book, you will have begun to let go of your labels and glimpse the self-love you have for yourself, recognize a part of yourself you would like to develop, or discover new ways or insights that help you get up every day and face it with a full heart.

I teamed up with my friend Michele Matrisciani, and over the past two years we have had a multitude of passion-filled conversations about our mutual respect and adoration for many published authors, experts, and everyday people we've met who live with shame and pain and who are learning how to overcome. The result is this book. We tell it in the first person of Melissa Moore because the central stories come from my life. Throughout this book, we use the word *storm* to refer to the challenge or painful experience that has brought you to this book. Our storms add depth and context and humanity and richness to our stories. It wasn't until I was writing my own memoir, *Shattered Silence,* that I could stop and give myself a pat on the back for something I once did well that I hadn't noticed before. Writing that book was also a time of reflection as I winced at errors in past judgments and actions. But the storms that we live through are a part of us only in that they have led us to *this* page, then that's where they stop. A storm functions as the critical backstory or the prequel to the legend that explains why the wicked witch became wicked in the first place. What *keeps* her wicked is entirely separate and absolutely *her* choice.

⤬

Throughout this book, you will see phrases like "according to" and "he said," "she told me," "research shows," and so on. I pulled together as much as I could from experts through original interviews and through tons of reading. This is how I learned to reframe the pain experience into the healing process, until we love ourselves so much that we can't help but feel WHOLE. The process is not perfect, but it's how I muddled through to my own understanding of myself, and I hope it will resonate with you. By all means, some discussions may come too early or too late in your personal experiences. I hope you will still find solace and strength in the book's ideas, no matter when or how you move through them.

⤬

Thank you to all the authors, researchers, therapists, and experts who provided interviews and other helpful insights regarding this book: Thom Rutledge; Rabbi David Wolpe; Pat Love, EdD; Fred Luskin, PhD; Anthony Scioli, PhD; Barry Vissell, MD, and Joyce Vissell, RN, MS; Daniel Rios; Marisa Minutoli; Pat Longo; and Natasha Shapiro. And to the brave women and men who shared their pain experiences and healing journeys with us. My intention was to bring them together and integrate them in a specific way as I learned to reframe my own pain experiences and make sense of my world and find a better place within it. These ideas have worked best for me. I touch upon them not in ways meant to be comprehensive, but to invite you to read about things that maybe you otherwise wouldn't have read and to consider learning more about the concepts that resonate with you.

As you turn the page, I hope you do so with the choice to watch, to heal, to open, to leverage, to elevate. I wish you to be WHOLE.

What's Inside:

Watch the Storm

THE WISDOM OF INACTION

You are the sky. Everything else—
it's just the weather.

—Pema Chödrön

In the movie *Deep Impact*, a comet hits the earth, causing a tsunami that devastates North America. It's pandemonium. A father and daughter, resigned to the fact that they will not make it to safety within the mountains, head to their most cherished place, the ocean. In a harsh reconciliation with mortality, the young woman buries her head in her father's collar. "Daddy," she cries. She is afraid, yet she looks up, watching the storm. Her father, ever so contemplative and protective of her until the end, closes his eyes and cradles her in his arms.

Cut to the next scene where others are succumbing to their better-known primal instincts, running and screaming in panic from the inescapable. Amid the chaos in the streets, a middle-aged couple ceases their escape attempt and acts on their last purposeful urge. They spend their final few moments gazing into each other's eyes, giving themselves the gift of an indelible image of strength and love.

Did the people running away from the inevitable somehow lose out on the preciousness of their few remaining moments? Was there something to be gained in the midst of their loss? Is it better to go down fighting than to go down possessing the moment in which you are taken? Now, I'm no philosopher, and I'm certainly not saying we shouldn't persevere over life's greatest obstacles, or at least try, but consider the wisdom in these characters' inaction. In the moments of taking their last breaths, the married couple, as well as the father and daughter, represented to me the importance of paying attention to the moment, to themselves, and to each other. They watched the storm. Of course, their fate was sealed by a natural disaster, and it's likely the storm you find yourself in won't have such a dire outcome. Nevertheless, there is great clarity and acceptance in the pause they take from fighting the conditions around them, and that's what I'm talking about here.

To do nothing, especially when something horrifying has happened, is probably the most difficult thing we could ever do, yet in many circumstances it can be our wisest choice. It's a place of acceptance and acknowledgment of all the turmoil before you forge ahead. If you don't take some time to assess what is going on, you can wind up like me and the millions of others who go in search of self-soothing only to adopt destructive coping mechanisms. My shame and avoidance manifested in an eating disorder, chronic depression, social anxiety, and panic attacks.

Why is the decision to wait to act—not firing off the angry e-mail, not begging the bank for a reprieve, not fixing our child's mistake, or not crying to the boyfriend to come back—so damn hard? Because in the face of extreme stress, there is fear, and fear signals our brain that there is danger. Doing nothing goes against our primal survival instincts and impulses to avoid said danger. If we win the inner war and stay "in the moment," our hormone-infused fight-or-flight responses take a backseat to sitting still as a stick, making us a blaring target for the impact. Some might call this passiveness, weakness, clamming up, or copping out even, but on second thought, is there anything braver than staring down something *despite* the certainty that it is about to wash you away?

Watching the storm is the early time in a pain experience when, instead of going into reaction or panic mode, you wait, pausing so that you can conserve what you will likely need later in the healing process: things like acceptance, clarity, and intention, which can sweep away self-doubt, denial, blame, guilt, and shame. It's an important time because if taken, it's a time of deep reflection, of permission to experience emotions, and of an objective assessment of the conditions of the storm. Taking a pause will not cause you to forfeit the facts; those will be the same regardless if you are frantic or not. But I have found in my own experiences, large and small, that stopping to validate the pain by calling it what it is—"a storm"—helps me to calm down and create conditions for clarity. Power comes to you when you identify the bad and consciously separate yourself from it. *This is not you, Melissa; it's another storm coming.*

When you are in a peaceful or calmer state, you will be able to access more resources and more facts that help crystallize a clear, motivated, purposeful response. Only then can we move forward with more intention than we would have if we didn't watch the storm.

Preparation and Contemplation

Sometimes we express ourselves most eloquently by not expressing anything—by allowing our presence, unexplained and unembellished, to speak for itself.

—Amy Cuddy, *Presence: Bringing Your Boldest Self to Your Biggest Challenges*

My life has been enriched by meeting people whose circumstances are nothing short of devastating and watching them persevere. I have seen how watching the storm acted as a critical time of preparation and contemplation responsible for their overcoming the aftermath of their storms. Unfortunately, I've also experienced firsthand how *not* waiting equated to nonacceptance, causing a cornucopia of issues—from addiction to clinical depression to suicide.

You are reading this book perhaps because you or someone you love is in pain and you want some perspective on what you can do. Something has gone wrong, nothing feels right—you're in the midst of your storm. What's my take on it? Pause.

I know what you're thinking. You just bought a book in the attempt to make strides, to try to "do something" for yourself, only to hear someone with zero credentials (that would be me) encourage you *not* to act, *not* to do something! Hear me out. Usually when we act, and especially if we're under pressure, we do the first thing that comes to mind—and without thinking about it. Therein lies the problem. We are reacting without giving honest thought about *how* we want to handle something. Our emotions and actions are being controlled by others, our own ego, and the environment. Operating in this state ensures that our power is swept away.

I have found there to be wisdom in inaction, in an accepting place I refer to as watching the storm. In holding your attention on the harsh elements and igniting your senses within the pain experience, you will see what I now see: *You can't control the storm.* Scary, yes. But it also can't control you. Deliberately watching the storm has the potential to stop us from taking

Reaction or Response? What's the Difference?

Reaction is a defense mechanism, while response is a support system. Here are a few ways to know whether you are in an adrenal reaction or in a conscious, purposeful response mode:

REACTION = INSTINCTUAL

Feels physical, even when it's not

Doesn't take very long

Usually only one type at a time

Feels good in the moment, but often feels terrible when coming off the adrenaline high

An easy release usually on an outside target

> Think about the last time you spoke rudely to someone or took out a frustration over a bill on an innocent operator at the other end of a call. You were angry long before the person on the other end admitted he couldn't help you.

RESPONSE = CONSCIOUS CHOICE

Takes longer

Can be multiple types at once

Considers options and ramifications

Depends on higher intelligence

Is in line with personal goals, ethics, and personality

Is a choice based on your best interests

---

things personally and interpreting other people's behaviors, opinions, or rejections as reflections of our self-worth. In the midst of a chaotic event, we can decide to give ourselves the gift of a pause, examine the situation, gain clarity, and choose better responses.

I've come up with a motto that I try to live by: "When the going gets tough, the tough stop and do nothing, *until* they are clear on how to proceed." Only when my thoughts feel stable and consistent am I confident that I can do stable and consistent things.

The Consequences of Nonacceptance

Doing nothing can be a very powerful action unto itself.

—Don Iger

When we are overwhelmed or confused, we forget to use the tools that we have that can allow us to process a new situation: acceptance, mindfulness, acknowledging emotion, embracing fear, and finally responding with intention and clarity. These are the conditions that create awareness. What happens when we do everything but that?

"I had a little problem with acceptance," Nickie said, recalling the weeks and months after her husband of five years left. "I couldn't fathom an existence without him, and, worse, I couldn't accept that he really meant his decision. It was such a breach of trust. Not accepting that living his life without me was what he truly wanted made me act in ways that are not only regrettable but were detrimental."

Nickie told me that she had incessantly called her ex until he changed his number. When she found out that he had a new girlfriend who was embraced by their mutual group of friends, she impassionedly e-mailed each and every friend, whom she had known for more than a decade, and "broke up with them." With her husband gone and her circle of friends in ashes, Nickie became depressed. Alcohol filled her weeknights, her career suffered, she stopped eating and started overexercising. She was scared and sad. Money was tight, and Nickie described being forced to move back into her childhood bedroom at her parents' house as the most humiliating experience of her life. This caused her self-worth to further plummet. "I became desperate, and I cringe at the actions that made me look like a lunatic," Nickie explained. "Not only did my ex have to have a threatening talk with me, but my parents and siblings had somewhat of an intervention. I couldn't get out of my own way."

Nickie's storm was swirling around her, and instead of understanding that she had the option of assessing the conditions of the storm and responding appropriately, she tired herself out—mentally, emotionally, and physically—

by attempting the impossible. "Getting my husband back was as futile as using my own breath to blow away rain clouds," she said. "What is the point of that?"

MY FIRST DIVE IN THE UNDERCURRENT

Sometimes the most difficult part of a situation isn't the struggle in the midst of it all, but the way in which it's dealt with afterward, as Nickie's "regrettable" behaviors illustrate. What's your next move? Where do you go? How do you move on? The world is spinning around you, and most likely, you either want to (a) crumble down into the fetal position and close your eyes until it all goes away or (b) run away as fast as you can without turning back. I know because when my first storm hit, I did the former, while my brother and sister ran off to the houses of random friends and hardly returned.

My first storm came when my father's mug shot was plastered all over the evening news, a harrowing juxtaposition with the framed Sears portrait of me and my siblings that hung on the wall above our television set. Our posed smiles mocked me as my eyes darted from the wall to the screen as the newscaster casually spoke my father's new moniker: Happy Face Killer.

My mother, instead of taking a mindful pause, banned all media from the house. This led me, a curious fifteen-year-old, to look for information about my father elsewhere and to assume I couldn't share with my mother the facts I uncovered and how I felt about them. Instead of my father's parents thinking before acting, their own shock and shame led them to completely cut themselves off from me and my siblings at a time when we needed each other most. If we all could have turned toward each other in our grief, and not run from it or deny what had just happened in an attempt to protect ourselves from *feeling* anything, I wonder how differently the rest of my teenage years would have played out.

Trauma: It's a Family Affair

After all, when a stone is dropped into
a pond, the water continues quivering even after
the stone has sunk to the bottom.

—Arthur Golden, *Memoirs of a Geisha*

Over the summer of 2015 a new name appeared on the front pages of most media news outlets—Dylann Roof. Accused of slaying nine black churchgoers in a racial hate crime in South Carolina, Dylann made headlines after his own sister, Amber Roof, recognized her brother's distinctive bowl haircut on TV and called the cops to tip them off. Police apprehended her brother in Shelby, North Carolina—just three miles from where Amber Roof's fiancé was living with his children.

Beyond the shock of her brother's hate crimes and the grief for the victims who lost their lives, Amber was faced with a choice that no wedding planner has ever considered: What do you do when your brother shoots up a church just days before you walk down the aisle on the happiest day of your life?

Of course, Amber and her fiancé called off the wedding and went into hiding. They were married weeks later in a secluded cabin, unable to salvage their original plans in their original venue. Amber and her fiancé have yet to surface. Solace and normalcy were stolen from her, her husband, and her stepfamily.

Months passed since the capture of her brother, but Amber stayed on my mind. What if I could help both the victims' family members and her heal? What if I can help her explain her sorrow for her brother's crimes and their own loss while she comes face-to-face with the family members? What good can be made of this senseless bloodbath? If any.

These curious thoughts stayed with me well into the fall, when I received an unexpected text message from Amber. She had read my message to her on Facebook and wanted to talk. "The real victims are the ones who lost their lives that day," Amber stated boldly. "I should not speak, as it may come off as if I am comparing my pain and loss to theirs." I disagreed. The nine people who were killed by her brother were indeed victims. But her pain was profound, and she was a victim too. I told her that her pain and their pain aren't on a scale to be judged, as we can't view our pain through a hierarchical lens. Denying your personal pain won't lessen other people's suffering. Denying your personal pain will only increase it.

One of the biggest reasons I ask people to sit with the storm, as painful as it may be, is because not doing so devastates families further. After the news broke about my father, it was everyone for themselves. This happens to families all of the time; many people are pulled away from each other instead of toward. And here's what grows out of that: denial. In his highly influential book *The Gift of Fear: Survival Signals That Protect Us from Violence,* Gavin de Becker describes denial like this:

> Denial is . . . a save-now-pay-later scheme, a contract written entirely in small print, for in the long run, the denying person knows the truth on some level, and it causes a constant low-grade anxiety. Millions of people suffer that anxiety, and denial keeps them from taking action that could reduce the risks (and the worry).

The save-now-pay-later scheme is so relatable to me. I can laugh at the times I skimped on the more expensive durable car for a cheap clunker that cost me thousands in the long run. Looking back, I was in denial that I had lost a father forever. He was away, but what did that mean? The long-term impact didn't sink into my brain because I was too busy clogging up the porous spaces with binge eating and schoolwork. I even purposely stayed in a school way out of town, which required me to commute four hours a day. When some teenage drama or dilemma appeared—whether it was being alienated from friends or grappling with my unhealthy body image—instead of dealing head-on with the fact that I couldn't work through it with a dad and finding a second-best solution, I bought more bags of chips and ate cookies in dark hiding spots. Riding away from my storm on the school bus and stuffing my heartache down with doughnuts are both habits that, to this day, I have to fight, but being aware of the fate brought on by the denial, which de Becker so craftily describes, has been more than helpful as I pursue my own wholeness.

As I grew older, I became mistrustful of men, and not just men who romantically pursued me. It didn't occur to me that I refused to get close because of the times my father dropped off all of our belongings after he twice left my mother and my family. I considered myself wise for not letting men in, which in hindsight was big fat denial. But underneath it all, I was afraid of discovering a massive flaw or secret about those men. After all, I hadn't seen my father for who he really was. I hadn't known about his other life, so wouldn't it be logical to assume every man had an alter ego, a secret life as heinous as my father's? On the flip side, I was afraid that the man would leave, just like Dad did, so I would always leave first—a surefire way of protecting myself but a horrible way to be in a relationship. By ignoring the patterns in my relationships with men, I ultimately destroyed relationships before their first bud.

The "Natural" in Doing Nothing

Silence is the sleep that nourishes wisdom.

—Francis Bacon

How can we overcome the compulsion to react in the face of tragedy? When I've met others battling a sense of turmoil, I have found comfort in their experiences—not because it's a relief to learn that I am not struggling alone, but because we all have a common feeling of helplessness and loss of control.

Understand this about doing nothing: It is as much a biological stress response as is fight or flight. Those latter two stress responses are a widely discussed phenomenon, gifts that lie dormant in the oldest part of our brain—the reptile brain—that make us capable of lifting cars to release trapped children or outrun a grizzly bear. It turns out, however, that the infamous fight-or-flight response has relatively recently received a new name: the fight, flight, or freeze response. According to psychiatrist, author, and UCLA professor Daniel J. Siegel, MD:

> This response is thought to have real benefits for an animal that is cornered by a predator. Collapse [freeze] simulates death, so an attacker that eats only live prey may lose interest. Blood pressure drops precipitously in a freeze state, which could also reduce blood loss from wounds. In any case, it makes the animal or person fall limply to the ground as they faint, which maintains precious blood flow to the head.

Depending on the circumstance, your body does many things, including reacting with autonomic responses like fight, flight, or freeze—yes, *freeze*, like a deer in headlights—and that's okay. Our bodies will decide *for us* when inaction is the appropriate action. Recently, a group of neuroscientists at the Karolinska Institutet in Stockholm defined the aptly named "stop neurons" as what make a person avoid getting hit by a car. I am oversimplifying this, but my point is not to be hard on yourself if you don't know what to do or feel paralyzed. It is a gift of nature, something that we humans have adapted over time to be able to endure the most hopeless cases.

When Peter Levine, PhD, a pioneer in pain and trauma recovery, gives lectures on surviving trauma, he demonstrates to the participants how the freeze response works by showing a video of a lion chasing a baby gazelle. In fewer than forty-five seconds, the lion is on the gazelle's tail. To the horror of the audience, the lion targets the neck, sinking its teeth in as it beats the calf's body into the ground several times. When the lion turns its back to summon its pack to feast on the kill, a miracle happens: The gazelle is "resurrected." It shivers, gets back up on all fours, and runs away. The baby gazelle's instinct to freeze created a situation in which it could survive.

It is my belief that when we feel cornered by our painful experiences, taking an emotional freeze in times of crisis can make sense. It's like having the power to look up at the cartoon cloud in your head and freeze-frame the whirlwind of emotions and thoughts so you can look at them with good measure. Think of it as putting yourself into a time-out before reacting, except you are not necessarily ordering yourself to "think about what you have done" but "think about how you *feel*."

Permit yourself to pause, or "freeze," in an effort to be objective, perhaps replacing yourself with someone else in your experience. What would you want to say to that other person in the circumstances that you are in now? When you remove yourself from the situation, what seems to be most important? Many books have described the inner child and how talking to our child selves can be soothing and eye-opening. How would you talk to your child self? What would you advise a friend to do, or how would you speak to her to console her? Use this pause as a method to keep rash judgments at bay and receive the wisdom of inaction. And then something miraculous happens: You come out of it, shaking like a gazelle but still very much alive, perhaps more so than when you started.

I would go back and tell the fifteen-year-old Melissa that the adults around her have made a fine mess out of their lives and that she is in no way responsible.

Clarity: The Result of Doing Nothing

Be still. Stillness reveals the secrets of eternity.

—Lao-tzu

Every *action causes an equal and opposite reaction.* I still remember that law of motion from my seventh-grade physics class. So therefore, it's logical to think that if you do nothing, then something *will* happen! For thousands of years, many different philosophies and religious traditions have taught the same thing in slightly different ways: The purpose of doing nothing is to wait for clarity. Only when we have clarity will the right response or path reveal itself.

Very recently, I was caught off guard by the news that my father would be the inspiration for a movie, in which David Arquette would play the Happy Face Killer. Aware of my father's narcissism, I cringed at the thought of how much being in the public spotlight would tickle him. He would feel glorified, while the rest of us in the real world would question how far we'd go in the name of entertainment. It was as if everything I had done to move beyond the stigma of being his daughter had been in vain. I lamented over how the families of my father's victims would feel. How on earth would they handle this?

Righteous indignation was my first response, followed by calling my husband in tears, whimpering "But it's not fair!" like a twelve-year-old begging her unwavering parents to get her an iPhone. I felt compelled to do something: Stop the show, write a letter, complain, call the president of the network, get a petition signed. Instead, I swallowed a dose of my own medicine (always bitter). I did nothing. I watched the storm of press releases and advertisements and trailers roll past me like white-capped waves. As hard as it was, I denied my inherent need to react and forced myself into a proverbial waiting room of contemplation and preparation until clarity came. And boy, did it.

The Taoists, as well as other Eastern philosophies and religions, teach this. The term *Tao* means "way," "path," or "principle." In Taoism, however, the "way" becomes clear when one is in constant meditation, with all thoughts subconsciously regulated outside the state of mental stillness. In my stillness, I was able to avoid a snap move that would make things much worse.

When the movie was released, I didn't do anything except go out to a nice dinner with my family. While I distracted myself by listening to my children's stories about how their school days went as well as to my husband's business accounts, the night slipped away—and so did my problem.

I thought that was the end of it until I received an e-mail from Daun Slagle, the sole survivor of my father's attacks. Daun and her baby were coerced by my father into his car, where he battered and choked her for several hours. Daun managed to escape and stands as the only survivor of my father's eight-woman killing spree. Daun had watched the made-for-TV movie and was disgusted at the way they used her likeness and misled viewers about her character. She wanted me to know that because she felt her reputation had been defamed, she was planning to sue the network. Over the next few weeks, Daun publicly spoke to the media about the movie and the wrongful portrayal of her. Typically when it came to my father's victims, I put the onus on myself to pay restitution and somehow get involved, or feel as if I should. Sitting with this guilt and thinking about Daun, I recognized that my first reaction to get involved was a part of me because of my faulty patterns of shame. When I let my knee-jerk reaction pass and really listened to my instincts, they told me to lay low and that none of it was my fight.

Weeks later, I received another e-mail, but this time it was from a production company. They wanted my assistance in developing a show that would showcase the ripple effect that serial crime has on the families of both victims and perpetrators. For the first time, I could move the spotlight off the criminal and onto the people affected. As we developed the show, we fell upon the idea of uniting both sides—the victim's family would meet the perpetrator's family. The show was a risk. Networks were nervous about taking on the show, except one. Guess which network was willing? Surprise, it was the same one Daun was suing. Had I joined in her lawsuit out of guilt for who my father was, which was not something I had any responsibility for, I would never have been invited to work with the network, which has given me the gift of making my dream come true—to unite the eight families filmed on *Monster in My Family* and provide a vehicle for them to gain the answers and solace they have been needing for decades.

In my case, the instincts for myself were right. Daun's instincts for herself were right too. We both created change in our own ways. For me, watching the storm meant leaning into the pain in quietness and waiting for the right wave so I could ride it home to my truth.

Clarity comes when we are calm enough and confident enough to accept that the storm will not go away on its own and to be alone with our emotions. I realize how difficult this can feel, but I received valuable insight from author Marci Shimoff, who suggests surrendering our trust to the universe to clear the mind. She researched "the Happy 100," a rare group of people she tracked down who exuded happiness from the inside out, for her book *Happy for No Reason: Seven Steps to Being Happy from the Inside Out*. What she found was that these people shared a common belief: "The universe is out to support you."

> [Happy people] don't believe the universe is benevolent only when good things happen to them—they take this approach all the time. When something bad occurs, they don't moan and groan, "Why me? It's not fair." They see all the events in their lives through the lens of "Ultimately, this is happening for my good. There are no mistakes. Let me look for the blessing in this." This belief in a friendly universe is the root of their relaxed and trusting attitude in life.

Your Storm Gives You Special Status

When people ask you, Why did this happen, it's always an
unanswerable question. I don't know why it happened, but I
know what I can do with it so that it is not just a loss.

—Rabbi David Wolpe

We are naturally built to handle crisis. However, we often act too quickly as a way of avoiding the crisis or distracting ourselves from it, instead of taking a pause to assess the situation and gain a fuller understanding of it before we act. This wisdom—to stop and do nothing until we achieve clarity—can be found in most traditions and belief systems, from Judaism to Taoism and Buddhism and even to tarot and astrology.

A friend introduced me to the work of Rabbi David Wolpe and a sermon he once gave about the ancient Jewish tradition of sitting shivah. This is the practice of mourning in which family and friends abide a period of doing nothing for seven days—"seven" being the translation of *shivah*. After reading his wonderful book *Making Loss Matter: Creating Meaning in Difficult Times*, I contacted him.

Just on time for our three o'clock meeting, in walked a man as warm and comforting as the Chesterfield sofa I sank into. I had reserved thirty minutes with the rabbi, so I was surprised that he wanted to talk about me first. It was obviously Rabbi Wolpe's nature to welcome and comfort the broken-hearted, the weary, and the lonely and to provide an attentive, safe place to fall. I found myself landing into his refuge of validating nods and frank wisdom. At moments I felt like a child listening to a bedtime story, hanging on to each of his parables of people who learned to make loss matter.

"A mourner has a special status," explained the rabbi when I asked him to explain the purpose of sitting shivah. "Between the death and the burial we don't sit shivah, because we are in somewhat of a twilight zone during that time. But after the burial, one goes back home and stays there for seven days. You can go to services, and when you are there, the congregation acknowledges you as a mourner, but then you go back home."

There is no work or social engagements or even concern with vanity. The person in mourning waits for visitors to come and determines the direction and amount of conversation. Pressing Pause for one week of life is a gift in many ways, he explained. "The gift in pausing is to allow the wave of shock to pass before you are forced to react to the world. When we take blows that are so great, you can't react. No one expects anything of you in those first moments. You are paralyzed, so whatever you would do wouldn't be you anyway. The pause allows you to recover yourself enough to figure out the process of integrating whatever the result of the shock is into your life."

I couldn't shake his earlier words, "mourners have a special status." When we are watching the storm, we are mourners, aren't we? Our storms change our life in some way, and part of what leaves us reeling is the sense that things will never again be what they were. Rabbi Wolpe teaches that change requires loss, and that loss is something we should give ourselves time to mourn. The idea of taking a mourning period to recover from every storm makes so much sense to me; we do what we are able to do, but we do not force ourselves to carry on as if nothing has changed and everything is fine. We can be kinder to ourselves and take heart that nobody expects much of us, except to sit and process. Maybe it's not literally sitting shivah, but we are entitled to the time—yes, *entitled*—to become aware of how our lives have been affected and allow a proper reaction to the shock to manifest. Only then can we respond instead of react.

As I mentioned before, doing "nothing" doesn't come easily to most of us, but after speaking to Rabbi Wolpe, I felt I had permission to allow myself time to do nothing in the midst of a storm, and I hope you see that too. With permission now granted, here comes the hard part: How on earth can we overcome the compulsion to react in the face of tragedy? When I've met others battling a sense of turmoil, I have found comfort in their experiences— and not because misery loves company, but because we share a common feeling of helplessness, a loss of control, especially when the storm brewing is a Category 5 hurricane. I found that bad things can be meaningful. Through trial and error, I learned to turn something inexplicable into a purpose for living—helping others.

Watching the storm is one way I have chosen to reframe my pain experience so I could reclaim my courage and produce a blessing. I am not suggesting that you should face whatever bad comes your way without feeling or expressing wild emotion; that would be asking the impossible. To the contrary, this is the time when you check in with both yourself and those around you regarding the turmoil that has you cornered, like the *Deep Impact* father and daughter on the beach or the married couple standing silent in the midst of chaos. You too can grab a moment of peace and serenity no matter how deep your impact.

Exercise: Meditation

Soren Gordhamer applies Zen and mindfulness-based teachings to our modern, networked lives in his book *Wisdom 2.0: Ancient Secrets for the Creative and Constantly Connected* and in his classes for groups ranging from business leaders to juveniles in detention centers to trauma workers. He calls for us to stop more often and *be*. But he recognizes that our inability to just press Pause is a stress in itself and stems from being uncomfortable with how we experience ourselves on the inside, what he calls our inner life. "The more out of touch and uncomfortable we are with our inner life, the more difficult stopping becomes," Gordhamer writes.

So yes, it's important to understand how stopping helps us gain the wisdom of inaction, but how do you practice it? Watching the storm becomes so urgent that Gordhamer instructs people to "don't just do something, sit there."

We love action, perhaps we may even be addicted to it. So we must learn to undo the action that propels us and that threatens to mess up our futures. "We think that when we are doing something—even if it is random, unfocused, uninspired doing—we are being productive," writes Gordhamer. "Often though we are doing a lot, we are getting very little done. In non-thinking, we do not follow the various associate thoughts in an attempt to figure something out. Instead, we let go of actively thinking and allow ourselves to receive information. Ideas come more as hits than as carefully thought-out decisions."

The trick is to create conditions that invite opportunities for nothing to occur. That's because these conditions are void of tension, which is what Gordhamer says is the culprit blocking right action and decision making. I know I can't make a decision in the heat of the moment, which is why I am not a police officer, a football quarterback, or an EMT. Only when a person is trained or practiced in subduing tension can something better and lifesaving emerge. Writes Gordhamer:

> "Until we can be at peace with nothing happening, in a strange way nothing really can happen since our actions will be an avoidance of non-doing.
>
> "It is through waiting and watching and listening to what wants to happen, making room for non-doing, giving time for the right response and answers to show themselves."

Friend and blogger Jenifer Joy Madden introduced me to the work of psychologist Elisha Goldstein, PhD. Dr. Goldstein's STOP technique, introduced in his book *The NOW Effect: How This Moment Can Change the Rest of Your Life,* is helpful when taking account of how to prioritize and think clearly in the face of a storm.

S: Stop what you're doing.

T: Take a breath. Make it slow and purposeful.

O: Observe what's happening around you and acknowledge how you feel inside. If you are thinking of something in the future or the past, bring your thoughts back to the present moment.

P: Proceed after asking yourself: *What's the most important thing right now that I need to pay attention to?*

A Mind-Set of Acceptance

Happiness can only exist in acceptance.

—George Orwell

I thought I had, in some stroke of genius, invented this idea of storm watching for myself. After all, for me it was a hard lesson that I learned only after a lot of trial and plenty of error. But when researching this book, I discovered the concept resembled something much more clinical sounding: acceptance and commitment therapy (ACT). Isn't that an ironic acronym? *Act*? When I watch the storm, I do the opposite of act: I wait. ACT is cognitive in nature, meaning it relies on the power of the mind to deal with stressors. It is based on the ability of the mind and our ability to use words to describe things to make sense of our stress.

According to Richard Blonna, EdD, the author of *Stress Less, Live More: How Acceptance and Commitment Therapy Can Help You Live a Busy Yet Balanced Life,* we can assess our stress and its potential effect on us, as well as our reaction to it, based on "space and time." I found this encouraging. It means that the degree to which we suffer in response to our pain experience is dependent on the time and place it happens and on our overall health. So what we find unbearable today could be less dramatic a decade from now. Likewise, what we found worthy of fretting over back in high school most likely won't warrant more than a shoulder shrug today. Dr. Blonna explains: "Not only will you be exposed to it [stress] at a different time and under different circumstances, *you* will be a different person and have the benefit of experience on your side."

ACT teaches you how to reframe your thoughts and feelings about a stressor instead of resorting to an outdated mind-set. Here is an example of how an ACT-trained professional might help me change the way I viewed a situation:

Melissa: "I want to be in a relationship, BUT I am too scared of being abandoned."

Social worker: "Melissa, you want to connect, AND you are scared about it."

Just a change in one word is the basis of acceptance and commitment therapy. Most of us focus on a desire to change how we feel about, in my case, abandonment by a romantic interest. But ACT says I can take action without first changing or eliminating feelings. "Rather than fighting the feeling attached to a behavior, a person can observe oneself as having the feeling but still act," according to an article in *Social Worker Today*. Instead of killing ourselves to change the way we feel, which usually creates more frustration and feelings of failure, it can be more effective to acknowledge and accept our feelings and then act, allowing change to happen in due course.

If you have ever been told to change your attitude in order to change your behavior, you have been primed for ACT. Changing a behavior (going on a date when you don't want to) may eventually result in a change in attitude or emotion (not all men are creepy serial killers). Focusing on changing actions despite the accompanying emotion is the key of ACT. In short, behavior and emotion can coexist and be independent of one another.

Not going on a date because I am anxious about being abandoned or finding out the guy has a deep, dark secret also makes it possible that I can go on a date while feeling anxious. ACT teaches that you can live with [insert emotion/fear here] and eliminate the control that emotion has on how you live or don't live your life.

Such a mind shift was apparent in a friend of mine who, upon announcing her second job layoff, admitted that it was a much less emotional experience than the first. While her first layoff was devastating and sent her into a deep and debilitating depression, leading to her losing precious time in her life, she had a different frame of mind after this layoff that prevented her from blaming herself or feeling worthless. She understood the necessity of the job elimination from the point of view of her boss (a compassion muscle she had gained, which we will talk more about in H: Heal Your Heart), and she had the perspective to know there would be life after the loss of this job (a universal trust, which we will cover later in the book). She had more energy and focus to scout jobs and network; she even thought of the downtime as a much-needed gift. It wasn't that she felt less sad about losing this job; it's that she was equipped now not to let the sadness be the only thing she felt.

Acceptance helps us not only to find the language we need to describe how we feel about our pain experience but then to use this self-knowledge to commit to the way we want to act moving forward. It's only in examining the usefulness of our thoughts, emotions, and reactions to our situation that we can figure out how to overcome challenges. This cannot be done if we spend time running from our feelings, our backs against the crest of the wave as it crashes to the shore.

"Commitment training teaches you how to stick to your plans while coexisting with your pain and suffering," Dr. Blonna writes. "It shows you that you don't have to eliminate your painful thoughts and feelings in order to move forward and get on with your life. As long as you realize that it's normal to have painful thoughts and feelings and to suffer, you'll feel able to cope with these issues. Stress comes from feeling threatened and unable to cope. You need not feel threatened by pain and suffering; they're as much a part of your life as the air you breathe and the sunlight that streams through your window."

Assessing the Conditions of the Storm

If you don't know where you are headed,
you'll probably end up someplace else.

—Douglas J. Eder, PhD

Would it make sense to board up your windows, stock up on canned foods, or abandon your home and move across the country when a weather forecaster threatens a little precipitation? We take in the conditions of the weather on a daily basis *before* carrying out plans. Will we need yellow ponchos for Disney World? Should the high school graduation ceremony be moved indoors? Is it going to be too muddy for a backyard wedding?

Underreacting and overreacting happen when you don't properly assess the conditions of your storm and you give in to the stress response. In his meditations, Roman emperor Marcus Aurelius wrote that the only way a man can be harmed by others is to allow his reaction to overpower him. Being highly reactive has been shown to make people prone to anxiety and aggression. In Buddhist meditation, stopping is one of the two elements; the other is deep looking. Deep looking can happen only once we have stopped. If you look at teachings on Buddhist meditation, you will find that once you achieve stopping, you become "solid and concentrated." Then you look deeply into your nature, or the nature of things, to find insight.

Emotions as Our Guideposts

Your emotions are meant to fluctuate, just like your blood pressure is meant to fluctuate. It's a system that's supposed to move back and forth, between happy and unhappy. That's how the system guides you through the world.

—Daniel Gilbert, PhD

Watching the storm is synonymous with the idea of paying attention to your feelings, acknowledging them, and accepting the conditions. If you skip this part of the process and instead go into denial or premature reaction mode, you miss out on an important part of the healing process—using emotions as guideposts.

We are emotional beings, and that's no accident. Emotions are not to be suppressed or a source of shame or hidden from others. They are our natural guides. Turning your back on them is like taking a hammer to your GPS when you find yourself lost in a foreign city (or in my case, in my own neighborhood!). To fear our emotions and then anesthetize ourselves against them will destroy our internal compasses. When we don't turn toward our emotions and allow ourselves to define them, articulate them, and then release them, our feelings become unresolved. India's ancient healing system of Ayurveda teaches that just as physical toxins, known as *ama*, can build up in our cells, we can also accumulate mental toxicity in the form of unresolved "anger, fear, doubt, cravings, compulsiveness, and emotional upset," according to the Chopra Center.

I saw these toxins of unacknowledged pain literally gush out of my friend Sasha when she, her husband, and their children moved in with us for a month. My dear friend from college had been a victim of the aftermath of the 2008 economic crisis. Her husband losing his job was the cherry on top of it all, as he was forced to file for unemployment and government assistance. After a five-year struggle, she and her husband ultimately succumbed to a foreclosure, bankruptcy, and homelessness. My husband, Sam, and I convinced them to stay with us until they could get back on their feet. Each day the kids would go to school, and Sasha and her husband would pound the pavement. We'd reconvene at dinnertime, surrounded by food and laughter. After two weeks, Sasha and I had settled into an evening routine of cleaning off the table and getting the kids ready for bed. And then one evening, she wasn't there to dry the dishes. I chalk it up to a female gut-instinct thing, but I headed straight to the bathroom door and heard poor Sasha vomiting.

"What is going on with you, Sasha?"

"Melissa," she said, looking at me with bloodshot eyes, "I can't take this anymore. I am so scared."

This was Sasha's storm, and I wanted desperately to help her, so I tried to make her feel safe enough to start listening to her emotions and learning from them.

"Okay," I said. "Let's think about this. What happened today? You have a roof over your head today, you have food in your belly today, your husband networked today and possibly made a good contact today."

Noticing a hint of an acknowledgment in her eyes, I continued, "Okay, what bad thing happened today? Did someone get hurt? Did someone get lost? Was someone bad to you?"

Sasha replied, "Everybody's okay today; my boys are healthy; I'm healthy; we're together."

I had done this form of Gestalt self-talk with myself when I developed severe anxiety as a little girl tossing and turning on the basement floor of my grandma's house. *What happened today?* I'd ask myself in the darkness. I didn't have to sleep at the shelter today. We are safe from my father today. I made a new friend today. I have a full belly today. It's a Pollyanna way of thinking, sure, but my father always accused me of having rose-colored glasses, so I decided to put them to good use. As I got older, however, I learned that while positive thinking and looking on the bright side are supported by science to enhance the mood and empower a person, one particular philosophy of stoicism was surprisingly helpful as well. Stoics are like the other side of the positive psychology coin, in support of negative visualization.

Stoics believe that it is a good practice to close our eyes once in a while and imagine the worst thing that could happen—to basically take our good fortune and imagine it away. The pain we feel through this visualization, what is revealed to ourselves, can be turned into power. Now, as bad as things can get, I can try to imagine them worse, and as in exposure therapy, I feel more capable of dealing with what I currently face and I can actually find gratitude for it.

Exercise: The Day in Review (What Happened Today?)

I end each day, no matter how happy or benign or damaging, with a day in review. I ask myself the same questions I asked Sasha when she was sick to her stomach over her economic situation. What happened today? When you do this exercise for yourself, answer the questions out loud and emphasize the word *today*, repeating it over and over within each new question and answer.

I had a roof over my head today; I made a new friend today; I helped someone with car trouble today; I handled myself poorly in front of my boss today; I cried today; I sent an unprofessional e-mail today.

Whether the day's review brings negative answers or positive ones is not the point. The emphasis on the word *today* is the meditative practice that aims to keep you in the present moment, which is all you have to work with anyway. At the end of the day, this line of questioning reminds me of one important fact: Today is about to end, as will the good and the bad things that occurred today. Nothing can make me feel more grounded about a new day to come than reminding myself that what's to come when I open my eyes is a clean slate.

This is similar to what in Buddhism is known as beginning anew or a beginner's mind. Beginning anew means to make a vow to try to not repeat your mistakes or negative behaviors. When we commit to living with more awareness and deeply looking at our storms to receive the insights they reveal, we can be born again. I vow to myself (over and over again, if that tells you something): "I am focused on doing things differently than I did before." I love the optimism and forgiveness that are etched in the notion of the beginner's mind, because it is truly compassionate and nonviolent toward my propensity to keep screwing up. My mantra: "Where there is a new day, there is a new mind."

LET IT ALL OUT

My coauthor, Michele, didn't know Marina very well, but on a bright morning in early fall, the two women began chatting after walking their small children to the elementary school doors. Marina commented on Michele's iPod, secured to her arm with a running band. Michele's stress levels had decreased since she began making running a part of her daily ritual, and Marina agreed that she too found stress release in exercise. Soon Marina's story of how stress affected her in the past came flooding out, and she and Michele were having a transformative conversation. Marina generously and without shame shared her story, which went something like this.

Marina wasn't much of a white-wedding girl, so when her then boyfriend proposed, she married quickly and settled into the routine of marriage. She and Elden headed to the gym together with the rest of the five-a.m. crowd and carpooled to the train station, where they'd say their goodbyes until meeting again for the ride home later in the evening. They ate dinner together on most nights and watched movies with Elden's friends on Fun Fridays. They loved watching Thursday-night football and lounging around in nothing but their Patriots jerseys on Sundays.

Until Marina got sick.

First, she noticed her sleep patterns disrupted to the point where she couldn't fulfill her obligations at work. Like clockwork, Marina would wake at three thirty each morning and jump out of bed. There was no going back to sleep, no matter what she tried. She began making frequent visits to her gynecologist's office for various infections, which she had never experienced before. Then she developed shingles on her face, which lasted months and caused tremendous pain. Finally, a night of intimacy with her husband sent Marina to the emergency room to treat a hemorrhage. When the cause was undetermined, her stumped doctor turned to Marina, asking only half-jokingly, "What are you, *allergic* to your husband?"

Bingo.

Marina hadn't told anyone about how bossy Elden was. Or how he treated her like a possession, making it difficult for her to see her old friends and get together with former coworkers. In fact, Marina admitted, for a long while she was in denial about it herself. She hadn't told anyone that when she mentioned she wanted to go back to work now that the youngest was in preschool, Elden accused her of being a bad and neglectful mother for *even thinking* about leaving the kids. She hadn't told anyone of the cold and rough sex, of the lipstick on Elden's collars, and of his arrogance that chipped away at her self-esteem day in and day out.

The truth in her doctor's question rang so true that Marina could do nothing but weep. After soul-searching with her therapist, Marina realized she was living de Becker's save-now-pay-later denial scenario—by keeping the peace and going along with her husband, she was paying exponentially in both her mental and physical health. Marina figured out that her subconscious had been telling her to get out of her marriage for as long as she remembered waking at three thirty. "It was as if my mind was telling me to get out of that bed where he was lying, but only my body was obeying," Marina said.

After she told her friends and family that she was unhappy and her marriage counseling failed to mend the broken relationship, Marina filed for a legal separation. It's been two years since she and the kids moved out and into a home of their own, and Marina hasn't needed to go back to her doctor for a single infection, her shingles haven't returned, and she is healthier than ever.

What's going on here? In *Opening Up: The Healing Power of Expressing Emotions,* James W. Pennebaker, PhD, shares his research, which indicates that purposely holding back or "inhibiting" our thoughts and feelings takes a lot of effort and energy. Exerting all of that concentration for the sake of being private actually weakens the body's natural defenses. Just as more commonly known stressors, like demanding work schedules or family illness, can affect immune function, heart health, bloodflow, brain, and nervous systems, so does inhibiting how we feel.

On the other hand, confronting our deepest thoughts and feelings can have remarkable health benefits, both long and short term. Through his probing, Dr. Pennebaker found that writing or talking in an act of "confession" can counteract many of the issues caused by inhibition. Even more, writing or talking about painful things can "influence our basic values, our daily thinking patterns, and feelings about ourselves." Marina agrees. Not only has she learned that her inhibition was making her physically sick, she sees how opening up helped her decide what she is willing and unwilling to accept in a relationship moving forward. To state it simply: Putting up a good front is not so good for us, while letting it all hang out can save our emotional and physical lives.

But to talk about issues isn't merely about "letting it all out"; it's also about taking things in. The process of sharing our most innermost demons or confessing our "sins" requires that we be ready to *receive* input that comes from our output. And some of that input might not be what we'd like to hear. In most cases, telling people how we feel as we grapple with recovering from trauma results in praise ("You were so brave"), identifying attributes ("You were able to think so quickly"), and solid advice ("I think the next step is to call her and apologize"), as well as healthy doses of attention, empathy, and assistance. And sometimes, just talking about things aloud helps *you* hear what you're saying more clearly than when ideas are moshing in the pit of your mind. How many times have you told a friend about a conundrum, only to figure out a solution yourself before you even finished speaking about it?

I grappled with getting up the nerve to speak myself. I didn't tell a soul about my father's crimes, or about that day I watched my mother being pummeled and emotionally battered by her new husband. Once I was "found out" by many of my teenage classmates and their families, I was the freak show to be avoided, as if I had inherited the rape-and-strangle gene. So once I made a new life for myself with my husband and small children in a state far away from Spokane, Washington, I dared not take the chance of having my children walk around with a scarlet letter. I was active in our church, played the dutiful wife, and even ran a daycare out of my home— but I didn't let anyone know about my past. Can you imagine what kind of uproar would have occurred if news got out that the community babysitter's father was incarcerated for a ten-year killing spree? *Mum's the word here,* I thought.

Even now, I cannot tell you to just jump in with both feet and tell the first person you see what's going on. But you can do what I did. Begin to write it all down. When I had nowhere to turn, I wrote almost a hundred thousand words. That's a lot of confusion and torment and anger and despair splattered on the page. But as I moved through the writing process, doing it almost on automatic pilot, other words began to emerge. Ones of strength, hope, creativity, and love. I felt exhausted after purging the sentences, but also freer.

It is said that when we are suppressing certain incidences or feelings, we remember painful experiences in a fragmented way, which means we don't have the opportunity to view the big picture in a manner that lets us come to terms with it. Writing down our stories assists us in confronting our trauma from a safe place, thus providing a sense of control over a narrative that has controlled us, perhaps for a very long time. Writing can pull the pieces together; seeing my life from early childhood to the day I left home as one long string of connected patterns and experiences helped me identify how I wanted to live moving forward. It also enabled me to see through adult eyes how little control I really had back then, which in turn allowed me to appreciate for the first time how much I had been able to accomplish with the few resources I could find. After reading back my story, I cried my eyes out, grieving for what I never had and what will never be, but also feeling relief for who I am now with a hope of whom I am yet to become. For the first time, I took a moment to have compassion for myself and forgive some of the dumb moves I made. We will talk more about writing to heal in E: Elevate Your Spirit.

In my opinion, though, the best revelation of much of the research conducted by Dr. Pennebaker is that you don't need to write with the intention of letting anyone read your story. It really is as simple as keeping a journal or writing letters to yourself. This is because, according to Art Markman, PhD, "the benefit of writing is not in disclosing this personal information to someone else but in creating a story that links together the emotional memories. Making these traumatic events more coherent makes memories of these events less likely to be repeatedly called to mind, and so they can be laid to rest."

And isn't that the point?

Michele, who obviously prefers to write, said that her strategy for conjuring up her emotions and laying them to rest was not in the form of writing them but in verbalizing them.

Michele's Story

This is going to sound crazy (because it is), but after my breakup with my husband, I used to walk aimlessly around Thirty-Fourth Street at lunchtime in search of a miracle. I was desperate to silence the demonic voices in my head who made it their mission to talk me into believing that my life had ended, that I was over, that there was no point in dreaming about the future. The best times of my life had passed, and I would just *exist* from here on out. (Talk about "mistaken certainties.")

The thoughts would march in at any given moment—in the shower, while eating dinner with my parents, and, most of the time, at the office. So as a futile attempt to exorcise the voices, each day at lunch I'd descend the eleven stories of my office building and head onto the bustling streets of Seventh Avenue.

Rain or shine, snow or sleet, freezing or sweltering, I'd head south on Seventh, all the while talking to myself about how desperate I felt and how lonely I was and how much I missed the damn guy.

But like wearing out the ear of a sympathetic friend, after a while I became completely bored of hearing myself—bored by my role of victim, bored by the apathetic state I had adopted, and bored by the fact that I had lost all interest in anything that wasn't about *my* feelings and *my* ex. I had accomplished one of the most difficult tasks of humanity: I actually repelled myself. But I didn't stop, mostly because I had created a bad habit—one that I had come to rely on to break up the day. Admitting that I wouldn't give up the nonsense, I was led to "mix it up" a bit by conducting a weird experiment, with my brain being the lab rat and my thoughts the stimuli. On one of my lunchtime strolls, I pressed Record on a handheld recorder (*waaaay* before smartphones) and began talking into it. Each day I'd ramble on and on, spewing my musings into the mike. Then every Monday of the following week, after taking the weekend off, I'd play back the previous week's entries. It was hard listening to myself—embarrassing, like reading my diary from high school. I wasn't embarrassed over my voice sounding unfamiliar or my Brooklyn accent being more prominent than I suspected; I was uncomfortable because I didn't recognize the person who was ranting and crying and whining and pining. I realized with a shock that I had emotionally traveled a long way since my first days of the divorce. I turned around and saw I had also physically covered much ground, striding way beyond the confines of Thirty-Fourth Street.

I don't think I would have realized I was healing if I hadn't really *heard* myself. I wasn't stuck in a rut after all or doomed to a perpetual state of depression. I began to feel hope. And the hope I gained helped me tell myself I was capable of growing from all this. Hope made it easier for me to hit Playback because I began to trust the tangible empirical evidence that I was already in a better place. I was literally *hearing myself heal.* Healing happened like a couch–to–5-K interval training program—a long period of walking interrupted by bursts of running until all we do is run. Nobody simply wakes up okay, just as we don't suddenly wake up a complete mess. Using time, distance, practice, and honest introspection (and maybe some crazy whims like taking lunchtime walks while talking to yourself), healing can be measured and heard if you only listen hard enough. ॐ

Exercise: How Does Your Storm Make You Feel?

Sitting with the pain can be . . . painful, but it is the beginning of opening up to awareness and growth. Ask yourself, *How does my painful experience make me feel?*

Embarrassed	Ignored	Invisible
Alone	Undignified	Foolish
Humiliated	Stupid	Disrespected
Guilty	Worthless	Other
Isolated	Used	

Can you write about it, or even talk about it?

Writing things down, or at least articulating the swirling sensations that can sweep us away, feels a bit like exposure therapy. It's less scary now that it's out there. Look at those lists of really crappy feelings. Now I look at them and think, *Big whoop.* Somehow they seem less scary, don't they? It's like lying in bed in a pitch-dark room for a few minutes at a time, until you realize that after a while, if you give them a chance, your eyes *adjust* to the dark, enabling you to make out shapes where none were, until you fall asleep in the light of your own peace.

You Are Here: A Course
in Mindfulness

You are here for life; and if you are here for life,
life will be here for you. It's simple.

—Thich Nhat Hanh

I always wanted to be able to say with absolute certainty which book I'd bring with me if I were to live out the rest of my life on a deserted island. Now I can! It's called *You Are Here: Discovering the Magic of the Present Moment* by Thich Nhat Hanh, one of the most widely known Buddhist monks and teachers. Some describe him as "second" to His Holiness the Dalai Lama. I know I'm a little late to the party . . . as everyone and their mother have talked ad nauseam about the power of the breath, being in the "now," and mindfulness meditation. It's a little embarrassing to be all giddy about the simple and transformative power of discovering that indeed I am here.

I love the plainness and magnitude of the book's title: *You Are Here.* I am here. Certainly. I *am* . . . here. How perceptive. But then I said the words again, still with mockery, as in *Duh, where else would I be?* Third time, like clicking my heels, the words seeped in. They became true, and they became powerful. *Holy crap, I am* here. *Which means, one day I won't be. Get with the program, Melissa.*

My brush with Buddhism, like many lifesaving tactics, came in the nick of time—like the ladder truck to the blazing apartment building or the lifeboat to the sinking ship. It occurred just a few years ago, when I was going through some rough times. I was having "adult problems," a far cry from the more internal grumblings I was used to dealing with. My husband and I and the kids had relocated to Texas only for Sam to get laid off; my son was having learning difficulties; my daughter required homeschooling because of bullying. Looking at each precious member of my family caused my heart to bleed with frustration at my helplessness to fix any of it. The pressure was driving Sam and me apart, often pitting us against one another like enemies instead of fusing us together like the partners we had once promised to be. Knowing how tumultuous one storm could be, we now had four circling our cabin, until ultimately we'd add another into the mix in the form of my own storm—panic attacks, feelings of numbness and apathy, resentment, and disillusionment. I was, to put it as aptly as I can, *languishing.*

But then I read the title of the book Michele told me about: *You Are Here.* And like I said earlier, I was a bit jaded, so in a fit of rage mixed with laughter, I said to myself, but also to Thich Nhat Hanh, *That's right, buddy boy. I am here. And it is the last place I want to be.*

But then, as if he were expecting such a reaction, Thich Nhat Hanh wrote:

> Buddhist practice is based on nonviolence and nondualism. You don't have to struggle with your breath. You don't have to struggle with your body, or with your hate, or anger. Treat your in-breath and out-breath tenderly, nonviolently, as you would treat a flower. . . .
>
> When you are dealing with pain, with a moment of irritation, or with a bout of anger, you can learn to treat them in the same way. Do not fight against pain; do not fight against irritation or jealousy. Embrace them with great tenderness, as though you were embracing a little baby. Your anger is yourself, and you should not be violent toward it. The same thing goes for all of your emotions.

I had watched each of us in my family struggle with pain instead of cradle it with tenderness. This idea of duality, that we are both good and bad, sad and happy, calm and anxious, shifted my perspective. Thich Nhat Hanh promises that the spirit of nonduality will put a stop to the war within us. "You have struggled in the past," he writes, "and perhaps you are still struggling; but is it necessary? No. Struggle is useless. Stop struggling."

So I decided to try.

Mindful simply means having good control over your attention: you can place your attention wherever you want and it stays there; when you want to shift it to something else, you can.

—Rick Hanson, PhD, and Richard Mendius, MD,
*Buddha's Brain: The Practical Neuroscience of
Happiness, Love, and Wisdom*

You Are Not the "I" of the Storm

The mask of shame will keep you from your
destiny. . . . You don't have to condemn yourself
for your mistakes. Take off the mask of shame. . . .
God cannot bless who you pretend to be.

—Joel Osteen

Obviously we all have storms. Some hit all at once, some come and go and leave us a bit different. One thing we know is that there will be plenty more storms in the future. In my earlier life, when I was still getting to know my own value and worth and had a lot of growing up to do, I had what English composition teachers call *I-itis*. Each storm was an extension of me; we were related until we became interdependent. Each storm had an eye, and it was *I*.

In what I believe is the vanguard of modern self-help literature, *The Ultimate Secrets of Total Self-Confidence*, author Robert Anthony, PhD, zeroes in on how identifying with our storms chips away at self-confidence and impedes the ability to find one's true north.

"Do you concentrate on your limitations, your failures, your blundering way of doing things, seldom stopping to think of what you might be?" he writes. "The problem is that you have been conditioned since childhood by false concepts, values, and beliefs that have prevented you from realizing how truly capable and unique you are."

That insight appeared in the opening pages. The book blew my mind, mostly because Dr. Anthony drove home the point that unless we perceive our own true worth as a person, we will be light-years away from ever achieving total self-confidence and self-worth. We can never be whole.

"Only to the degree that you can truly acknowledge your own unique importance will you be able to free yourself from your self-imposed limitations," he says.

Michele made me laugh when she used the phrase "the *I* of the storm" because it's so accurate. When we identify so closely with our experiences, we create what Dr. Anthony calls mistaken certainties, things that we are sure are true but that, in fact, are not. Like, "If I date men, I will most likely get hurt," or "I was a terrible student in elementary school, so I should go ahead and get a GED," or "My parents lost all their money in the stock market crash of 1929, so I keep my cash under my mattress because I don't trust banks," or "My divorce was so painful, I would never get married again." These mistaken certainties are generally based on wishful thinking, Dr. Anthony explains, which distorts reality and leads to self-deception. "We want things to be as we would like them to be rather than as they are. We look at the world through the filter of our beliefs, which blinds us to what is real." This goes for the bad stuff too.

Because my mind has been programmed or conditioned to accept false and distorted concepts and values, I am vulnerable to falling into the trap of developing a lifestyle to justify them. Perhaps this is the case with you as well. In *Buddha's Brain: The Practical Neuroscience of Happiness, Love, and Wisdom,* Rick Hanson, PhD, and Richard Mendius, MD, describe this phenomenon by saying, "As you go through life, your brain acquires expectations based on your experiences, particularly negative ones. When situations occur that are even remotely similar, your brain automatically applies its expectation to them; if it expects pain or loss, or even just the threat of these, it pulses fear signals."

It's a question of awareness, Dr. Anthony says. We must get through our thick skulls that everything we accept, relate, or reject is based on our present level of awareness. And if the level of awareness is faulty or distorted, as many of us in the midst of crisis experience, then our ability to be whole is jeopardized.

Dr. Anthony says, "Your number one priority in life is the expansion of your awareness. To discover that many of the things you thought were true are the things that, in reality, are not true."

For all of us, that means . . . *We are* not *the I of the storm.*

Earlier, I mentioned how being in the moment, even the painful ones, helps us to feel the pain and burden of our circumstances while creating a separation between what is internal in us and external in the world. Think back to acceptance and commitment therapy. We separate our feeling from our behavior. The same holds true with identity. If we can remove the assumption that we are defined by the events that happen around us, we can expand our actions and behaviors to become the whole person we would like to be—full of self-confidence, radiant power, love, and fulfillment. I admit, it's a lofty wish list for sure, but we deserve all of it and more. We just have to know how to get there. Watching the storm is about raising our awareness to be in touch with the good, bad, and ugly that make up life itself without internalizing the storm as the only definition of who we are. The importance in doing so is that even when we don't like the reality of a situation, and even when we can't help the way we feel about someone or something, awareness leads to an acceptance that allows us to have *control over our actions and reactions*. That's all we are trying to do here in W—to get a firm grip on it all by taking stock. When we do that, the real healing can begin.

I didn't learn this overnight. My own negative self-image was keeping me from knowing and utilizing my potential because I held mistaken certainties. I let things that had happened to me define who I was and who I was meant to be, and that could have been my downfall. When we live this way, Dr. Anthony likens it to being like a bird in a cage, "which has no idea how much space exists outside."

My father had written me from time to time from prison, beginning when I was fifteen years old. Usually his letters were filled with rage, hate, and guilt-inducing accusations about me, his own family, and the women he had killed. When I was seventeen, I began to have my best friend Tania open the letters for me. On one particular day, I knew I needed her not only to open it but to read it to me. I knew it would be an important letter because it was a response to a letter I had sent to him a few weeks earlier in a moment of desperation. I was lost and in need of a parental figure, guidance, attention, and love so badly that I actually thought my *best* option was to write my father for advice.

My home life was a wreck. I was sleeping on a cot in my grandmother's moldy, unfinished basement with a raging madman as a stepfather, my mother physically and emotionally unavailable, my brother and sister seeking refuge at the homes of various friends, on welfare, and with a newly diagnosed deaf baby half-brother. I explained to my father that I was sexually assaulted at the age of fifteen, in the middle of his arrest and conviction, and how the traumatizing act of violation had created a pregnancy. Tears stained the page as I went through the account of having an abortion and how being all alone through it had affected me: I was afraid, beyond repair. Could he help me, I asked, figure out a way to stop the nightmares I had every night, the crying spells, the shame, and especially the way my heart panged every time I looked at my mother's son, my half-brother, who was the same age as my aborted child would have been. Finally I had told someone.

As Tania opened the letter, she scanned it first and then indignantly told me I was never to read it. Despite my better judgment, I insisted. Though she resisted me at first, finally she tossed the letter over, moving across her bed-room with tears in her eyes. At first I thought they were tears of anger toward me for being too stern with her, but soon after I knew she was crying *for* me. So I begged her, "What does it say?"

"He says you are a murderer too, and that you deserve to be locked up in a cell right next to him."

Ralph Waldo Emerson said, "We are what we think about all day long." When I read that quote, I felt like he was talking directly to me. All day long I thought, *I am poor white trash.* I thought, *I am a murderous girl who neglected to care for a gift from God.* I thought, *I am a slut for not being a virgin,* despite the fact that my virginity was stolen. I thought, *I am bad for still having a wanting for a father who is nothing short of the devil himself.* I thought, *I am despicable for being the daughter of such a man.* I thought, *I have a mother who is a fool. I am bad, I am his sins, her sins, and my sins, all wrapped up in one giant mistake.* I thought these things All. Day. Long. And in my mind, that is exactly who I had become.

The problem with identifying so much with your storm is twofold: You don't know how to be anything other than your storm, and you are denied the gift of getting to know your true self. In that way, Emerson is spot on. You become who you think you are.

Building Strength by Finding the *How*

Start by doing what's necessary; then do what's possible;
and suddenly you are doing the impossible.

—Francis of Assisi

When it comes to watching the storm, I try too hard and lose too much sleep anticipating what is to come, as if my mind's eye is a crystal ball that reveals the degree of future pain. My favorite line from William Goldman's classic novel *The Princess Bride* is when the evil count says, "One of my theories is that pain involves anticipation." I can laugh at myself now at how silly my actions have been when I spent so much mental energy worrying about things that didn't happen. I caused myself pain in just the anticipation of what would be. When we anticipate future pain, we are not watching the storm—we are forecasting. It's pretty safe to say that even our favorite meteorologists have been known to be wrong about tomorrow's weather. Watching your storm is being in the moment. This moment right now.

Even if this moment is the most painful or repugnant event of your life, the important thing is to trust that the feelings will change. You may think the feelings will consume you, but you can learn to wait them out. Each time you remain still and nonreactive, you become a bit stronger, and you do not allow the moment to infiltrate you. Each time you are able to bear the pain of your feelings and see that they didn't kill you, or each time you keep yourself safe until you can reach out for help, or each time you accept help that is offered, or each time you find a way to show self-care or self-love in a single moment, you build strength. Then one day in the distant future when you see someone you care about going through the same storm, you will be able to help her navigate her moment. Just as I witnessed in Chillicothe, Ohio.

WATCHING THE STORM IN CHILLICOTHE, OHIO

I drove past the cornfields and the baby blue water tower splashed with the town name, CHILLICOTHE, and reached a Craftsman home with a wraparound wood porch. Everything looked normal and serene from the outside, from the American flag to the black Labrador retriever greeting me. But as I got closer to the wooden-screen front door, a different picture emerged. Taped to the door was a sun-faded missing person's flyer. It was the reason I was there. I was meeting Yvonne, the mother of one of the six women missing from the small town. I was scheduled to interview her for *Crime Watch Daily* to bring awareness to her missing daughter, the murders of four other women, and yet another disappearance.

Grief has a distinct look, and Yvonne had been wearing hers for quite some time. I mirrored her somber expression as I thanked her for inviting me into her home. Inside she had her adult daughter's pictures and her grandchildren's photos on every available wall. The house was a shrine to her daily devotion.

"I go to sleep thinking of Charlotte and wake up thinking of Charlotte," Yvonne told me. I asked what helps her continue from moment to moment.

"Along with the other mothers of the missing women, I've started our own support group. We share updates from the police, we cry together, we can talk to each other in a way no one else understands. It's not like being a widow, a label that adopts you in order to tell the world you have buried a husband. When you lose your child—there is no label for it." Perhaps that is no accident, as it is a way of life unfathomable and unspeakable.

For Yvonne, watching the storm meant taking in the awareness of the grim circumstances and then mindfully connecting with her small community to find answers. She would never stop looking for her daughter, but she was trying to take a thoughtful approach that used her skills and didn't leave her more vulnerable. Yvonne was uniting with the media to gain attention and resources for the search for her daughter. The alternative was to fret in silence and passively wait for answers to come to her from the authorities who, sadly, had already written off her daughter as being dead from her high-risk lifestyle. That latter kind of stillness is *not* watching the storm; it is burrowing deeper into your sense of helplessness and fear. Yvonne was able to contemplate the conditions of her storm, gauge the reality, and look within herself for a true answer to the question of what might get her through. Reaction turned to response, which helped her see other ways to look for her daughter, such as inviting me and the media to place a bright spotlight so that the FBI would assist the small town's sheriff's department by providing DNA analysis and other tools to which Chillicothe didn't have access.

In the meantime, solace would come from the scent of her daughter's clothes as Yvonne waits for answers and justice.

"I've seen many people who have sat with the pain until they could create something beautiful out of it. That's part of healing—to help other people," Rabbi Wolpe told me during the transformative interview I mentioned earlier. "I see this as part of my own healing. That's how we work. Because my son died, I am a better rabbi, a better human being, an author. It doesn't make what happened worth it, but it makes something meaningful out of something meaningless. When people ask, *Why* did this happen, it's always an unanswerable question. I don't know why it happened, but I know what I can do with it so that it is not just a loss."

Rabbi Wolpe really made me think. *Why* indicates a focus on something that happened, that was likely out of our control, or had nothing to do with us in the first place, and is over and done with. *Why* is a question that doesn't require action. But *how* is different because it forces a person into a mode of power and conquest. A first responder using the Jaws of Life to pull a molten car door off a burning car doesn't ask, *Why did this car hit the oil tanker?* He asks, *How do I get this family out?* When we watch the storm, we commit to ourselves in the now, grabbing our own tools to rescue our troubled soul. Try it yourself and see how you can go from a passive *why* to an active *how.* When I changed my own question from *why* to *how,* I automatically was shifted into the present moment, gifting me with the ability to press Pause on my irrational thoughts and futile questions.

I am sure if you asked therapists and credentialed experts why you should watch the storm, they would tell you a host of fantastic, interesting, and helpful things. Why do *I* do it? Because bad stuff comes back to haunt us when we try to avoid it. It bites us in the butt if we try to run away. I know this because I lived it over and over. Whatever I don't deal with now will *deal with me* later. Watching the storm gives me a way to experience my pain without being swept away by it: I might as well recognize this as a storm, name it, acknowledge it, accept it, find clarity, form better thoughts and patterns, and then kiss it goodbye with 99 percent certainty that there won't be a surprise visit from my suppressed feelings years after I could have addressed them.

> If you're ever feeling lonely, depressed, overwhelmed with emotion, or overwhelmed in general, share with the universe: "Universe, while this may not feel good to me, I trust it is good for me." Inspired by Marci Shimoff's writing, this mantra can help bring you back to yourself.

OPEN YOUR EMOTIONAL STORAGE BOXES

Have you ever been in the mood to clean house? Even for the most disorganized person, a good overhaul of the basement, kitchen cabinets, closets, and dresser drawers can be a therapy like no other. The desire usually strikes unexpectedly. One minute you are ignoring bills and watching TV surrounded by junk mail so old that there's actually a *TV Guide* at the bottom of the pile, and the next minute you are rummaging through stuff at warp speed. What is that about? What triggers us to get up one day and start going through our crap?

My friend Sally has the most enviable habit. When she has a bad day, she immediately comes home and whips out a garbage bag. The snapping sound of the thick black plastic is a signal that she's about to make her day all better, wiping the slate (aka countertop) clean, controlling the feelings of anxiety, stress, despair, being overwhelmed, whatever, by channeling them outward. "At least I can put them to good use with a positive spin," she explains. I get what she means; I feel so satisfied when I finally decide to go through my own stuff and put it in storage. My wall of cardboard cubes, each labeled with a Sharpie, is neatly stacked so I can see it when I want but stored masterfully enough that I can easily forget about it.

Perhaps my propensity to pack things up and put them away is why I love *Antiques Roadshow*. I mean, here you have people who weren't like Sally, who didn't recycle the family vase, who had the wherewithal to go back into their wall of boxes and reexamine their "stuff." The episodes I love to watch aren't the ones that showcase the couple who picked up something at a flea market but the ones where people were moving home and were forced to go through boxes of things that they had forgotten they owned. When you start to look more closely at something, seeing it anew, maybe you decide it's unique enough or meaningful enough or even troubling enough to take it on the road for a spin. On *Antiques Roadshow*, people have experts examine their item, telling them what they see and why it's wonderful regardless of its monetary value, and then offering an opinion as to its estimated price.

What I've noticed is this: When the person discovers that what was boxed up actually does have extrinsic value, she is always happy about it. And when a person discovers it's just something that belongs in a box somewhere in an attic, valueless, she is never *unhappy* or *regretful* she took it out for that spin. Why? Because she determined after all that the object had value *to her*. She saw a purpose in taking another look at it, maybe discovering that with a different frame of mind she actually loved it, that it went with her decor, or that it could be useful now or in the future. Perhaps she's a different person now than when she first boxed it up. Maybe packing it was an impulse reaction and not a good response in the first place. More likely, the experience will prompt her to go through the other boxes she labeled oh so long ago to sort out what else she can use today or, at the very least, to offer it to someone else who may find it useful or delightful.

Watching the storm is very much like this process of going through boxes, except you're tackling emotional storage. Perhaps the storm happened some time ago and you labeled it and put it away for good—your mental Sharpie marking it DO NOT OPEN! DEPRESSION, DEATH, REJECTION, BANKRUPTCY, ILLNESS, ABORTION, DRUG ABUSE, ALCOHOLISM, RAPE, DOMESTIC VIOLENCE, GUILT, REGRET, SHAME, BLAME, FEAR.

But watching the storm is about slowing down and taking time to mindfully reopen the box, examining, like an expert on *Antiques Roadshow*, the intrinsic value of your item. What happens most of the time is that you wind up like the person on the show—admitting the object is owned by you and is therefore something that you can control the value of.

This is what happened to me when we were relocating to California. I knew I had a lot of packing to do, and walking around the house, I saw our belongings in a new light—as cost on a moving truck. Bulk and multistate shipping fees became my new measurement of value, that is, until I walked into the garage and saw the cedar hope chest I received for my high school graduation. I could never get rid of it, I knew, as it holds my first communion dress, my children's first baby blankets, and my inheritance of teacups from my grandmother placed atop high school artifacts. Curious to explore the bottom layers, I grabbed a chair and began to dig, letting the cedar aroma take me on a nostalgic recap of my milestones.

"Oh, I forgot about that!" I squealed in delight to no one. Then I felt the warmth of tears after seeing pictures of my children, plus a bit of anger at the passage of time that prevents me from blowing raspberries on my children's chubby baby bellies. How independent they are now. In the corner between my daughter's first pair of shoes and a card from my husband for my first Mother's Day, I spied a folded sheet of ruled notebook paper with ballpoint-pen doodles bleeding through and tattered holes where the page had been torn from a spiral notebook. The writing was not mine. It was from a boyfriend I had hoped time would erase.

Should I just close the chest? It would be so much easier and faster. After all, it was thirty days to moving day. Opening that letter could open the hurt. Yet this time I told myself the letter represented a storm in my life, but now I was safe, a grown woman, in a loving relationship, and opening a letter I honestly don't recall ever reading would not change my life for the worse in any way. I tried to separate myself from the storm. I told myself it wasn't me, it was something that had happened, a fact I cannot change, but it was not indicative of who I am or who I was going to become.

"I'm sorry for not listening to you," the letter began, "and for forcing myself on you. I just didn't get lunch in, and you know how I get when I don't eat. . . . "

The nerve of this boy! To blame me for raping me. I thought about the abortion, as I did often, but this time through the lens of calmness and compassion for a very troubled girl. I recalled how young and alone I felt. I wouldn't blame my daughter if she were in this predicament, and now I could finally melt away the judgment with which I had burdened myself for far too long. I decided I'd do the deed that I had promised myself I would never do. I forgave myself.

What came of the letter? I threw it away because there is no room for it among the gifts of life preserved lovingly in my favorite cedar chest.

To watch the storm is to trust in ourselves, in the face of pain, that we will know what to do when our open wounds are stung with a saltwater wave. Once we have taken stock of our wounds, as I tried to do when opening my cedar chest, H: Heal Your Heart will explore the choices we have in front of us on our path to becoming WHOLE.

What's Inside:

Heal Your Heart

THE PLACE YOUR VOICE RESIDES

*We have the power to live with joy
and contentment by responding to our
suffering with kindness.*

—Kristin Neff, PhD

While I watched the storm inside me, I began to identify and pin down what had been bothering me all along: the intense sorrow and mourning I had over the loss of a more typical childhood, of a father-daughter relationship, of a grandfather for my children. Then something interesting happened. That sadness was crowded out by pure and absolute anger.

I felt robbed, undignified, and incomplete. A good part of me realized I had never reached my true potential. I was angry that my father forced me into hiding, to be ashamed of my last name and fearful of the very blood that coursed through my veins. I was so mad at him that I thought I'd go get myself an apology because he ruined my life. But *he* didn't make me feel any of that. *I* did.

That realization has caused me to become intrigued by anger. It's like a chameleon, taking on so many different forms. Like sweet little Grandmother who is really the Big Bad Wolf, anger can not only blow your house down, it can implode your world.

I'm so angry, I could cry.

I'm so angry, I could spit.

I'm so angry, I'm telling! (That one is from my son.)

I'm so angry, I feel sick.

And on and on.

And sometimes it masquerades itself as something completely different.

I'm so depressed, I don't know why.

Here's the big reveal about anger: It makes a person feel the urge to retaliate. According to the American Psychological Association, "Twenty-five percent of anger incidents involve thoughts of revenge such as, 'I'm going to spread rumors about my boss to get even,' or 'I'd like to just bump her car to put her in her place.'" Interestingly, anger is experienced through interactions with people we like or love, including children, spouses, and close friends.

Isn't that why we are here? Recovering from a painful experience in which either someone we love or like has made us feel inadequate, afraid, ashamed, unloved, pissed off as all hell? And that person could even be ourselves.

How long can we go on being angry? Anger is related to the fight-or-flight stress response we talked about in W: Watch the Storm. This part alerts us and others that we feel threatened or have witnessed an injustice. It's a function that helps us identify what we are willing to put up with and when our dignity is being attacked, and helps us communicate something urgent as a matter of safety, such as when a mother finds her lost child at a county fair and yells, "Don't ever walk away from me again!" Anger should be acute, lasting only a short period of time, and yet the problem with the anger that many of us experience is that it lingers far beyond the moment.

For a long time, I was afraid to face my anger, so I turned the anger inward and became depressed. My anger went right into the long-term "chronic" phase. I wallowed in self-doubt until the easiest resolution became isolating myself. When we live with unresolved anger, we shut down a large part of ourselves and go into hiding. I used food to express anger that I had swallowed inside me.

I noticed when my coping mechanism got even worse. It was after my boyfriend, Sean, had forced me to have sex and I was left alone to decide about the baby that had been conceived. I felt I was in the worst possible situation any girl my age could ever face, with no way out: pregnancy; an impoverished, abusive home; an abusive relationship; a father in jail for murder. These thoughts made me want to cry, but I saved my tears for my nighttime pillow. Earning my diploma was my only hope of getting out of poverty, and I knew that having a baby would put an end to that prospect. It was after Sean tried to beat the hell out of me to kill the baby that I decided to abort the child. After the abortion, I couldn't forgive myself. Nobody knew about my situation, which made it worse. My heart felt tied in knots all the time. I found myself gorging on everything I saw, even when I wasn't hungry. Food gave me comfort for a brief period, but it didn't feel good being full and bloated only to be lonelier and more despondent than before. The first time I remember purposely soothing my pain with food was when we moved to Grandma Frances's house, where my mother and we kids slept in the basement on cots with shoeboxes as dresser drawers. Pulling the light bulb string revealed the cold, cramped cement-floored cellar we were now forced to call home. Soon my uncle would also sleep there, and then my mother's husband, Robert, and my first baby half-brother.

In the meantime, my father would toy with us, saying he was coming to visit and then not show up. I'd shove instant potatoes, along with all my emotions of anger, sadness, and humiliation, down my throat. Instead of visiting us, my father had chosen to be with his mistress, the woman he had left us for so suddenly.

When he did finally make the trip, my father, appalled by our bare cupboards, would take us grocery shopping. We'd fill the car with five-gallon buckets of ice cream to make sure we'd have plenty long after he left. In a way, sugary foods expressed a sense of security, ever so temporarily.

My anger was fueled by:

- Not admitting my emotions as anger
- Not expressing it to anyone
- Not believing I had a right to express anything to anyone
- Not having the sense of self to give credence to anything I felt
- Other people's opinions
- The media

Most of all, my adult anger stemmed from the fact that nobody told me as a child that I didn't have to feel so much guilt. Even as a child, I was never told that the circumstances that encroached on my life—divorced parents, poverty, abuse, rape, abortion, inability to stop my stepfather's tirades, not protecting my younger siblings, etc.—were *not* my fault. The people surrounding me, from my grandparents to my mother to my teachers, didn't notice me or my pain, and if they did, nobody did a damn thing to help. That imprinted on me the message that I wasn't worth noticing and that my pain and shame should be suppressed because neither of these emotions was worthy—I wasn't worthy—of tender attention and repair. Messages like this, according to the theory of physician Donald Winnicott, might lead people to replace their true self with a false self designed to protect the true self from the pain and self-loathing it experiences. I can only say with certainty that this was true for me. Before I worked on meeting and loving my true self, the one that existed before all the garbage piled up in my life (a process we will discuss more in L: Leverage Your Power), I was shy, withdrawn, insecure, private, afraid of my own shadow, full of guilt, and incapable of trusting others, especially boys and men.

One of my favorite books of late is *Unworthy: How to Stop Hating Yourself*. If I could hug Anneli Rufus for authoring this guide, I would. She explains that the human brain has the capacity and preference for "negative bias," meaning we remember the worst of times over the best of times, and that when this happens, we rewire our brain that way. We learn from those bad experiences, in the sense that we retrain our thinking, our habits, our beliefs, but the problem is that what we learn is faulty. We believe we are bad and unworthy and adopt coping strategies that take the form, she says, of "so-called personality flaws" in order to protect ourselves from ever feeling unworthy again. Through lying, adopting phony personas, indecisiveness, and excess apologizing, we try our best to keep from being vulnerable and achieving deep interpersonal connection or even, like me, trusting another person. Letting someone see the "real self" would risk showing them something they could hate as much as you hate yourself. We can have none of that.

Michele can remember the entire high school cafeteria jeering, pointing, and laughing mockingly as she fell to the floor off a chair that had been unscrewed and rigged as a practical joke on "senior day." It was the same day she found out she had been accepted into her first-choice college, but humiliation trumps pride any day; she can't quite recall the "feeling" after opening her acceptance letter, but she definitely remembers her humiliation. Just like fight, flight, and freezing, our ability to retain negative messages over positive ones is a biological survival instinct. To use Rufus's analogy, "It is far more useful for an evolving creature to remember *Hungry lions bite* than to remember *Flowers are pretty.*"

Has your pain experience left such a lasting impression that you are like Michele, who is not able to remember any joy from achieving one of her biggest goals in life? Has what you've been through caused such a negativity bias that you can't stop hating yourself or feeling guilt and hopelessness? Take solace from knowing it's not your fault. Remember you are wired to attach to the negative. Rufus emphasizes what we know about brain plasticity—the ability of the brain to change itself and for new thought patterns to be created, which is good news. But what I love most about Rufus's message in *Unworthy* is that we don't have to beat the negativity bias by swinging in the entirely opposite direction and saying nice things to ourselves and trying to lure out our true self by dangling a honey-glazed carrot in front of its steel prison door. We simply have to stop being mean to ourselves.

"You might not, and you need not, ever love yourself," Rufus declares in her book. "You might not, and you need not, ever call yourself Genius, Gorgeous, or Fabulous. You might not, and you need not, ever call yourself anything nice at all. Just stop calling yourself bad words. Put down the razor blade. Resist. Refrain. Is that so much to ask?"

Well said, Ms. Rufus. Well said.

The Wisdom of the Wound

*Do you not see how necessary a world of pains and troubles
is to school an intelligence and make it a soul?*

—John Keats

I used to think that complete healing might never be possible for the depth of my pain. Have you ever wondered the same? Maybe like me you thought the pain and the circumstances could never be healed or reconciled.

Healing in and of itself poses a paradox, something I learned from David Knighton, MD, in his unprecedented book, *The Wisdom of the Healing Wound*. Dr. Knighton founded the Wound Healing Institute at the University of Minnesota Medical Center. He is committed to his medically holistic approach that helps people heal from nonhealing wounds of the physical, emotional, and spiritual varieties. He calls it simply wound care.

"Wounding is every bit as essential to life as healing," Dr. Knighton writes. "In fact, the two work together in an immensely intricate biological dance that permeates all of nature. The processes of evolution and natural selection are all about wounding and healing. The organism that heals most effectively survives to reproduce."

Intrigued by this puzzle, I read on and discovered an entirely new way to think about my pain experiences—by labeling them as wounds. That's when the light bulb went on—that is exactly what they are! I look back and see that my emotional wounds are not all created equal. Metaphorically speaking, the scars left from growing up poor seem now like cuts that required stitches, while living with an abusive stepfather moved into the realm of a stabbing, and then there was the internal bleeding left by my rape. Dr. Knighton describes how people who have suffered these and other types of physical wounds have gone on to heal. And if wounds heal, as Dr. Knighton says they do, and they are a necessary component of life itself, then I don't have to force myself past my wounds until they've healed naturally.

Like a child who needs only to touch a hot stove to learn never to touch it again, our emotional wounds are a form of memory. They enable our bodies to store vital information about where danger lingers and when we need to exercise caution. I found so much comfort in this idea of my wounds—their utility and purpose—that they began to feel like living, breathing extensions of myself. Not tightly wrapped balls of emotion, but lightweight fireballs of energy—my energy, which I can move in any direction I wish.

"A wound can be memorialized in another form as well: a scar. Each scar is a visible—and visceral—reminder from our body, telling us, 'Don't do this again!'" writes Dr. Knighton. Our psychological scars inform us in the same way. Like physical wounds, he says, psychological wounds are about "disruption of structure and function." And that is exactly how I had been feeling all of these years—disrupted; I just didn't have the right word! Being able to articulate it in that way made all the difference to my moving forward. I felt less afraid of the strange sensation now defined as disruption, because disruption does not mean permanence; it's not something I was stuck with, but a pause in my life cycle. Maybe my brain had been a little bruised up, but now I have the wisdom of those healing wounds, which Dr. Knighton describes like this:

> Wounds teach us about who we are, where we have been, and what we need to do in the future. Our wounds thus make us wiser, better able to survive and thrive. Their lessons stick, in part because of the pain of healing, in part because the cost of not learning their lessons can be life-threatening.

H: Heal Your Heart is about learning how to let your wounds heal, and learning how to embrace them as complex but beautiful wisdom. In many ways, this is the hardest part of the program. Why? Because the concepts are not as tangible as, say, writing an action plan or practicing meditative breathing. These practices are choices that first we exercise in our imaginations and mind's eye and then use precision and purpose to bear their energy outward and onward, sharing a part of our inner selves with the outer world—a world that has hurt us. The only way up is through the hurt, so believe in yourself. Let's get started.

The Courage to Be Afraid

Sometimes you gotta get through your fear
to see the beauty on the other side.

—Poppa to Arlo in *The Good Dinosaur*

Now that my dream of helping others has come true, it brings to mind the saying "Be careful what you wish for." That's because my job now requires me to speak in front of large groups of people—not my cup of tea, to say the least. I can relate to and be friendly with a person one-on-one, but in a group . . . forget it! For years I planted myself as a wallflower, observing everyone. Until I heard other women tell me their stories at speaking events, it didn't occur to me that others had the same debilitating fear. My anxiety around mandatory speaking appearances sent me begging the doctor for magic pills that would quiet my palpitating heart and steady my trembling hands. More often than not, my solution was to decline speaking events. The breakthrough didn't happen until I zeroed in on yet another paradox: "Courage is doing what you're afraid to do. There can be no courage unless you're scared." Eddie Rickenbacker, a World War I hero, is credited as the author of this wise gem. And while less than 1 percent of us actually serve in the military, we all have had experiences that have felt like a personal war— when we felt threatened but somehow walked through the fire regardless. We had the courage to do what we were afraid to do, whether that meant quitting a job, leaving an abusive spouse, disowning a child, or training for a marathon. We are bound together by such vulnerability that enables us to be afraid and do it anyway. In W: Watch the Storm, we described the necessity of sitting with the fear and other emotions that accompany painful experiences, becoming familiar with unpleasant feelings, learning not to act upon them, and not avoiding situations that invite conflict or pain.

Despite the necessity of fear, we are diametrically opposed to it. From fear of the boogeyman hiding in the closet or our children being abducted or getting cancer, we are afraid of it all. The problem is that fear doesn't serve us, especially when we're trying to heal our heart.

I wanted to understand more about the notion of embracing fear and how it facilitates healing, so I sought out Thom Rutledge, author of several life-changing books, including the bestselling *Embracing Fear: How to Turn What Scares You into Your Greatest Gift*. He was kind enough to e-mail me, exclusively for this book, his perspectives on how we can use fear to heal ourselves emotionally; what he has offered is nothing short of invaluable. I wanted to know if there is a common denominator when it comes to fear; I wondered if there is one thing at the core of it, no matter what the catalyst or the person experiencing it.

"YES!" wrote Rutledge via e-mail, using all caps for emphasis. "At the basis . . . UNCERTAINTY. We humans are afraid of uncertainty and we hate change. Here comes the irony: The only thing certain about life is . . . yep, CHANGE."

Just as I was about to reply with a thank-you to Rutledge, my inbox dinged with more:

"The fear of uncertainty is a side effect of human self-consciousness. My old dog does not worry about getting older, knowing that with each day she is that much closer to death. She is a Zen master—in the here now, just as excited to see me at the end of the day as she was yesterday and the day before. I, on the other hand, have this wonderful thing called self-consciousness—so I can be afraid of all kinds of stuff. We are so afraid of uncertainty that we will very often opt for a negative certainty over living with uncertainty. Who we are, the kind of people we will be, individually and collectively, will be determined by one thing: how we relate to fear."

So we need to take cues from our fears and do something with them—after we've sat with them for a while, that is. But what do the next steps look like? What exactly are we doing during that process, if it is a process at all? How does simply feeling what we feel help release guilt, shame, and anger? I typed out these questions, hesitantly pressed Send, and then freaked out a little. *What would he say? Maybe I missed the whole point.*

"This is about awareness," he replied. "We humans naturally are not big fans of awareness when it is about tuning in to thoughts and emotions that make us uncomfortable . . . we need to find our way to feeling safe enough to feel our fear. With this work, we are being clear that feeling safe is not going to be the absence of fear. Safe means 'I know that whatever this is, it is not going to destroy me. I am safe enough to sit here in the middle of this room and observe all of these emotions around me.'"

Alecia's Story

After the birth of their second child, Alecia's husband, Will, became withdrawn. He didn't hold her hand, cuddle, engage with her or the kids; it was upsetting to her. But because she wasn't sure what the exact problem was, she didn't know how to talk about what was upsetting her. So she'd throw a tantrum, ranting and making biting remarks. Will would then say her dirty fighting was what led him to be withdrawn, so Alecia ultimately came to the conclusion that she probably had postpartum depression. She was put on antidepressants, kept her desire for closeness to herself, and went back to work.

Alecia and Will lived a lifestyle that was pretty businesslike, operating under the guise that these days working families can't expect much more than being two ships passing in the night. Even if their physical intimacy had been sucked out of the relationship, along with the emotional part, it was easy to blame it on the chaotic schedule, the sleep deprivation, the demands of the kids.

Finally there came a point where Alecia knew they couldn't keep feeding themselves such bullshit, and she suggested marriage counseling. Will declined.

So Alecia went into therapy. She told the therapist she was afraid she might be bipolar, or she had some sort of personality disorder, or (her husband's theory) her mother tore out her self-confidence as a child and that resulted in an unrealistic view of what a husband can give to a wife. She was making her man crazy, abusing him emotionally, and driving him away. She needed to get help, needed to fix herself and *fast*, before the worst thing possible happened and Will decided he wanted out of their marriage. As the therapist listened and listened, he concluded, "Clearly there are issues that need to be addressed, but Alecia, I will tell you I *know* you are not bipolar."

"Oh my God, Doc. Am I . . . an alcoholic?"

"No, Alecia."

"Then what is wrong with me?"

All her therapist could say was "Time's up."

Determined to find out what "label" she fell under, Alecia switched therapists, and while her husband continued to refuse intimacy, she looked for solace in food, slept a lot, and insisted on blood tests to check her thyroid, as her weight had skyrocketed. When her thyroid function came back spot on, as her new therapist predicted it would, Alecia took some comfort in statistics that told her 20 percent of marriages are considered sexless.

Alecia had been in therapy off and on for several years, and on a rare evening without the kids home, Will asked if Alecia wanted to watch a movie. "Honestly, I wasn't even disappointed or shocked that he didn't want to use our alone time to be intimate. It had become our way of life."

So with a glass of wine in one hand and a fistful of her son's Halloween candy in the other, Alecia followed her husband to the living room to find a movie. Three glasses later, she was "happy" enough to get up the guts to make a move on him. When Will rejected her, she thought, *Of course, I was trying too hard. Thank goodness there's more Halloween candy.*

Alecia thought back to when she and Will first met, when she was the girl who could speak to an audience of salespeople and get them laughing, clapping, all fired up for the creative line she was pitching. She remembered that saucy brunette—yeah, her, the old her. The one who flew off to Ireland on a whim; the one who always knew she was a good mother without needing reassurance it was true.

"In that moment, I hated the pathetic person I had become," admitted Alecia. "The one who felt like she couldn't be skinny enough, smart enough, successful enough, good enough, who was jealous when former colleagues got promotions or accolades, who started taking politics way too seriously. All my life I had considered them theater, but that had changed about me too. There wasn't much left of the old me, the real me who had to still be in there somewhere, and as I dug deeper than I had in a very long time despite all those hours in therapy, I suddenly wondered, *Has this man who claims to love me, whom I adore, somehow made me a lesser person? Has he made me more like him? And have I allowed it?*"

After years of feeling like an alien in her own body, caught in some cycle of self-destruction that orbited out to her loved ones, Alecia suddenly wasn't afraid anymore. For so long she had let fear control her. She had always thought, *I need to get help, I need to fix myself, and I need to do it before the worst thing possible happens and he decides he wants out of our marriage.* For the first time, Alecia began to think, *Just maybe it isn't me.*

When she eventually spoke with her husband, not shouting at him from behind a haze of wine but really speaking honestly, Will finally confessed, "I don't want this life with you. I haven't for years. I love the kids, but I don't want to be locked down, trapped in a marriage. It's not my nature to live like this, to be faithful, to be traditional, all the pressure to be something, someone I'm not. I feel like I'm suffocating. I want out."

Deep down, Alecia knew the truth all along but worked hard to deny that Will was insensitive, detached, and negligent toward her emotionally and physically for reasons she could not control. "It was easier to focus on myself and take the blame than to hear him give voice to what I had feared most all along," she said. "That he did not want me or our marriage and there was something broken that could not be fixed: him."

Armed with the facts, Alecia was able to face the future in a way she couldn't before. "I feel sorrier for him than angry," she said. "As for me, I have a lot of work to do. I don't know what happens next, but I know what's *no longer going to happen next.* Funny how the worst thing we think that could possibly happen can turn out to be the best thing that ever did." ❧

When I became frustrated by my own stagnation and mistaken certainties, I would bounce back to doing what I thought was the only way through my fear—to somehow, someway muster the strength to close my eyes and clench my jaw and jump into boiling lava. But Thom Rutledge taught me that what we really need to do before we act is create conditions of safety. This reminded me of what I did with both my children when I helped them learn to walk, turned off the lights when they went to sleep, or left them on their first day of school: I made them feel safe. I made them feel at ease by telling them it's okay to be afraid, and that everyone feels that way once in a while. And then I witnessed them having the courage to do what they were afraid to do.

Exercise: Feel the Fear

Here's a practice from Thom Rutledge to get you going.

"Imagine you are sitting in the middle of a big room. For each of us the room is different, of course: personal, safe, familiar. This room will soon fill up with your emotions, but first you create some kind of protection as you sit there. Maybe a transparent, impenetrable egg. Maybe Plexiglas or a warrior's armor. Maybe you invite the image of someone you trust to be strong and protective to sit next to you. Allow your imagination to do whatever it wants as long as the result is feeling a bit safer in the middle of this room surrounded by your feelings.

"Next, from your position in the middle of the room, with your protection there, look around to see what is in this room. There is no right way to do this. Totally subjective. Again, we are letting our imagination work. All I am telling you is that these are your emotions, your feelings. See them in any way you see them. Feel them in any way you feel them. And nothing more. With this image, you are literally sitting in the middle of your emotions. Just sit there, just imagine this until you have had enough, and then dismiss all the images of emotions and let the imaginary room go. It belongs to you—you can bring it to you any time you think it might be a good idea to practice being aware of your emotional self."

In their book, *Buddha's Brain: The Practical Neuroscience of Happiness, Love, and Wisdom*, Rick Hanson, PhD, and Richard Mendius, MD, say that to face fear, we should bring mindfulness to it. They compare fear to any other mental state, explaining that is all it is: a state created by our mind. "Recognize fear when it arises, observe the feeling of it in your body, watch it to convince you that you should be alarmed," they advise. "Notice how awareness which contains fear is itself never fearful. Keep separating from the fear; settle back into the vast space of awareness through which fear passes like a cloud."

The Freedom of Forgiveness

Forgiveness is giving up the hope that the past could have been any different.

—Oprah Winfrey

One of the most difficult questions I am asked by the media is whether I have forgiven my father—if my healing and moving forward depended on this difficult act. It's hard because it took me a long time to figure out exactly what forgiveness would mean—for me *and* for him. Before I would even consider forgiveness, I needed to understand what kind of commitment I would be making if I decided I had it in me to forgive.

In 2005, I was a new mother, and with not much of a social life, I spent my daytime hours glued to an ongoing televised investigation of a triple homicide and a search for two children, Shasta, age eight, and Dylan, age nine. What law enforcement knew was that in May, Shasta and Dylan's mother, her boyfriend, and their thirteen-year-old brother, Slade, were murdered in their home. What they didn't know was who did it and where in the world the two other children were.

I never imagined that ten years later I would be a correspondent for *Crime Watch Daily* and have the opportunity to sit down face-to-face with Shasta, who has grown into a beautiful, fine young woman. I wasn't sure how I felt about the task. Shasta's young face stayed with me for more than a decade. I often wondered what happened to the little girl. Did she ever feel safe again? Was she happy, and could she ever be after trauma beyond any of our imaginations? On the one hand, I felt invasive and sensational; on the other hand, I took the job because I knew I wanted to give voice to people like Shasta, who have lived through trauma so horrid you might want to skip this section all together. But to offer a true perspective on what it takes to heal one's heart without talking about the details of Shasta's horror story would be like writing a cookbook without mentioning the flame of the stove.

In a conference room at a local hotel, the lights were set and the camera panned to Shasta sitting across from me. *How do I ask about the worst day of her life? And is it okay to?* I let Shasta guide me into her hellish nightmare that began in her home in Kootenai County, Idaho. Inside was a gruesome scene. Shasta then began to speak to me about the initial entry into her home, when Joseph Duncan attacked and murdered her older brother as she was forced to watch from a chair, hands zip-tied behind her back. Duncan carried her away in his red Jeep and sexually assaulted her. Shasta proceeded to share the details of the day Duncan murdered Dylan—again, in front of her eyes—with a gunshot to his stomach and head. Both of us now in tears, she pressed on. Shasta was forced to help Duncan place pieces of her brother's body on a tarp and then watch as he poured gasoline on top of the nine-year-old's body. Even though he was dead, Shasta thought she heard him screaming. She was helpless, and she wandered into the woods in silent numbness.

Alone with Shasta now, Duncan drove to a nearby Denny's to grab food while on the trip to a new secret location. Shasta cried as she passed the billboards with her picture next to her brother's. An astute waitress on the graveyard shift recognized Shasta—the girl on all the posters and billboards. Calmly, the waitress called the authorities while stalling Duncan and Shasta in their booth. When the officer arrived, he approached the child and said, "What is your name?"

I was stunned at Shasta's composure as she relayed her story. All I could think was, *How do you recover from that? What joy or even will to survive can grow after witnessing that level of trauma?*

I pressed on with the interview. I asked Shasta, "Today, what would you say to the killer of your family, if you could say anything?"

"You don't control me anymore," she said with confidence. "I won't let you take one more piece of me or my life away."

And then she added this.

"I forgive you."

The old me—the one who was hurting, living in secrecy and shame, and fearful—would have thought, *Yeah right. What a crock! What you have just described to me is the definition of* not *forgivable.*

But the new me—the one who has searched and studied and practiced forgiveness myself—now sees what Shasta means: that healing your heart and taking a step into a fulfilling, bright future requires understanding exactly what it means to forgive and doing it when you are truly ready.

It does not mean that when you think of heinous actions against you, or the ones you have committed yourself, your blood pressure doesn't go up, or that you are happy all the time and the slate is clean. It doesn't even mean that you want your violator to get into heaven or get out of jail free or ever be happy.

But here is what forgiveness does: It provides the freedom *to no longer waste energy* wishing someone would go to hell or fantasizing that he rots in a hole without food and water or pricking a voodoo doll with needles to make sure he is never ever happy.

Forgiveness isn't about the other person at all, you see. It's about you. All about *you*.

> *To forgive is not just to be altruistic,*
> *it is the best form of self-interest.*
> —Archbishop Desmond Tutu

Shasta is not saying she will ever forget his crimes, but she accepts the loss of her family as a fact that she cannot and never will change. In the face of that grimness, forgiveness gives Shasta a good chance of being unstuck in her past. Forgiveness has allowed her to let go of hope for a different outcome, to live on in spite of what happened, and to make a future for herself that is not defined by her past.

The topic of forgiveness is a crazy one. I've read many books and had the opportunity to speak to thought leaders and researchers on its power, and still it was hard to wrap my head around when I was raw in my pain, in resentment, in despair, and in jadedness. Maybe you have felt that way before, or maybe you feel that now. But you haven't shut the book just yet, and for that I thank you. It's good to know there is a little part of you that is curious about whether or not you can forgive, or if you even want to, right?

I took this conundrum of struggling to forgive to one of the leading researchers of forgiveness, Fred Luskin, PhD. I devoured his book *Forgive for Good: A Proven Prescription for Health and Happiness,* which boasts on its cover the warning: "Holding a Grudge Is Hazardous to Your Health." He should know, as he is the director of the Stanford University Forgiveness Projects, which are responsible for much of his research on the power of forgiveness on the mind, body, and soul. I couldn't believe Dr. Luskin agreed to take my call when I needed help further understanding the fundamentals of forgiveness and its trade-offs and benefits.

In *Forgive for Good,* Dr. Luskin writes, "In careful scientific studies, forgiveness training has been shown to reduce depression, increase hopeful-ness, decrease anger, improve spiritual connection, increase emotional self-confidence, and help heal relationships."

"Forgiveness is not necessary to heal," Dr. Luskin explained to me during his busy Los Angeles commute. "It's like taking the express lane. When you forgive, you are saying, 'I made peace with my life. I understand that life can be very difficult, so I'm not going to let this ruin me. There is goodness in the world, so I am going to find it. I'm going to tell a story of overcoming.'"

WHY FORGIVENESS IS SO HARD TO SWALLOW

In the faith I was raised in, when a person in a state of sin is genuinely sorry and repentant, they are "absolved" of their sins. To achieve a state of abso-lution, you do a penance and then basically are forgiven by God. The way it was taught to me, once I did my penance, I would be working with a clean slate from God. Where I went wrong was confusing absolution with forgive-ness, which is not at all about acting as if the sin was never perpetuated. I took that version of what I was taught about faith and turned it toward the several transgressions in my life: my father, my mother's absenteeism, and even my abusive stepfather. In the context of absolution, I fell flat on my face. If I forgave them, would that mean I'm saying we're square? The dic-tionary defines *absolution* as "a freeing from blame or guilt; release from consequences, obligations, or penalties." *Whoa,* I thought. *So if I were to forgive them, would I be communicating that they are free from blame or guilt and don't require consequences?* No wonder I decided forgiveness wasn't for me. That's a huge undertaking.

But, Dr. Luskin explained, "You forgive so you are not captured by a piece of your life. Your brain's real estate is taken up by a very, very bad parent. You forgive so your parent occupies less of your brain as your life moves forward."

When people don't forgive, the lack of forgiveness is a crutch for why they are not living the right life. "It's not a good thing," Dr. Luskin told me, "because you want to get over stuff with whatever time you have left; you want to do good in the world. When you don't want to heal, you need an enemy, you need an excuse. Let's just say you are a crabby person. It's so easy to say, 'Well, I'm crabby because my father ruined my life.' Or else you will be stuck doing the work that you need to do to stop being a crabby person. Once typical grief runs its course (say, over a few years), all you have left is your life. You have to figure out how you want to live it most success-fully. It doesn't matter what happened."

Before I had the opportunity to talk with Dr. Luskin, I had always thought of forgiveness as an act. When you are trying to *do* something that doesn't require *doing*, it trips you up. When I asked Dr. Luskin what kinds of steps I could take to start to forgive, he helped me see that forgiveness is not an action at all; it's an inner state, an experience.

"Let's use happiness as an example," Dr. Luskin said. "If you're happy, it doesn't matter whether you are happy over something that happened to somebody else or because the Yankees won the World Series or because you like yourself. The feeling of happiness is the same. The trigger of what made you happy doesn't matter so much. Similarly, when you forgive, you are aiming to be at peace, not blaming, and having a story you can live with. Like the happiness analogy, it's no different if you are aiming forgiveness toward something you did in the past or something someone else did. You are looking for the experience of not being or feeling whatever it is that you've been feeling for so long.

"The thing that makes me concerned is the people who just get so lost in their stories, there's no way they could experience the state of forgiveness. 'Oh, you wouldn't believe what happened to me fourteen years ago,' they say. Yet in the fourteen years, fifty million people had terrible things happen to them! It represents an asphyxiation of compassion in the culture, and it sucks the air out of things. When you forgive, it's like you pump air back into the system."

Dr. Luskin took a lot of pressure off of me during our conversation, and I am forever grateful. I had put so much onus on my inability to forgive that it almost made me feel insufficient, adding to my cycle of guilt, shame, and the "what's wrong with me?" syndrome. But, he says, as does Thom Rut-ledge, that healing from painful experiences doesn't *require* forgiveness. Therefore, I didn't have to worry that I would have to write this book trying to preach that everyone should forgive and that if you can't, you will never be whole. His wisdom made me think harder about my own philosophy on the matter: Forgiveness is a state humans are capable of; the absolution part remains so powerful only God can do it.

A lot of things can help you heal. Time, clarity, friends, hope. Forgive-ness is like taking the express lane. Doing so demonstrates we have made

What Forgiveness Is Not

It is not pretending that what happened didn't happen.

It is not saying it's okay to your injury.

It is not easy.

It is not equal to being weak.

It is not forgetting.

peace with life, believe there is goodness in the world, and possess a willingness to go and find it, despite our suffering. Forgiveness is an inner state that tells a story of overcoming rather than of victimhood.

All along I thought forgiving is something done for the person who hurt us. But it's not about that person at all. It's about us. As Dr. Luskin put it, "It's not 'I release you from your crime'; it's 'I release *me* from your crime.'"

Don't we owe it to ourselves to at least try forgiveness? If we don't, our bitterness may destroy us. Forgiveness can offer us the hope that we need not be limited by anything that happened to us. For a lot of people, not forgiving can become a modus operandi. Being "the serial killer's daughter" kept me in a cycle of shame, which in many ways gave me permission to hide out in my house and not apply my college education toward making my secret dreams come true. Letting go of the shame, owning my identity, and forgiving the past, however, released and unleashed me into a whole new world, one that demanded I toss my crutch if I wanted to remain in it.

One of the most compelling ideas Dr. Luskin left me with is that forgiveness should not be a religious matter but a secular one. It's an issue of mental health, no different than any other mental health issue we grapple with, one that asks, "Can forgiveness help life be more fulfilling?"

In *The Book of Forgiving: The Fourfold Path for Healing Ourselves and Our World*, Archbishop Desmond Tutu and Mpho Tutu lay out two models of forgiveness, one that the authors describe as the better-known model of "strings attached" forgiveness and the other as the less conventional model of "forgiveness as a grace, a free gift freely given." Attaching strings to forgiveness goes something like this: "You stole five dollars from me, and when you pay me back, I will forgive you." The more meaningful and lasting model resembles this: "You cheated on me, and even though you can never give me back the trust in you I used to have, I do not wish this pain on you. And I will not immediately distrust every man who wishes to be with me, because of this."

The Tutus write, "There is history, and we are not served by forgetting our history. There is always a risk when we forgive that everything will not turn out all right. Just as we take a leap of faith when we make a commitment to love someone and get married, we also take a leap of faith when we commit ourselves to a practice of forgiving. We do not forget or deny that we are always vulnerable to being hurt again, but we leap anyway."

Exercise: Tune Your Humility Key

In *Buddha's Brain,* Rick Hanson, PhD, and Richard Mendius, MD, offer an exercise that helps keep my humility key in tune, called the Ten Thousand Things, which I have adapted as the following:

With a relaxed and steady mind, breathe slowly and deeply until your focus is on just the breath.

Consider someone who has hurt you or crossed you; that person can be you, i.e., you acted out of accordance with your own core values and have let yourself down.

Dr. Hanson suggests there could be ten thousand things that have caused this person to act in the way he or she (or even you) did! Can you imagine those ways, and consider how these things, whether biological, situational, or personal, affected that person? For me, I think back on my mother's own marriage to a distant man and being the daughter of an emotionally closed-off woman. What affected my mother? What pain, temperament, or even level of intelligence played factors in her upbringing and in her circumstances? I was mad at my mother a lot for being a victim, for allowing herself to stay with my stepfather, who abused her terribly. But I remember the ten thousand things that have led her to be so complacent and unprotective of herself and all of us. She didn't have a father to nurture her self-esteem, raising her to believe she is a princess to be loved and respected by her husband. She lacked a mother to be a role model of strength, and she was let down by a mentally deranged first husband.

Reflect on the situation someone put you in that eats you up now. Are there ten thousand different things that could have led him or her to act in that way?

Consider the realities of this person's life: race, gender, class, job, responsibilities, daily stress.

Consider whatever you know about this person's childhood, like how my father's father was an alcoholic. Consider major events in her life as an adult; is she the insecure, shamed daughter of a serial killer, for instance?

Consider this person's way of processing conversations, criticisms, and daily interactions. What kind of personality does this person have, what fears, dreams, hopes, pet peeves?

Reflect on the historical events that may have been ingrained in the DNA of this person, even if the person didn't experience the event, i.e., a grandchild of a Holocaust survivor or the child product of a rape. Now turn inward to yourself once more. Do you feel any differently now about this person? Do you feel any differently about yourself?

EVERYONE HAS A STORY

It seemed to me that my dad had lived with two fathers: one before he quit drinking and one after. My dad seemed to carry the scars of that emotionally. While I had never seen the scary side of my grandfather to its full extent, I had seen my giant of a father belittled to bits and pieces, spoken to like a child instead of a grown man. But as Grandpa became a Christian, his demeanor became more relaxed and even loving at times, once I came along.

Observing my father and his family made me wonder about my mom and her own family. She was very loving and caring deep inside, but she had a hard time showing this emotion. For thirteen years she was married and primarily a mother and homemaker, but once my father left her for another woman, she was forced to work outside the home for the first time since she was a young teenager. I could tell from the bags under her eyes and the extra work she took on to try to make ends meet that this was all very hard on her.

My mom was raised in a Byzantine Catholic home in Indiana. After her father left, her mother had to raise six children on her own during a time when this carried a social stigma. My grandmother did what she could to survive and carry on. It made her tough and resilient but emotionally unavailable to her children. I realized she had learned from her family not to talk about issues or express emotions. My mother's side of the family didn't hug, greet one another with enthusiasm, or say "I love you." Now I witnessed my mother going through the same thing. I knew this had to be hard for her, especially as she further withdrew from us.

I grew up in the belief that we are to be forgiving of others' trespasses. I used to assume that meant accepting people's behaviors, regardless of their violating act. Now I know that forgiving and forgetting are not the same thing. We can forgive by moving forward with our lives, but we don't have to continue to live with abusive actions. To forgive allows me to take care of myself, to take care of the loved ones I have in my life. Continuing in shame, secrecy, and victimhood would not serve my children nor help me be the example I deserve to set. Therefore, I am the mother who has shattered her own silence, and I am no longer a victim.

This reminded me of my conversation with Rabbi David Wolpe, who reflected on self-pity and victimhood. "I am always amazed by people who have traumatic lives and have no self-pity. They don't ask, 'Why me?'" Rabbi Wolpe said, as I nodded in agreement, thinking of all the remarkable people I have known who have made suffering look so easy, if they showed suffering at all! Most of us, when something tragic happens, ask, "Why me?"

"Why did I get a flat tire?" "Why was I born poor?" "Why did I have to bury my dog?" But when something great happens, Rabbi Wolpe points out, these same people don't stop and count their blessings.

The measure of your sorrow is the measure of your blessing.
—Rabbi David Wolpe

Rabbi Wolpe shared a story about how he started in with the "woe is me" bit when he broke his leg as a kid during summer vacation. "I thought it was the worst thing in the world because for the entire summer I couldn't swim."

The time he would've spent swimming, he spent reading instead. For two straight months, Rabbi Wolpe reveled in the stories of other people, which ultimately planted the seed of his becoming a writer.

"Breaking your leg," he said, "becomes the prelude to a story that actually turns out to be good."

Reframing what happened, whether it's by reframing the story of the person who hurt you or the situation itself, will result in a different ending to the story. The past just became a prelude to your future. This is not to be confused with denial or even justifying bad behaviors. "We simply don't want to give energy to things that suck energy."

Self-Forgiveness

*Be gentle first with yourself if you
wish to be gentle with others.*

—Lama Thubten Yeshe

As difficult as forgiving others is, it is still much more common to let others off the hook than to move on from our own mistakes. Ralph is the perfect example of this phenomenon.

Ralph couldn't take one more day of his job as creative director at a large public relations firm. For a decade, he had played "the corporate game" and planned to quit. But with two small children, he tacked on another five years plus weekend freelance gigs to make ends meet. His wife, Mariah, hated seeing him go through the motions and encouraged him to put his happiness first. So before Ralph finished his sixteenth year at the firm, he quit.

Ralph used money from savings and poured it into his dream—a microbrewery. Beer had been his passion since his grandfather taught him how to make mead using local honey when he was growing up in Northern California. Now, living on the East Coast in a small upscale town, Ralph was excited to introduce his beer to market. But Ralph soon learned that beer making need be less an art and a passion than an actual business. Lacking the acumen for entrepreneurship, Ralph had misallocated his resources to the point where he had to "borrow" from the children's college funds to keep the beer taps flowing. It was time for Ralph to admit the reality of his situation, which included coming clean to Mariah. Ralph was depressed, embarrassed, and forlorn.

❧

If Ralph were your best friend, what would you tell him? I know I would tell him it is preposterous to beat himself up for taking a worthy risk in life. I would tell him that he had the support of his wife, the will to succeed, and the talent and craftsmanship for beer making. He also had a terrific idea and enough money in savings to support his family for an entire year as, around the clock, he single-handedly navigated opening, marketing, and operating his microbrewery.

But we all know how easy it is to be nice to others—to possess the ability to shine a light on someone else's crappy situation; to root others on when they are running out of breath at the twenty-fifth mile. But when it comes to *our own* screwups, misfortunes, bad decisions, whatever, we say we deserve what we get, and that includes *not* being forgiven. Suffering like this is the way we show others that we take our "crime" seriously, know how bad we are, and don't need to be told how pathetic we are because clearly *we know*. Our inward self-loathing and self-blame are outward messages that scream we are unlovable, sucky people—and that's the end of the story.

When it came time to file bankruptcy, Mariah explained that he was not to blame, but Ralph couldn't get past the situation. When she told him he was a good example to his children, teaching them to be brave and believe in themselves, he answered that he acted "selfishly." When Mariah pulled up the biographies of some of the most historically successful inventors and businesspeople, which were filled with tales of failure after failure, Ralph just rolled his eyes.

If you have ever tried to tell loved ones to "look at the bright side" while they were down in the dumps, you know how hard it is to get through to them. And in Ralph's case, Mariah unsuccessfully reminded him that they weren't homeless and the bank would work with them, and he could always go back to freelance work or get a regular job, and many other things, including the old standbys: "We have our health, the children are still young, I love you." Still, Ralph didn't pay any mind to these truths. He refused to see what he was doing to himself and how he was making things worse. He had inner resources that he was turning his back on because he decided instead to spend his energy hating himself.

Ultimately, Ralph stopped communicating with Mariah, completely shutting her out. At night she'd head to bed alone, and he'd open up a bag of peanut M&M's and chase them down with vodka. (The sight of beer made him physically ill.) At one point, Ralph even told his wife that he thought she should leave him because she didn't deserve to be with such a loser. He withdrew from the children, gained weight, avoided his infant son, and was quick to snap at family members and friends.

"We have not a pot to piss in," he said. "I will never forgive myself."

Ralph regretted his decisions, and that regret seeped into every aspect of his being until he finally chose failure over forgiveness. If I could do anything for Ralph, it would be to ask him to heed the advice of Marcia Cannon, PhD, who in her remarkable book, *The Gift of Anger: Seven Steps to Uncover the Meaning of Anger and Gain Awareness, True Strength, and Peace,* says mistakes are a given if you are human, and sometimes a mistake can be catastrophic. "Each mistake can become a healing tool, helping you to grow in awareness, strengthen emotionally, and deepen your sense of inner and interpersonal peace," Dr. Cannon writes. "As you take the steps to make that happen, you may find that you are growing in acceptance and appreciation of yourself, as well as more fully accepting and appreciating those around you."

Dr. Cannon says that when we dissect the word *atone*, it becomes two words: *at one*. Therefore, she defines atonement as "at-onement," the state of feeling at one with yourself and with others in your life. She says, "In preparing to take actions to meet the needs of any relationship, whether it's with yourself or with another, you are really asking yourself, 'What needs to happen in order to feel at one?' . . . As many have learned, this is actually a question worth asking periodically: 'Am I feeling at one with myself and with the world around me now? If not, what needs to happen for me to feel more positively and peacefully connected?' Ask yourself this question and act on your answer."

Love and the self are one and the discovery
of either is the realization of both.

—Leo Buscaglia, PhD

I spoke to Thom Rutledge, author of several bestselling books, including *The Self-Forgiveness Handbook,* a book so robust with raw truth and insight that I couldn't help but see myself in every page and, ultimately, in a very different, positive, and gentle light. Rutledge knows about the topic of self-blame and living in a perpetual state of self-punishment. As a recovering alcoholic himself, he has a laundry list of transgressions he has made amends for, and he does the hard work every day of reminding himself he is worth loving, respecting, even trusting.

People like Ralph are no strangers to Rutledge, as he treats clients like him in his private therapy practice. For one reason or another, these people don't feel they are worthy and so choose a form of self-punishment. From

How to Make Amends with Yourself

PRACTICE THE FIVE T'S

1. Take yourself at face value. Accepting yourself and your flaws helps you remember that mistakes and failures exist to facilitate growth and improvement.

2. Terrible is *not* your middle name. Remind yourself of your good intentions and that you are not a bad person.

3. Tell someone. Talk it out with someone you trust, who will tell you all the reasons why you are loved and worthy of love.

4. Talk to your internal "committee," and tell it to take a hike. Labeling your flaws as an entity themselves and addressing them are helpful steps in recognizing they are not a true part of your identity and are not in line with your core values. They become easier to dismiss.

5. Turn the tables. Ask yourself what you would say to someone in need if that person were in your position.

addiction to eating disorders and commitment phobia to OCD, poor self-esteem is a breeding ground he's familiar with.

I figured Rutledge would know why we are quick to forgive others but so unforgiving of ourselves, even to the point where people who have been forgiven by their "victims" *still* can't forgive themselves. This is what he had to say:

> "Forgiving others is taught and preached to us from the moment we arrive on earth; not much mention is given of self-forgiveness or self-compassion. We are taught that considering ourselves is 'selfish.' The word *selfish* is powerfully charged with negativity—with shame. Certainly no one teaches us that there is such a thing as positive selfishness. Yep: *positive selfishness.* I have a definition for that one: Positive selfishness is self-focus and self-care that not only does *not* harm others, it actually benefits others.
>
> "I think something that makes forgiving ourselves harder is that we tend to associate self-forgiveness with letting ourselves off the hook of responsibility. When I am

working with someone in need of self-compassion, more often than not, the most important thing I need to emphasize is that self-forgiveness has absolutely nothing to do with absolving us of responsibility; self-forgiveness does not stop me from experiencing my guilt when I really have done something wrong. (As opposed to guilt I can feel when I have done nothing wrong—that's a whole other story.) In fact, healthy self-forgiveness is very much connected with the healthy (deserved) guilt when I have done something wrong—put the two together, and then you have the way to genuinely make amends."

A note about the word *amends*. Rutledge told me that someone in Alcoholics Anonymous once made a most excellent point: "Amend" does not mean apology—it means "to change." If you apologize without moving forward toward the change necessary, the apology is superficial, empty, and has nothing to do with practicing self-compassion.

"When I apologize and then do nothing to change, the apology becomes part of the mistreatment, part of the abuse," Rutledge told me. "A therapist once said to me, 'You know, Thom, your bringing flowers home to your wife the day after you were so out of control is every bit as much a symptom of your alcoholism as throwing the vacuum cleaner across the room last night.'"

We don't want to treat ourselves like crap, only to make empty gestures to ourselves. Self-forgiveness requires making amends with ourselves but *following through* with corresponding change, or else you practice nothing more than self-abuse. Self-forgiveness is a promise you make to yourself that you will support yourself while working hard to make a change. It is saying to yourself, *I forgive you,* thereby freeing up your energy to be spent on making change that is true and permanent.

Guilt and Self-Hatred

*Mistakes should be treated like a speck of dust in
the eye. As soon as you identify the problem, don't condemn
yourself or feel guilty for having it. Just get rid of it. The
sooner you do, the sooner you will be free from the pain
it is causing you. Only then will you be able to live a
creative life, build self-confidence, and express
your unlimited potential.*

—Robert Anthony, PhD, *The Ultimate Secrets
of Total Self-Confidence*

Negative beliefs about ourselves will block our ability to forgive ourselves every time. So much of our work on self-forgiveness focuses here. When talking about self-forgiveness, the goal is not so much to answer "How do I forgive myself?" but to address the more discerning question: "Am I a forgivable person, worthy of compassion and love?" Says Thom Rutledge, "We cannot forgive ourselves when we are living from the dangerous double standard of '*you* deserve good things but I don't (because of who I am).'" For instance, instead of believing he deserved to take his shot as a microbrewery entrepreneur and that in striving for a fulfilling career he was acting as a good role model should, Ralph chose to believe that being a married father meant "my life is irrelevant, and I should sacrifice all of myself and my ambitions in service to the security of my family." This is erroneous. Although he faced some financial setbacks, his life was far from over, and as we will see through some of the powerful testimonials in L: Leverage Your Power, the quality of our lives becomes exponentially more critical when others are depending on us, not the other way around.

We all have thought negatively about ourselves at one time or another. Where do those negative, erroneous beliefs live, and why do they thrive on keeping us soaked in our guilt and far away from any semblance of self-forgiveness?

"Guilt is a value judgment placed upon us by an outside authority figure," explains Robert Anthony, PhD, author of *The Ultimate Secrets of*

Total Self-Confidence, among other books. "Guilt is one of the most common forms of stress in our society. The world is full of guilt-ridden people. Unless you are one of those rare individuals who have overcome this destructive emotion, you probably share a variety of unnecessary guilt feelings with the vast majority."

I, too, struggle with an excess of guilt without enough self-forgiveness, and hearing Dr. Anthony talk actually made me feel better. I figure this means we're all in this together, which means there must be a way out of this together. Since most of us have been conditioned to feel guilty whether through religion, family, friends, society, teachers, coaches, and so forth, it stands to reason we can lift each other up and show each other how worthy we are of forgiveness. Dr. Anthony implies this is so, but he cautions that we have major work ahead of us, calling these outside judging forces "guilt machines."

"Guilt is the master tool of the manipulator," Dr. Anthony writes plainly. "All a person has to do is make us feel guilty and we feel compelled to get back into their good graces as soon as possible." While this is true, it's a discussion we will have in depth in L: Leverage Your Power.

For now, we know there are several kinds of guilt, from parent-child to child-parent to societal, but the one we will focus on for purposes of becoming WHOLE is self-imposed guilt. Dr. Anthony says, "The most destructive form of guilt is that which is self-imposed. This is guilt we gift ourselves when we feel that we have broken our own moral code or the moral code of society. It originates when we look at our past behavior and see that we have made an unwise choice or action. We examine what we did—whether it was criticizing others, stealing, cheating, lying, exaggerating, breaking religious rules, or committing any other act we feel is wrong—in the light of our present value system. In most cases, the guilt we feel is an attempt to show that we care and are sorry for our actions. Essentially what we are doing is whipping ourselves for what we did and attempting to change history. What we fail to realize is that the past cannot be changed."

There is a difference between feeling guilty and learning from the past. "Going through a self-inflicted guilt sentence is a neurotic trip you must stop if you want to develop total self-confidence," states Dr. Anthony. "Feeling guilty does not build self-confidence. It will only keep you a prisoner of the past and immobilize you in the present. By harboring guilt, you are escaping the reasonability of living in the present and moving toward the future."

Those words brought me back to Alecia, who had tied herself in knots trying to get through to her husband only to realize that he simply didn't want to be a husband to her anymore. Alecia's values were emotional intimacy and physical connection in her marriage. When she no longer had either, she found it much easier to beat herself up for not living up to her own value system. She also had locked herself down to avoid facing her fear, and she was caught in a blame cycle for supposedly "breaking her own moral code." She had succeeded in adopting false selves in order to feel "in control," unknowingly thinking, *If I'm flawed, then I can actually fix my flaw and all will be well.* They all intersect—fear, resistance, shame, guilt, self-loathing. This combo renders a person incomplete, impartial, broken, and impaired—or more simply put, not whole.

Guilt always brings punishment, and for many of us that punishment is the refusal to forgive ourselves and invite in new opportunities for growth. So to mitigate the guilt, we tend to start doing penance and never stop. The punishment may take many forms, including depression, feelings of inadequacy, lack of self-confidence, poor self-esteem, an assortment of physical disorders, and the inability to love ourselves and others. Dr. Anthony says that those who cannot forgive others and hold resentment in their hearts "are the same people who have never learned to forgive themselves. They are the guilt-ridden people."

With these words, Dr. Anthony answered the burning question I had concerning the difference between self-forgiveness and forgiving others, other than that the first is much harder. There is no difference between them, it seems. Clearly, if you can do one, you are capable of the other. Choose one, and make the other a little less painful. That's a good prescription in my book.

Exercise: What's Your Return on Suffering (ROS)?

We live in a value-driven society. *Yes! Really!* From the physical dwellings in which we live to the quality of our friendships to the interest we earn at the bank, we are concerned about what kind of value-adds specific things have to offer. In the business world, a similar concept is one called return on investment (ROI), a popular metric entrepreneurs and companies use to measure performance of a certain investment. I'll spare you the formula because the world knows I am no spreadsheet fanatic. As I learned to heal my heart, however, I also learned that a lot of my own negative and erroneous beliefs were the giant equivalent to a life of suffering, which devalued my own performance and therefore my healing process. I concluded: *My suffering gives very little return.*

We all want our investments of time, money, energy, friendships, and any other pursuit to benefit us in *some* way. Why is this different when it comes to self-inflicted suffering? If you can determine that your ROS, or return on suffering (cute, right?), is basically nil, would that help you think differently about what you are doing to yourself and consider a change? Figure this to be some warped thought experiment, if not a total stretch of the imagination. If you are paying $200 a month for a gym membership but have put on five pounds this year, perhaps the $2,400 investment isn't well spent. Likewise, if your guilt and self-hatred are preventing you from applying for a job, enjoying a more fulfilling love affair, going back to school, or saying you're sorry, or otherwise limiting you, perhaps they're not a good use of time or energy. *Note:* For this exercise to help you, it takes total honesty and accountability. Are you sabotaging your growth by, as therapist and author Pat Love, EdD, says, "falling in love with your pain"?

So I'm no accountant, but that didn't stop me from making up my new rule, which is to look for a high ROS. If I want to puke during spin class, for instance, it's the kind of suffering I'm going for, especially when my mood and energy levels are raised for the rest of the day. If I spend my day worrying about what some TV producer thinks of my show pitch, well, my ROS is low. What did I get done that day by obsessing over something I can't control?

Decide right now that even if you want to continue hating yourself or keeping yourself on the hook for one of your less-than-shining moments, you can at least be a bit more cognizant as to how it is devaluing you— which, frankly, is just not good business!

Try a Little Tenderness: A Word on Self-Compassion

*We can't stop our judgmental thoughts, but we don't
have to encourage or believe them either. If we hold our
self-judgments with gentleness and understanding, the force of
self-contempt will eventually fade and wither. . . . We have
the power to live with joy and contentment by
responding to our suffering with kindness.*

—Kristin Neff, PhD

I'm belaboring this point, and I'm not sorry. Self-forgiveness is one of the best and most important ways you can treat yourself, but it is also one of the hardest things to do. Until you learn how to truly let go of the grudges you hold against yourself, once you have cleared the path to truly make amends, you will miss out on the critical tool you need to mobilize and take action when the time is right (see L: Leverage Your Power). Compassion is an emotion. Compassion literally means "to suffer with." Among emotion researchers, including Kristin Neff, PhD, associate professor in human development and culture at the University of Texas at Austin, it is defined as the feeling that arises when you are confronted with another's suffering and feel motivated to relieve that suffering. In short, you really want to help. Add the prefix *self-* in front of *compassion*, and it's still an emotion. Now the term simply means that we feel motivated to relieve our own suffering—to help ourselves. Isn't that a nice concept? Why is it so hard?

Dr. Neff, who pioneered self-compassion as a field of study more than a decade ago and has written bestselling books on the topic, says this atrophied practice is a better and more effective path to happiness than is developing high self-esteem. Talk about a hot-button issue. It's so in vogue to strive to be our "best selves," it's almost a little too much to take. So here we are going around playing like ostriches, denying our flaws (which aren't going anywhere, by the way), and we beeline straight to how to feel good about ourselves, to push ourselves to new challenges, and to say yes to what we fear most, even when we are doubtful of our capabilities. But really what we wind up doing is nothing more than flapping our self-esteem flags in a proverbial parade of pretend pride, without completing the prerequisite to self-esteem: *being kind to ourselves.* It's like we signed up to take nuclear physics without first learning the periodic table of elements. That's just backward, and in college it's not even allowed!

In a 2011 article, "Why Self-Compassion Trumps Self-Esteem," Dr. Neff explains, "I realized that self-compassion was the perfect alternative to the relentless pursuit of self-esteem. Why? Because it offers the same protection against harsh self-criticism as self-esteem, but without the need to see ourselves as perfect or as better than others. In other words, *self-compassion provides the same benefits as high self-esteem without its drawbacks.*"

So what does Dr. Neff recommend doing? She says so much that I can only highlight some of my favorite wisdom from her. She describes three essential components of self-compassion.

- **Self-kindness**: You know the Golden Rule: Do unto others as you would have them do unto you. I say we upgrade it to a Platinum Rule: Do unto yourself as you would do unto others. You accept your loved ones in spite of their imperfections (heck, some of my loved ones' imperfections are downright lovable!), so this involves identifying your own imperfections and failings and giving yourself a break by being kind with yourself. Dr. Neff puts it this way: "It [self-compassion] requires *self-kindness*, that we be gentle and understanding with ourselves rather than harshly critical and judgmental."

  Overslept and didn't catch the train to work? Your adrenalized head rush need not be a catalyst for self-deprecation; instead it can act as a stimulus for self-kindness. Maybe you need to get more sleep, or maybe you are taking on too much these days.

  Horrified that you forgot your best friend's birthday? Let that heart-sinking feeling become a reminder of how comforted she was last year when you remembered her mother's one-year anniversary of losing her battle to Alzheimer's. See . . . now you are only *half* bad.

- **Common humanity**: As much as you may not want to admit it, you *are* human, and as one of the human beings, you are required to share

The Benefits of Self-Compassion

When you practice self-compassion, you will . . .

- **Build resilience and decrease stress.** *Psychological Science* published a study that revealed higher levels of self-compassion are related to improved emotional recovery after marital separation and divorce.

- **Increase productivity.** I don't have a research study to point to, just logic. You have more energy and intentional focus on the things you want to get done when you aren't spending your brain matter criticizing what you can't get done. Words have wings, they become things.

- **Foster better body image.** In 2012, *Body Image* published a study that found that people who practiced self-compassion were less obsessed with their appearance, were not as preoccupied about their weight, and appreciated their bodies more.

- **Decrease mental health issues.** A 2012 study in *Clinical Psycholgy Review* showed a decrease in anxiety and depression in people who practiced self-compassion. The study also found that a self-compassionate view reduces the harmful effects of stress.

- **Live happier lives.** A brain-imaging study led by neuroscientists at the National Institutes of Health showed that the "pleasure centers" in the brain—the parts that activate when we experience things like chocolate, cash, and kissing—are also active when we are compassionate to others. Why should this not be the case when turning compassion inward and showing kindness and generosity to ourselves?

suffering and feelings with the rest of us. As a daily practice to cut myself some slack, I remember that if I feel low, most likely someone out there feels like garbage too, maybe even worse. And when I'm celebrating, I remember someone probably just hit a bigger jackpot . . . or just got bad news. We do not suffer alone, nor do we bask in joy alone! Anyone who received a promotion and had nobody to share the news with can attest to what a killjoy that is. As Dr. Neff puts it, we need to feel "connected with others in the experience of life rather than feeling isolated and alienated by our suffering."

- **Mindfulness:** We covered this topic back in W: Watch the Storm, and you'll notice mindfulness peeks its wise head in throughout most of this book. If you allow yourself to experience your emotions without judging them or suppressing them, and instead simply pay attention to them without commentary or judgment, you will feel so much freer. Why? By allowing yourself to experience your emotions fully without judgment, you naturally become more compassionate. By letting go of judgment, you can consider what "ten thousand things" might have led you to behave or react in whatever way caused you to now be displeased. Then your guilt or remorse or shame can pass through you and resolve. Mindfulness is one of those things that you just can't take anybody's word for; it's more like "you had to be there to get it." You must give it a whirl and see for yourself how it manifests in your healing. If you lost your cool with the school principal and think maybe that confrontation didn't fare well for your kid in the long run, don't judge what you did by beating yourself up or avoiding the school from now on. Be more mindful of your action; dig deeper. Did someone not come to your defense when you were a child? Were you feeling patronized by the principal's words? Did you feel intimidated or threatened during the conversation? The feelings will become less life threatening, and the practice usually results in a powerful shift in perspective. The goal is that "we hold our experience in balanced awareness, rather than ignoring our pain or exaggerating it," explains Dr. Neff.

Exercise: Silence Your Inner Bully

The work of author Byron Katie has been a great influence on me. She offers an effortless plan she calls "the Work." Through her strategies, I was able to put a muzzle on my inner bully. Her process to silence the critic within, which you can view on her Web site (thework.com), is called inquiry. It involves four questions you ask yourself whenever you find that negative words are live streaming through your mind. Katie advises that whatever the judgment is, ask yourself in response to it:

1. Is that true?
2. How can you possibly know that is true?

3. How do you react when you believe that thought?

4. Who would you be without that thought?

This sequence of questioning has saved me so many times. I remember when I first started appearing on television, I dreaded watching back takes. Television is new to me, and so is interviewing people for a living . . . well, at least with lights blaring, cameras rolling, producers and directors standing around with their arms folded across their chests, and my inability to anticipate how the person is going to take my questions or answer them.

Anyway, instead of having compassion for myself and patting myself on the back for jumping feetfirst into an industry in which I had no formal training, I played the compare-and-contrast game. It's so easy to do: Everyone on television—everyone whom I have come across, at least—is gorgeous, poised, articulate, and just freaking good at what they do. So here I come, former hairdresser and makeup artist, trying to play the role of Giuliana Rancic. First of all, I hated my voice. I hated how slowly I had to pronounce each word just to trick my mouth into believing it went to voice-over school. I looked fat. I made weird faces when the other person was talking—the "I am intently and actively listening to you and I have empathy and compassion for you" expression. Why did I even make such a face? I truly do feel empathy and compassion for these people. Wouldn't my face naturally exude it? No, this was Hollywood, a place where, when you are a graduate of beauty school and usually answer to people on set hollering "makeup!" you tend to overcompensate . . . just a tad.

The first time I saw myself on-screen, I felt like crap. I was embarrassed by myself and for myself and decided this career was a big mistake. What the hell was I thinking? Worse, if *I* thought this, could you imagine the people who have actually put in their ten thousand hours of television work? What must *they* be thinking of me, insulting their craft like this?

And then . . . inquiry.

1. Is it true?

Well, I'm still here.

Positive Self-Talk

We have to learn to be our own best friends because we fall
too easily into the trap of being our own worst enemies.

—Roderick Thorp

A mother and father and their six-year-old boy hugged goodbye on the first day of school. He was in first grade, so this drop-off was different from starting kindergarten. Little Johnny knew the drill now: where to line up, who his teacher was, and even the smiling faces greeting him. First grade was the real deal—reading, writing, arithmetic, and even daily homework!

When Johnny got home, he sat down with his math sheets and writing journal. His parents sat with him while he tackled the first math problem. He got the answer all by himself, but to his dismay, it was the wrong answer, off by one.

"Well, Johnny," the father turned to him with a sigh, "it seems you are just not good at math."

Does anyone else reading this agree that these parents should be smacked? Should I even insult your intelligence by telling you how this story ends?

Well, the good thing is that I made the story up, but the point is, we go around telling ourselves we suck at things every single day. Having poor Johnny ripped of his potential through the ignorant assumptions of his parents is downright abusive, so why is it okay for you to do this to yourself? To *abuse* yourself?

Any one of us who has tried to look in the mirror in the morning and force a smile and a "Good morning, Gorgeous" knows that talking nicely to ourselves is harder than sticking to a no-carb diet! Somehow we've learned to believe we are subpar, especially if we have been through or are going through a painful experience.

Husband cheated = "I'm ugly and fat."

Daughter got arrested = "I had no right becoming a mother."

You burned the cookies you baked for the PTA fundraiser = "Everyone's going to hate my kid."

Being my own bully started for me at an early age, when I lived in a trailer while friends lived in houses; when friends sported designer jeans and I wore whatever I could dig up at the consignment shop; when girlfriends got asked to dances and I didn't. "I'm poor, I'm dumb, I'm fat and ugly, I'm plain trash."

I said those things so much to myself it's still a habit I'm working on breaking to this day. Now, being on television, I find I'm even harder on myself, but thankfully, I know how to stop it. And the secret, as Anneli Rufus suggested, is to just . . . stop it.

It is said that pessimistic people are more negative toward themselves than optimists. They say meaner things and are eager to self-blame. The venerable Martin Seligman, PhD, in his bestselling book *Learned Optimism: How to Change Your Mind and Your Life*, explains that optimists not only see the world as a "glass half full," but they look at setbacks as temporary and not condemnations of their existence. Pessimists, on the other hand, think their misfortunes are permanent states and representative of their self-worth. Compared to optimists, pessimists give up more easily, have poor health, age faster, and die earlier! I don't know about you, but personally I have enough problems to deal with than adding to them with negative thoughts, which by the way, on rare days when I feel rational, I know aren't even true!

I've searched high and low for the answer to why we do such mean things to ourselves, and while I have found helpful strategies and great workbooks and have listened to a ton of infectious Joel Osteen sermons, I decided to make this simple: Force myself into kindness. Just like I force myself on a treadmill (once in a while). When I wake up and the first thing I want to do is bully myself, I literally stop. I say out loud, "Stop it!" (Kind of like I do when I'm yelling at my kids.) "Today, I am going to be nice to myself." If I need to, I look at the note on my mirror imploring, "Stop it!" And to reinforce my commitment for that day (because I can't make any promises for any day past today), I tell other people what I'm up to. For example, at a birthday party for my daughter, when one of the neighbors said something along the lines of her not looking forward to her Caribbean cruise because she had gained weight, I stopped her. "You know what I decided, Farrah? I decided today we are going to be nice to ourselves. No more talking like that *just for today*." It was that easy. No book, no therapy, no happy pill, just the choice. My neighbor was happy to oblige, as if she had acquired a workout buddy, except our workout was to exercise our atrophied kindness muscles.

If you treat the voice inside your head as something separate from you, as the false self that masks the real self, it's easier and more natural to come to your own defense. Think of that inner voice as Johnny's parents saying really dumb and unhelpful things, and you as the person who comes to Johnny's rescue each time you decide to stop it.

When you are attempting to heal your heart, it is imperative to *stop* intercepting your power by saying stupid things to yourself that are mean, untrue, and frankly not productive. Your power is synonymous with your value. Once you take away your power, you diminish your value, and that's not doing anyone any good.

Your power, your value lies within your flaws, your vulnerability, your story. But when I ask people, from relatives to friends to strangers, what gifts they have, how they think they add value to the world, they're usually stumped. And I hate it every time. Could there be anything more frustrating than seeing someone who was put on this earth for good reason (and I believe we all have been) squander her existence because she talks badly to herself? Not to me. I lived in a house of squalor with a mom who was a victim of domestic abuse, with two grown uncles who needed respite under their own mother's roof, a grandmother who was closed off and alone, and a stepfather who felt so poorly of himself that the only way he could feel powerful was by beating up my mother. I've seen the fallout of "I'm not enough." Two things arise: Either you live in squalor, or you get up and say, "Not today. *At least* not today."

What's Inside:

Open Your Mind

POSITIVE EXPANSION

*"What happens when people
open their hearts?"*

"They get better."

—Haruki Murakami

Welcome to O: Open Your Mind, the empty yet transitory space in the WHOLE journey where a person begins to change from suffering in WH to thriving in LE. It's literally in the middle of your journey—awkward and unfamiliar. With your internal grumbling and past emotions confronted, I hope you find your mind quiet enough to get a glimpse of your future self. But it's unclear what this middle stage is, where it leads. Famed mythologist Joseph Campbell called this phase of the hero's journey "the belly of the whale." The belly of the whale represents the moment of separation between the hero's known world (trauma) and self. By entering this stage, the person shows willingness to undergo metamorphosis. I know that you, like me, are willing.

After I worked so hard and long to change my impulsive reactions and accept my emotions while tackling the frustratingly difficult tasks of forgiveness and facing my anger and fear, I felt winded. The exhaustion was the kind I imagine someone training to climb Alaska's Denali mountain would experience after a weekend training session up a four-thousand-footer—warmed up and inspired by the view, but nowhere near the top of the world.

Feeling some of the freedom of healing, I got greedy. I wanted more. When was the last time I had laughed at anything—myself included? Dreaming and hoping, those survival skills for my child self, had become wastes of time in my adult life. Could I regain them? Now that I have allowed myself to become vulnerable within my own story, how would I continue to write it? What would define me now that I no longer identified with my storm or held the crutch of resentment toward the people I believed had screwed up my life? For the first time, I felt more open—open to what, I wasn't sure— and I wanted to dip my toe in some of the oceans that were missing in my life, so I began to open my heart to what could be in store for me next.

In his book *The Road to Character, New York Times* columnist David Brooks discusses the common denominator of people who made tremendously positive contributions to the world: They all had to go down in order to go up. Brooks writes, "When they had quieted themselves, they had opened up space for grace to flood in." This is precisely what happens in the O stage of WHOLE. With fear, self-doubt, blame, and despondency out of the way, what remains is a wonderful vastness—an open space that we can fill however we choose, a space that longs to be filled by our own grace and inner character now open to a multitude of resources. Brooks continues:

"Before long, people who have entered the valley of humility feel themselves back in the uplands of joy and commitment. They've thrown themselves into work, made new friends, and cultivated new loves. They realize, with a shock, that they've traveled a long way since the first days of their crucible. They turn around and see how much ground they have left behind. Such people don't come out healed; they come out different."

O: Open Your Mind is about throwing yourself back out there—into work, friendships, and even love and laughter. It's about changing attitudes toward the unknown and reframing the way we think and feel about ourselves and our circumstances. Here we take that vulnerability and use it to fill our open spaces with joy and fulfillment. Without the distraction and disruption of our pain, we can take an unbiased look at our stories and find value in our flaws. We change the way we tell our stories to ourselves and others—maybe even stop telling the old stories altogether! Open Your Mind is also where we engage in thought experiments that take our curiosity to the next level, revealing hints of where we want to go next, even when we don't think we have a clue. It's a deeply contemplative stage where we infuse our character with reminders or explorations of our core values, creating a system of beliefs that we will use as our guideposts from now on. We are wise enough now in our journey to know that our goal can never be to come out healed, but to come out different. And that is more than enough.

The Value in Vulnerability

Vulnerability is strength.

—Cheryl Strayed

Once upon a time in a kingdom far, far away lived a lovely queen and her adoring king whose baby girl had just been born. The little princess was just as the queen had wished—with hair as black as ebony and skin as white as snow and lips as red as roses. One day the queen pricked her finger. "Ouch!" she exclaimed. The queen's servant got her a Band-Aid and all was well. The queen and king spent their lives raising their daughter to be virtuous and kind, which made the stunningly handsome and talented prince of a neighboring kingdom fall hard for the princess. And they all lived happily ever after. The End.

Once upon a time there lived a wealthy widower and his beautiful daughter. They were each other's soul companions and made a happy life together despite the sudden passing of the gentleman's kindhearted wife. After a few years, the gentleman brought home a new wife, who had two teenage daughters of her own. The gentleman's daughter jumped for joy over having a new mother, who often took her on lavish shopping sprees, but was especially grateful for her two new sisters. Together the threesome shared secrets of budding romances and borrowed each other's clothes and shoes. Not a day went by when they didn't feel blessed that they were granted the complete blended family they had wished for without the help of any fairy godmother. The End.

Okay, last one (this is way too much fun). Once upon a time there lived a brother and sister whose father was a woodcutter and whose stepmother was a kind and charitable woman. When a great famine settled over the land, the woodcutter's second wife took the children into the woods in search of nuts and berries to fill their aching bellies. When they returned home empty-handed, the stepmother gave the children the last piece of bread and began a prayer circle. Together they realized that while they were starved for food, they were not starved for love. The End.

Believe me, I'm a big fan of happy endings, but somehow they don't seem as satisfying without the part of the story where the hero walks uphill to school (both ways) in a snowstorm with no shoes on. There is virtue in a little struggle, in deflecting evil doings, in the righting of wrongs. Healthy doses of growth and perspective are what come out of a teensy touch of the sleeping death, don't you think? The Brothers Grimm certainly did. And Walt Disney must have agreed that there is no point in storytelling unless a hunter kills a mommy deer, a long-eared elephant is enslaved by a traveling circus, or a wooden puppet is trapped by his impossible longing to become a boy. Heck, the Greeks had cornered the market on suffering long before anybody else joined the bandwagon!

It turns out it's human nature to enjoy watching a warrior embark on a quest to deal with his crappy hand. With no obstacle to overcome, no nemesis to fight, no vulnerability to come to terms with, what's the point of turning pages?

I decided to own my personal tale of woe by choosing to look at it through the lens of a well-crafted hero's journey—the story of a girl with a less-than-ideal upbringing who overcame hardship and tapped her hidden potential in order to bestow gifts onto others. Along the way, the story gets as meaty as a grim story can, with a nemesis father, an evil stepdad, an impoverished home life, and eventually a Cinderella ending.

We often mistake our struggles for the reasons we feel worthless, when the opposite is actually true: It is our flaws, the kryptonite that makes us feel our most vulnerable, that reveal our true worth. Through the hardships in my life, I have learned to be a heroine who knows how to get out of the ties that bind, who kicks some major ass. After all, what lessons would I have to pay forward to my daughter if I didn't struggle with the guilt and shame of a rape and an abortion? What kind of love could I offer my husband without the knowledge of what it is like to live without affection? What kind of advocate would I have been for my son if I hadn't lived without a counselor to lean on? What kind of education would I have given myself if I hadn't been desperate to pull myself out of poverty?

It's like when you hear those people who have lost limbs or thrived after bankruptcy or served time in prison for gang violence say, "I wouldn't change any of it if I had the chance." I'm not yet able to say I would not change the way my life played out if I had the choice. I am still working out whether or not I truly feel that way. However, I could say with certainty that if my own fairy godmother appeared with the promise to grant me one wish, I certainly wouldn't waste it on undoing my struggles.

Rewrite Your Journey

Perhaps some of us have to go through dark and
devious ways before we can find the river of peace
or the highroad to the soul's destination.

—Joseph Campbell, *The Hero with a Thousand Faces*

If our value is found in our vulnerability, then where do we go to dig it up? To our own stories. We are the heroes within our own journeys, to cite the concept created by Joseph Campbell in his iconic book *The Hero with a Thousand Faces*. My perfunctory understanding of his "stages" of the hero's journey is that Campbell identified a common pattern in which mythic stories are told. Imagine which stage *you* are in now, or if you recognize any from the past. Putting yourself in the center of a fantastic story can help distance yourself from how you have personalized and internalized the pain experience. This is an expanded version of what we discovered in H: Heal Your Heart called the ten thousand things—the many different variables Rick Hanson, PhD, says influence people's bad behaviors. The stages of the hero's journey drive a character through his or her experience. We see evidence of this in Hollywood movies like *The Lion King, Beauty and the Beast*, and *Fight Club*, thanks to a book written by Hollywood development executive and story consultant Christopher Vogler. His *The Writer's Journey: Mythic Structure for Writers*, the go-to book for mediums and writers of all genres, explores Campbell's work in a twelve-stage version for writers. So with that in mind, which of the following stages of the hero's journey have been driving you to move through your pain experience in the way that you have, and where in the journey have you created or been afforded the opportunity to turn the corner and emerge triumphant? I'll go first.

Your first step toward finding your value is realizing that what you are concealing is your actual gift, and that each struggle or "stage" serves a purpose. For me to deny who I am—the offspring of a sociopathic murderer—is pointless and does an injustice not only to me but to the world. When I stopped hiding my flaw and shared it with people, I owned my story

(continued on page 96)

Stages of the Hero's Journey, as Summarized by Christopher Vogler, and How I Relate My Journey within It

1. **The ordinary world.** The hero, uneasy, uncomfortable, or unaware; there is a stress or dilemma (trauma).

   Here's an example of my ordinary world. I bought my first house, had two children, and married the man of my dreams. Life was good, except for the secret I didn't want anyone else to know about.

2. **The call to adventure.** Something shakes up the situation, either from external pressures or from something rising up from deep within.

   My six-year-old daughter, Aspen, creates her family tree and sees a hole—my daddy is missing. Aspen comes home eager to fill in the slot with her grandfather's name. She wonders who he is, and I wonder how to tell her. The secret is now a problem: How do I tell my young daughter that her grandfather is the Happy Face serial killer?

3. **Refusal of the call.** The hero feels the fear of the unknown and tries to turn away from the adventure.

   Not wanting my secret to be public, I ponder how I can address my daughter's question without rocking the boat. I go to libraries and look for resources, but none are found. It is too scary to go public, but I wonder how long I can keep my daughter's curiosity at bay.

4. **Meeting with the mentor.** The hero comes across a seasoned traveler who gives him or her training, equipment, or advice that will help on the journey. Or the hero reaches within to a source of courage and wisdom.

   I watch Dr. Phil on television advising a family in crisis and see that he may know how to help me, but it would take all the courage I have to come out publicly, as my secret is heavy and I am scared of how it will affect my life. I go to Los Angeles and meet Dr. Phil. My secret is coming out.

5. **Tests, allies, and enemies.** The hero is tested and sorts out allegiances in the special world.

   I experience people's friendship and compassion, then I also see people judge me for my secret too. I quickly learn who is standing next to me and who is judging me. I start to form a support team and let go of people who are hurting me.

6. Approach to the innermost cave. The hero and newfound allies prepare for the major challenge in the special world.

    I write my first book, *Shattered Silence*. At home alone, vulnerable, I gather my stories and my experiences and place them on the page.

7. The ordeal. The hero enters a central space in the special world and confronts death or faces his or her greatest fear. Out of the moment of death comes a new life.

    My memoir, *Shattered Silence*, goes out into the world. I appear on *The Oprah Winfrey Show*. Critics say everything I feared people would say, but I soon realize that my fear dissipates as I confront it. I now emerge free to be myself.

8. Reward. The hero takes possession of the treasure won by facing death. There may be celebration, but there is also danger of losing the treasure again.

    I take my freedom to be myself and hold my head with dignity. My life is mine without the burden of carrying the secret.

9. The resurrection. At the climax, the hero is severely tested once more on the threshold of home.

    I take a leap of faith again and create the Lifetime Movie Network show *Monster in My Family*. Other families just like me now must cross over too with their secret being revealed. I walk with them as we face the world, not knowing how we will be perceived.

10. Return with the elixir. The hero returns home or continues the journey, bearing some element of the treasure that has the power to transform the world as the hero has been transformed.

    After facing the world alone, scared of people's judgments about my secret, and then again with a group of families, I learn that we are being healed with our disclosure and honesty with ourselves. The suppression is lifted and all are freed. Now the world knows there are more victims in a crime—the direct victims and the people around the perpetrator.

and inspired others to own theirs. Most of the beloved characters in our favorite fiction and nonfiction stories triumphed thanks to their flaw and the overcoming of it. Once I realized that, I returned to my life with my own elixir: freedom.

I had the pleasure of speaking with Barry Vissell, MD, and Joyce Vissell, RN, MS, founders of the Shared Heart Foundation (sharedheart.org), about the power of finding value in our flaws. They open each of their couples' workshops with an exercise in vulnerability, explaining that coming right out with the worst of our stories loosens up the group and makes everyone more relatable to each other. To encourage participants to do this, Barry and Joyce take the lead, introducing themselves by beginning with Barry's confession of his own infidelity (among other things)! I can imagine what the workshop attendees are thinking as they wait for Joyce to bop Barry on the head. Instead, she sits tall next to her husband, smiling and nodding. You would think this therapy couple would be selling some sort of marital bliss story—two free-spirited geniuses coming of age in the sixties, working together and building a practice and a family over forty years—but the first thing they do is burst that bubble!

But their big reveal is that the flaw is not a turning point in their journey but just another pace: Marriage is about screwing up and living to tell about it *together.* Maybe you're screwing up too or feel you're about to. Do not be afraid.

"When you're vulnerable, you can't help but connect, and that connection makes you more human," Dr. Vissell explains. "And when you are human, you are acting from a place closer from which we have come, and that's really divine," adds Joyce Vissell. "Our purpose is to get closer and closer to our divinity."

I remembered a pivotal moment of vulnerability when I was a teenager and saw in hindsight how helpful it was to my not feeling alone and shameful. I had slept at my friend Stephanie's house the night before, and on the morning news program, I saw my dad's face. Fascinated, Stephanie and her mother stopped what they were doing to watch the coverage. I was so embarrassed and humiliated. I thought they knew. I began to tremble. The secrets I kept—all the shame and guilt—had been called out by the national news anchor. Steph and her mom were going to ask me about him . . . they were going to judge me.

Stifling a cry, I ran down the hallway and stubbed my toe on the door. I hurdled onto Stephanie's bed and soaked her pillow with my tears. I told them what happened and who my father was. And in that very process that the Vissells described, my admission resulted in Stephanie's sharing with me something terrible that had happened in her own family. I knew I wasn't alone. I didn't have to be.

Exercise: Go "Lite" on Your Life

At the beginning of the chapter, I recounted watered-down versions of some of our favorite fairy tales—Once upon a Time "Lite." They were completely uninteresting and made no impact whatsoever, leaving readers asking, "Who really cares?" Try to rewrite your pain experience as if it were the most ideal version, i.e., the watered-down, "lite," *uninteresting* version filled with trumpets and rose petals.

I'll do mine first: I was born Melissa Jespersen, raised by loving parents who, to this day, are passionately in love. My home was large and custom built, and it had expansive views of the mountains, which I would hike with several friends during the summer and ski in the winter. I went to college on an academic scholarship, won a competitive internship, was later hired, got married, had two kids, and well, here I am writing this book. The End.

Water down your story and maybe you will see that without the crap that you've endured, the stuff that keeps you awake at night, or the bull you've had to deal with, you aren't who you were meant to be—interesting and flawed. You are not nearly as "divine" as your vulnerable self.

FLEX YOUR VULNERABILITY MUSCLE

Barry and Joyce Vissell believe that the only way to intimacy, with a lover or a friend, is through vulnerability. The only real hope of having a loving, fulfilling, dynamic relationship is through showing another person *all of us*—not just our strengths.

"In our workshops, Joyce and I teach and invite vulnerability," says Barry. "As each participant becomes vulnerable, he or she becomes more beautiful and attractive to all of us. In addition, each person's vulnerability opens our hearts to our own vulnerability. This is the truth about vulnerability: When you share your human frailty, you become accessible, more lovable, and you give permission for others to not have to act strong all the time."

So how do you flex your vulnerability muscle? This sounds simple, but it's quite difficult to do. We are busy and stressed, and some of us simply don't like to be alone. But this is an exercise worth pursuing. Don't be afraid of alone time! Sometimes I walk and just be with my thoughts and feelings, and I even make myself laugh, thinking this person Melissa is nice to be around. Sitting with my own vulnerability has helped me tremendously. Knowing where I have been and how hard I have hurt is one thing, but processing how I feel and think about these things is transformative and happens only with alone time. Seeking the value in my vulnerability has helped me set better boundaries and identify my core values, without which I would never have discovered the path forward.

The Subjectivity of Success

We think we know what success means. Money. Renown.
You can't be successful at everything. You can't have it all.
Work life balance. Accept the loss, where we aren't
succeeding. Make sure what we want is what WE want.
Make sure our ideas of success are truly our own.

—Alain de Botton

The biggest lesson I learned from my vulnerability was how scared and unfulfilled I had become in my adult life. All that hiding and all the shame and guilt and secret-holding and denying who I was: That prevented me from reaching my potential. It wasn't until I had the courage to be vulnerable that I could realize how tragically small I had made my life. The problem didn't end there. Once I admitted to myself and others how disappointed in myself I was, I shut down again. On Facebook I fancied postings of people who were doing great things, including authors and inspirational gurus who didn't know me from a hole in the wall. They were successful; they were happy, put-together enough to be sending *me* inspirational quotes every day or sharing excerpts from their latest TED talks or published books. Those people, my "friends," didn't squander their chances like I had. I had what Michele jokingly called Marlon Brando moments, walking the floors of my home thinking, *I could've been a contender.* With regrets like these, who needs enemies?

First things first. I had to get my head clear and define what success meant to me. It certainly didn't feel successful to be keeping tabs on everyone else's lives and walking along my proverbial waterfront shouting and crying about how my life ended up. I had to get a grip. I wasn't even thirty years old at this point. And then I met the wisest little boy, whose wisdom was like a bucket of ice-cold water thrown into my face, and I was stunned awake. *Success was* mine *to define.* This is the point where I realized that maybe I didn't have to think I was unworthy. Opening my mind manifested a blank slate that I would strategically and deliberately fill with things I wanted, and that included a personal definition of success.

Matteo's Story

Six-year-old Matteo had a playful grin on his face. He finally had control of the ball. With both hands, and with his tongue hanging out of his mouth, he dribbled the ball clumsily down court as spectators yelled his name. "Matteo! Matteo!" The court was wide open, nobody covered the net, and Matteo ran beneath the basket, shot the ball up underhand, and scored! His first basket EVER! The crowd went wild as little Matteo, drowning in his yellow jersey, met his dad courtside to receive his high-five.

"Matteo, you know that was the wrong basket, right?" his dad asked, rubbing his forehead.

"Yeah!" Matteo answered, even more lit up. "But I *still* got it in!"

On that note, the little boy ran off to assume his position with his yellow-shirt teammates, who all celebrated with Matteo. ༃

Success to you and me might be scoring two points for the *right* team. Matteo was there to make baskets; everything else—defense, offense, fouls, people jeering—was arbitrary. Matteo was having fun; his dad screamed from the sidelines, biffing his forehead to death.

How we define success is subjective. It's highly personal. And as we've seen with Matteo and his teammates, that definition makes the difference between having fun and feeling humiliated by failure. Success is an attitude. We should all take a lesson from Matteo.

As we turn our pain into power and move toward tangible change, our problem becomes how we define what we consider success. If it is so personal, then why do we feel so much pressure to achieve "accepted" goals or specific measures of success?

As important as it is to know what you want to pursue in your new life, whether it's a tangible goal, an idea, or a state of mind, equally important is knowing how you will determine when you are successful. What does success mean to you?

Our culture's temperature changes on this issue as quickly as Twitter trends. It also seems to change generationally, depending on the political, social, and economic climate and the priorities born out of it. One thing is for sure: We seem to focus on extrinsic measures of success like—you guessed it—cash and celebrity.

Who better to argue the meaning of success than Peter Buffett, son of the most successful investor in the world and, as of this writing, the third richest man in the world, Warren Buffett. "True success comes from within," Peter writes in his book *Life Is What You Make It: Find Your Own Path to Fulfillment*. "It is a function of who we are and what we do. It emerges from the mysterious chemistry of our abilities and passion and hard work and commitment. True success is something we earn privately and whose value we determine for ourselves."

I figured Peter was being quite vulnerable when he wrote these words, considering he must have known many skeptics would berate him for being disingenuous. I mean, how can a man whose father's net worth, according to Forbes.com, tracked around $66.5 billion in 2016 have the audacity to speak out against our culture's obsession with wealth? Talk is cheap, after all. But Peter won me over with his story of how he and his siblings weren't given much in terms of money from their father. Warren Buffett's gift to his children was for them to gain the satisfaction of making their own way and finding their own success.

"Money should be the spin-off of success, a side effect, and not the measure of success itself," posits Peter.

So if success doesn't equal having our own reality show or even being well paid, then what does it mean? That's something only you can answer. In terms of helping us figure out what would make us feel successful, Peter Buffett asks readers to consider what makes us "personally legitimate." He writes: "In my own view, success should be defined with reference to the substance of a person's achievement. What is someone actually accomplishing?"

It is such an obvious question, yet I personally have never asked it of much I have done. I created two children, a home, and a family. Beyond that, everything else I had done before I went public seemed to be less empirical, and thus I didn't take the time to consider what I was actually accomplishing. Instead, I lived vicariously through other success stories I heard on the news, online, and in my own network.

Other, more philosophical questions Buffett says to consider: "Is she helping others? Is he living up to his potential? Is there passion and originality in her approach to life and work? Is there fundamental value in what he's trying to do?"

Wealth does not bring about excellence, but excellence brings
about wealth and all other public and private blessings.

—Socrates

Perhaps this is why it isn't outlandish to hear the story of the Google exec who quits to help underprivileged children, or the surgeon who moves to Africa to offer free medical care, or the actress who leaves Hollywood for Montana to raise therapy horses, or the Wall Street guy who moonlights tutoring inmates. What happens to the success once the money is gone? Peter Buffett asks, "Does the success vanish as soon as the money spigot is turned off? If it can be undone so abruptly, how solid could it have been in the first place?"

It takes courage to go against societal indoctrination that sets wealth attainment as a primary life goal. To paint our own ideas of success, to forge ahead to make our life what we want it; these call for things that are little spoken of these days: imagination and curiosity. With an open mind, you are better able to make moves that will permanently enrich your life and fill it with meaning.

Personally, I didn't feel successful until after I connected with a community of people, strangers actually, who wanted to share their stories of shame and victimhood. Sharing my story with Oprah opened up my true meaning of success, and it had to do with telling my story, taking ownership of it, and using it for good. I would have never dreamed that kind of vulnerability would have led me here. Just living in the moment without expectations led to an organic growth in what I am called to do. To me, nothing is more rewarding than a heartfelt "thank you" from a stranger or the pride my children have in me. It's the closest thing to a legacy. No lottery can create a lasting legacy.

The Curiosity to Continue

*You don't have to be Thomas Edison. You don't have to
be Steve Jobs. You don't have to be Steven Spielberg. But you
can be "creative," and "innovative," and "compelling,"
and "original"—because you can be curious.*

—Brian Grazer and Charles Fishman, *A Curious Mind:
The Secret to a Bigger Life*

We've summoned the courage to feel the fear and vulnerability that we have been running from. We might even have made some attempts at self-forgiveness and compassion for those who have trespassed against us. We understand that talking nicely to ourselves carries over into all aspects of our lives. Now that we are (hopefully) reconciling with the junk that has filled our hearts and possessed our minds, our heads should feel lighter, with more space to fill now with cool stuff. An open mind is an open heart, and both are necessary when figuring out what comes next.

So are we done? Au contraire! We're just getting started.

Getting started with what? Who knows? Who cares? That's not to worry about right now. Not when we have our secret weapon, the gift of all gifts: curiosity. Not feeling it? Well, then that's perfect, because that's when curiosity is at its height! Because by nature, curiosity is directionless. We can relate to being directionless, can't we? Who hasn't experienced the sensation of drifting along a deserted highway without a GPS? What I love most about the art of curiosity is that it's something of an oxymoron. The more you guide it, the more directionless it seems. But that's an illusion, because when you guide your curiosity, you are guided by it in turn, and it will lead you to your destiny.

Developmental psychologist Peter Gray, PhD, says curiosity is our best teacher, the foundation for learning. Curiosity requires play, and play, curiosity. They are interdependent, and they are what children use to retain knowledge. It is all they need to self-direct their learning—and learn they do. My son certainly learned more about physics by riding his bike up and down hills than he did in school. And it's no different when we grow up. In his book *Free to Learn*, Dr. Gray further explains: "The drive to play freely is a basic biological drive. Lack of free play might not kill the biological body, as would lack of food, water, or air, but it kills the spirit and stunts mental growth." Since most of us are seeking information about our healing for the purpose of fulfilling our spirits and spurring mental growth, I vote for more play and curiosity in our plans. If lack of play and curiosity can be stunting and harmful, then it's logical to assume that both are the antidotes to our confusion and questions about what our lives can be like moving forward.

In her inspiring and uplifting book *Big Magic,* Elizabeth Gilbert credits curiosity with being the secret to finding inspiration when you aren't sure what you want to do next. She tells a really cool story about being in between projects and not having a sense of what she would write about next. Instead of panicking, she followed her sense of wonder about gardening. Becoming curious about the plants and flowers she was growing led her down a rabbit hole of information, what she calls a scavenger hunt, as she followed the trail of curiosity. She read books on subjects she never knew existed, simply because she kept on being curious about things she was learning along the way. The result was *The Signature of All Things*—a novel about a family of European botanical explorers.

When it comes to big magic, you might not get any bigger or more magical than legendary Hollywood producer Brian Grazer, who is on Team Gilbert when it comes to curiosity. He wrote an entire book about curiosity and its importance in our lives. In *A Curious Mind: The Secret to a Bigger Life,* a title that puns his Academy Award–winning movie, *A Beautiful Mind,* starring Russell Crowe and Jennifer Connelly, Grazer urges a call to action to return curiosity to the forefront of our culture. We need more in schools, in careers, and in relationships, he posits. In fact, he credits curiosity as the basis of the greatest success, fulfillment, happiness, and growth in the world. To think something so powerful is naturally possessed by all of us—from the beautiful people who walk the red carpet to isolated scientists locked in research labs to families sitting around their kitchen tables. Curiosity makes the world go 'round.

Imagination underpins every uniquely human achievement. Imagination led us from caves to cities, from bone clubs to golf clubs, from carrion to cuisine, and from superstition to science. We create through imagination.

—Ken Robinson, PhD, *The Element: How Finding Your Passion Changes Everything*

"Curiosity isn't just a great tool for improving your own life and happiness, your ability to win a great job or a great spouse," writes Grazer. "It is the key to the things we say we value most in the modern world: independence, self-determination, self-government, self-improvement. Curiosity is the path to freedom itself."

Grazer's ode to curiosity didn't mention those of us who seek help recovering from painful experiences. He did, however, lay blame on the lack of curiosity for causing entropy—in creativity, in achieving goals, in education, and, surprisingly, in our most important relationships.

Yes, we need to be curious to have rewarding, deep, reciprocal, everlasting relationships with friends, family members, and life partners. Grazer writes that "when our curiosity about those closest to us fades, that's the moment when our connection begins to fray. It frays silently, almost invisibly. But when we stop asking genuine questions of those around us—and most important, when we stop really listening to the answers—that's when we start to lose our connection."

I can't thank Brian Grazer enough for dedicating a chapter to this truth. Being curious about what success meant to me, and even more curious about whether or not I could truly help people, has enabled me to reengage with the world, and that is more important than ever when you're coming back from a difficult experience. Curiosity inspired me to make the effort to connect with my husband beyond the family business issues and housecleaning items we get stuck discussing most of the time; it's made me a better, more active listener when I interview guests on my show, a skill I persistently strive to improve. My mothering style is more attentive and my children talk to me more because I'm interested in meeting them on their terms and on their level. Most important, I try to make a habit of being more curious about myself—what I want, how I feel, why I do or don't do or say things. It's a way of probing without the pain of the actual probe. When motivated by curiosity, it is a gentle and kind way of giving myself attention and the respect of listening to my responses. It is an idea that lets me better understand myself and be open to the fact that I am changing every day.

No longer closed off by our fear, our emotions, and our pain, we can be open to the vastness of our curiosity, something we were meant to exercise. The more we are conscious of our curiosity, the more our curiosity can feed our consciousness, and a wonderful, expansive cycle ensues.

ART AND HEALING

Creating art can be a natural way of letting your curiosity unfold in a safe, controlled way. In a recent four-year study, researchers at the Mayo Clinic found benefits to painting and making ceramics. They reported that people who took up creative activities in middle and old age were less likely to suffer from memory loss. Several books published recently suggest that creativity in art—whether as adult coloring, Zentangle (a form of meditative drawing using a pen and square paper tiles), writing poetry, directing one's own movie via iPhone, or sketching—has the same holistic benefits as spending two days at a luxury resort and spa: lifting self-esteem and untangling stress.

What exactly is art therapy? It's certainly misunderstood, according to Natasha Shapiro, psychotherapist at Tribeca Healing Arts in New York City, where she practices several forms of therapy, including art therapy. Her studio is a wonderland of watercolors, an organized chaos of canvas, crayons, and creativity. You *will* want to make art there, even if you have never picked up a paintbrush.

Shapiro herself is a professional artist, but her art is kept separate from the therapy she offers to clients in her studio. Art therapy can incorporate many mediums, including music, poetry, photography, collage, sculpting, painting, drama, dance and movement, and on and on. It's a way to use language, metaphor, and movement to understand yourself, connect to parts of yourself you didn't know exist, and share and learn to trust and be vulnerable to a practitioner.

As Shapiro explains, art therapy activates creativity, but as a result of the process, people also learn to become more creative in their responses and reactions and coping mechanisms as they move forward in their healing journey. The creative aspect of art therapy changes the brain because clients are engaging in multifaceted activities and are making their own choices—and someone is respecting those choices. It becomes a way of expressing curiosity that is outside of other parts of your life, and it can allow you to strengthen your curiosity muscle in a soothing and healing way.

For me, active curiosity has become a great mindfulness practice. There's no better way of staying in the moment or "being aware of being aware" than by curiously pursuing something or someone and mindfully acknowledging to yourself that you are doing it. Being inquisitive feels (to me, at least) centering, relaxing, and ultimately transformative. When going deeper in for second and third looks, instead of taking something for granted or believing I don't have the time or energy to stop my busywork of the day, I feel connected and as if I am navigating my way through my day and life in the way I have been built and am supposed to.

I remember being in the green room at Harpo Studios in Chicago, waiting to go onstage with Oprah Winfrey, the queen of talk. *Nervous* is not even close to how I was feeling. To momentarily distract myself from my nausea, I asked a producer why the beige room I waited in was called "green." The answer was interesting, so I asked other people about this foreign world of entertainment, about the host, about the producer herself. The more I scratched my curiosity itch, the less intimidated I felt.

Every time I met with television producers, I asked more questions. They explained who the show's key players were: Executive producers ran the show, producers created the content, supervising producers ran the details of the content, and so on. Learning this vernacular helped me understand the operation in which I was briefly a player.

Before long, my curiosity let me into a world where I hadn't expected to belong. After all, I didn't have a celebrity pedigree, a New York University film school degree, or even a communications degree! But still I ventured deeper into this "members only" industry until I felt ready to barge right through the doors, without using the secret knock.

Eventually, I ended up at Warner Brothers/Telepictures interviewing people affected by crime on *Crime Watch Daily*, and I coproduced A&E's *Monster in My Family*.

Brian Grazer says that every conversation can be a "curiosity conversation." How can you have such a conversation with yourself? This process isn't to be confused with self-analysis. In fact, keeping the conversation light might reveal much more than any armchair therapist could uncover. Just as it is more exciting to a child to answer the question "What was the word your teacher said most today?" rather than "How was your day?" you too can encourage yourself to be a tad bit more interested in what makes you tick.

I asked my friend Carol, one of the most creative and imaginative people I know (thanks to her genuine affection for people and her infectious curiosity), how she engages in inquisitive self-talk. Here's what she told me:

When I am feeling an emotion, I let myself experience it; then I accept it. But instead of leaving it at that, I let myself become curious about it. *Why did that person's tone alone spike my heart rate? How come the unreturned phone call is making me scared? What would I feel like if I just pressed Post on my blog without reading it over for a third time?* And then I flip the question. What if my answer were different? What would I do or think or feel then?

Carol's flipping strategy was a eureka moment for me. That is what curiosity is—examining things from every which way. From asking myself *What if I liked vanilla better than chocolate?* to *How would I respond to my son if he were female?* I can rescue myself from the pigeonholed view I have about everything from dessert to child-rearing. With the blinders off, I can truly see the error of my ways, the small victories I have achieved, and the way in which I will choose to respond the next time.

Being inquisitive requires the vulnerability to feel free enough to ask

Five Conversation Starters

The goal is to move beyond the mundane "What do you do for a living?" or "Do you like to travel?" Here are some ideas that have worked for me as icebreakers. You'll see by their nature why trust is so important; these aren't surface questions. By asking things in this manner, you are asking interviewees to share a piece of themselves.

1. Do you like what you do? (Many times I ask this of people before I even know what they do.)

2. What's the most surprising thing you have discovered about mothering, teaching, lecturing, writing . . . ?

3. Do you think you can do something better than what is already being done? How would you do it?

4. What moment in the last week would you replicate if you could?

5. What's your opinion of music (or television, media, radio, movies, YouTube, books, etc.) these days?

questions and to bare a bit of yourself, which is helpful in generating a more interesting and revealing conversation. Trust in the interviewee is important. But having him trust you as someone coming from a pure place of interest and caring is even more vital to facilitating a rewarding conversation for the both of you.

> *It is because your heart is open, and because you enjoy the questions, not because you have answers to these questions. From the moment that you enjoy the questions, then you have an open door to life.*
>
> —Paulo Coelho, *as told to Baptist de Pape*

Exercise: Curiosity Is Just a Click Away

You go online in search of a recipe for apple pie only to find yourself reading about . . . *forestry?* Every time you see a wiki entry that piques your curiosity, all you have to do is click on a word to know more. Curiosity in life need not be very different. Just as a search for *apple pie* led me to click on *ice cream,* which led me to click on *beet sugar,* which led me to *chard,* then *cultivar,* and finally to *forestry,* so can clicking on the ideas and images of outlandish possibilities that bounce around our minds guide us to something we might not have thought of if we didn't allow ourselves the freedom to mentally play around. Curiosity to explore ourselves more deeply prevents us from dismissing things that could be bona fide clues about who we really are and where we want to be heading! What we would normally pooh-pooh as a "crazy thought" is now permissible, thanks to curiosity. Forestry conjured the image of the redwood trees I once visited in Northern California, which in turn reminded me of an old friend who, thanks to apple pie, I have now reconnected with on Facebook!

What you want out of your life as you move through your pain experience can come to you through being playful with your curiosity.

It might sound ghoulish to say I was curious about the women my father had murdered. But it's the truth. Who were they? Were they anything like me? Would we have been friends? Did they like the same things, laugh at the same jokes, listen to the same music? What did they look like, what was in their hearts, what goals and dreams did they have? Who was their family? All these questions nagged at me until curiosity no longer sufficed. I had to turn the curiosity into action, so I mustered the courage to contact the families of my father's victims. What felt like a macabre fascination about lives that were extinguished led me to an understanding of what I was really after, what my true motivation was and still is: to shine a light of dignity on people who impacted this world greatly and in many special ways. It became something of a calling. I wouldn't have begun to explore my belief that every soul has a purpose and each soul is connected if I had pushed away thoughts of my father's crimes—advice, by the way, that I had received from so many people.

Knocking on the doors of victims' families who would see me, combined with my insatiable curiosity about television, led me to where I am now: bringing together families of other violent crimes all over this nation. And it all began with allowing myself to ask, "Who was she?" "What did she like?" "Where did she see her life going?" Simple questions that showed me how naturally we crave the search for answers. Although it's important not to obsess or get weighed down by these searches, we shouldn't feel ashamed about our curiosity to know about hard things. It might not help everybody to dig up the past about people who have created hardship in our lives, but if we're able to entertain the question, spend a little time looking for an answer, and then move on, the process is working.

Core Values

Following my curiosity connected me to my heart's values—the core values by which I live day in and day out. When you open your heart to others' stories and to the vulnerability and trust required to connect in an inquisitive way, you reap an unexpected side benefit: You further redefine who you are and where you are headed. Examining my desire to meet the families of my father's victims shed light on two of my core values, which I hadn't been able to articulate previously: We all matter, and we are all connected.

I define my life by these core values. They are the rules in my personal playbook. When I feel astray or am unsure of something, I consult the playbook. It tells me how to behave, how to act and react, what risks to take, whom to surround myself with, what I am willing to sacrifice or salvage, defend or admonish. And that's just the beginning. Core values are there for you in thick and thin, during times when you are forced to ask the questions "Do I really want this?" "Can I really do this?" and "Why am I acting this way?" Core values are simply the system you live by that reminds you and communicates to others what's important to you. They are a representation of what you stand for and what you would like your life to stand for.

If we don't know what's important to us, we spend a lot of time wandering and wondering what we should be doing. There is tremendous power in discovering and living according to our highest values, and experiencing inner peace is the natural consequence.

Clarity about my personal values has assisted me in making decisions more quickly. Better yet, I've found greater satisfaction in the decisions I make. I first learned about the importance of identifying and living by a belief system from renowned psychologist and bestselling author Pat Love, EdD. She explained that overcoming the effects of trauma, individually and as a family, depends on a person's core value system. In fact, our core values, as I have come to understand them, are a panacea for most of our problems. Could our solutions be that accessible to us?

"Because we are innately designed for the brain to survey the environment and to mark, anchor, and note salience—anything that is important—the brain marks [situations] with emotion. Therefore, in the future, it is the emotion that tells us what to do," Dr. Love explained in a phone interview. "When the same [situation] happens, the marker comes up to help us in the situation. Many of us, because of trauma that wasn't handled expertly, did the best with what we had, but the strategies that saved our lives as a kid have become highly inconvenient in adulthood and are not good for us now. What do we do when we know we are doing it wrong? Choose the response that always brings us back to our core values. What do you do when you are already programmed to fight or take flight or manipulate or freeze? All of these coping mechanisms are in the same room with you. What do you do with the diversity? Take note of your strongest feelings, and trust they will help you act in alignment with your core values. When you are dead and gone, how do you want to be remembered, what do you stand for? What are the characteristics you want to embody? What makes you *you*? You've got to bottom line it. For so many people, it's about managing the coping mechanism, and this is how to do it.

"In circumstances when I have to make a decision that requires an action of some sort, I ask myself, 'What would a supportive or kind person look like in this situation? How would a kind and supportive person act right now? What would a kind and supportive person say?' Now imagine that the person or situation that I am facing is not so kind and supportive, which is probably why I am questioning my response in the first place. The easy and reactive solution would be to be unkind and unsupportive back, but leading my life by my core values of kindness and support reminds me which way to respond—in a kind and supportive manner." The important thing to remember is this, said Dr. Love: When you act out of your core values, the situation may not work out the way you want, but in the end you don't have regret or remorse—two reactions that make you feel yucky.

After talking to Dr. Love, I wanted to speak with my family about defining our family core values, which Dr. Love suggested any family do to help come together in conflict. Each member of the family, being in agreement with core familial values, will act and react to issues in the household in alignment with those core values. Fairness and generosity are my family's values. Now when my teenage daughter argues her case with me, I can ask myself, "How would a fair and generous mother respond?" I expect my daughter to ask herself the same. This not only eases conflict but also opens our minds to new solutions and communication styles that keep us united and not torn apart.

Exercise: Prepare Your Own Playbook

Values are who you are, not who you think you should be to fit in. I'm not talking about morals, which are defined by society. Values are the backbone of life. They are the beacons on your path—in your personal life. When you identify and get clear with your values, something magical happens: They come alive in ways you haven't imagined and illuminate and nurture your entire life from the inside out. When actions and values are aligned, life feels content, in harmony with your purpose; you have peace of mind, even in challenging times.

But with that said, how do you figure out what your core values are? Again, for me, curiosity and saying yes to the thoughts and images in my mind, no matter how outlandish they seemed, helped a lot. If you are stuck, consider the following prompts to engage your curiosity and dig deeper into your heart and soul. Then begin making a list.

1. Remember the last time you felt bad about someone's behavior toward you. What was at the heart of your pain? Did you feel you were treated without dignity or respect? These values might be what you believe are most important to live by and to defend in yourself and others. Add them to your list.

2. Is there a story that brings tears of joy to your eyes no matter how many times you hear or read it? Is it a story about redemption or acceptance? Perhaps these values are a lead. Add them to your list.

3. Is there an action that you define as intolerable, no matter who takes it? Is there something so bad that someone's doing it immediately turns your stomach? Is it lying or cheating? If so, add truth and honesty to your list.

4. Has someone treated you or done something for you in a way that transformed you, made you believe in humanity again, or altered the course of your life for the better? Has the person shown

unconditional love, relentless support, or generosity by opening their home or wallet to you? Add generosity and love to your value list.

5. Do you wish your parents gave or did anything different? Do you want to emulate any of their behaviors? Did they abandon you or neglect you? Expect too much or hover? Add loyalty and trust to your list.

Now look at your list and eliminate, two at a time, the things you could live without if you were forced to. The process of elimination is hard, so this is where you can exercise some of that curiosity. Put yourself in situations and imagine what you could live with and what you just aren't willing to submit to. Keep doing this until you have arrived at your remaining two values. Make a commitment to look at your pain experience through the lens of these—*your*—core values. Your mind will open to new possibilities.

Be Accountable to Your Values

It is wrong and immoral to seek to escape
the consequences of one's acts.

—Mahatma Gandhi

To open our minds, we need to dive deep and reclaim our values, put them to use in our lives, and be accountable to them, so we never again stray from them or make them vulnerable to people or things interested in tearing them down.

Anthony Scioli, PhD, hope researcher, author, and professor, whom we will meet more in depth later in this chapter, has created the following exercise to help us define our core values, stay true to them, and remain in a power position when it comes to painful experiences and challenges.

STEP ONE: WHAT ARE MY VALUES?

Values are important ideas and beliefs that we follow to live our lives. Here are six things that you should remember about values.

1. **Values are parts of your personality.** You will be known and remembered by your values.

2. **Values are like a personal treasure**. Values are your most important possession.

3. **Values work like a compass or GPS.** Values guide your actions and your choices in life.

4. **Values make you feel happy.** You feel great joy when you live according to your values.

5. **Values work like muscles.** Values give you the strength to do your best work.

6. **Values are a badge of honor.** You feel pride when others learn about your values.

The Two Kinds of Values

1. **Rules for living my life**: We call these instrumental values. We can use values like musical instruments to play the song of life. To use values in this way, it is best to think of them as rules or ways of living. An example: "I value hard work because it will help me to reach my goals."

2. **My biggest life goals**: We call these terminal values. *Terminal* means the end or goal. These kinds of values represent goals that we hope to reach. An example: "One of my valued goals is to live a comfortable life."

How to Identify Your Personal Values

1. You can select only a *total of six values*.
2. You must select *two values from each group* (two from A, two from B, and two from C).
3. You would live by these rules *even if nobody was watching you*.
4. You would *put up with some pain or sacrifice* to live by these rules.
5. You would *not let fears or doubts stop you* from following these rules.
6. You would *not let other people change your mind* about following these rules.

Put an X next to your six most important values. Remember, pick *two from each group*.

GROUP A (PICK TWO)

◯ **1. Equality**: I want to stand up for equality and opportunities for all people.

◯ **2. Helpful**: I want to help those who are needy, poor, or in trouble.

◯ **3. Real love**: I want to find or be with my soul mate.

◯ **4. Loving**: I want to be affectionate and gentle with those I love.

◯ **5. True friendship**: I want to be trustworthy and generous with friends.

◯ **6. Loyal**: I want to remain loyal to those I care about.

○ **7. Social recognition:** I want to be respected and admired.

○ **8. Ambitious:** I want to be hardworking and set goals for myself.

○ **9. Wisdom:** I want to be wise and have a deep understanding of things.

○ **10. Capable:** I want to be really good at a job, career, sport, or hobby.

○ **11. Sense of accomplishment:** I want do something great and be remembered for it.

○ **12. Courageous:** I want to be known as brave.

GROUP C (PICK TWO)

○ **13. Self-controlled:** I want to have self-discipline and not be seen as impulsive.

○ **14. Family security:** I want to be able to care for family and keep them safe.

○ **15. Freedom:** I want to be independent and have a lot of choices in my life.

○ **16. Health:** I want a healthy body and a healthy mind.

○ **17. Salvation:** I want my soul to go to heaven or somehow to have eternal life.

○ **18. Peace:** I want to live in a world without war or fights between nations.

STEP TWO: MY RECIPE FOR SUCCESS
(NUTRITION AND DIGESTION)

We get our values from other people. Like food, these values have to be digested and absorbed so we can use them or live them in our own way. From whom did you get each value? Was it one person or several people? How will you use or live these values for yourself?

My Values	Mother	Father	Friend	Neighbor	Teacher	Hero/Famous Person
I value hard work	*She took care of six kids.*	*He worked two jobs.*				*My favorite soccer player practices hard.*
How I will use/ live this value	*For me, this means I will practice many hours to play the guitar well.*					
1.						
How I will use/ live this value						
2.						
How I will use/ live this value						
3.						
How I will use/ live this value						
4.						
How I will use/ live this value						

Example

STEP THREE: STAYING ON COURSE

What habits of mine can help me live according to my values? What habits of mine might interfere with my living according to my values? Are there internal (personal) obstacles like doubts or fears that may prevent me from living according to my values? Are there obstacles (people or situations) outside of me that might get in the way of my values? Who or what can help me live according to my values?

LAUGH IT OFF

Because as a child I seldom laughed, I would never have thought that one of my core values would include finding the humor in most things, but after looking back on my life and all my ridiculous misfortune, finding humor in bleakness has become one of my saving graces. Now, in adulthood, I don't leave home without it.

At first, making self-deprecating jokes or laughing with my husband privately about things outsiders would never consider humorous seemed ordinary enough—like the private jokes we share with those we are truly connected to. But then I dug into the use of humor and found it is a beneficial way of using an open mind to ensure healing keeps happening. Humor is a form of communication, and as long as you keep talking about "it," all is good. For many people, communication is difficult, and thus the option of exercising humor, especially dark humor, could be the sole way these people continue to keep their minds open. We all have to laugh to keep from crying, as the saying goes, which is what the next story is about.

Penny's Story

"Growing up, Vietnam was like a long-lost sibling I would never meet," Penny told me. "I knew 'she' was there, monopolizing my father's thoughts and dreams, but didn't know what she looked like, how she smelled, what she hoped and dreamed for. My older 'sibling' by four years, Vietnam stole my dad from his eighteen-year-old life in 1969 and left him a private, reserved, and sleepless man by 1973, when I came along. Everyone in the family knew about Dad's service, but he preferred to keep his draft a

My Values	My Habits That Will Strengthen This Value	My Habits That Can Interfere with This Value	Possible Internal Obstacles	Possible External Obstacles	Possible Help
I value hard work	I get up early every day.	I watch a lot of TV.	I fear I may forget parts of the music if I perform.	My friends hate music, tease me about guitar.	My music teacher; listening to more music
1.					
2.					
3.					
4.					
5.					
6.					

Example

secret to many acquaintances and old neighborhood friends who, upon his return from war, asked about his absence. 'I was in prison,' he'd answer, because back then incarceration was more acceptable than 'Nam.

"As Dad grew older, and so did we, he spoke a little bit more about his tour in Southeast Asia, treating it almost like nostalgic high school days. He'd pass around pictures of himself and his 'brothers' on R&R in Hong Kong, telling about the time his cousin back home smuggled pepperoni and vodka in care packages to his base, and reminiscing about money wired from his crazy uncle to fund Dad's more indiscrete 'expenses' of war. We didn't even know he had earned a Purple Heart; it just didn't seem to come up in the midst of Dad's lightheartedness about the kind of buffoonery that went on in the barracks filled with teenage boys.

"He'd tease my mother while she grimaced at the sight of my father in the photo—he was wearing a shit-eating grin, and a beautiful young Vietnamese girl sat on his knee. 'Don't be jealous, Susan,' he quipped. 'She reminds me of you; I didn't understand a word she said either! *Ba-dum tsh*.'

"It wasn't the first time my father eluded to the infamous and rampant prostitution that I had only learned about from seeing the musical *Miss Saigon*.

"At the holiday dinner table, surrounded by extended family and some of my college friends, Dad would react to the unexpected ringing of the doorbell by crooning, 'Uh oh, kids. That might be one of your long-lost Vietnamese sisters and brothers coming to claim your inheritance.' We'd all look at him as if he were a little twisted and then laugh riotously. And I'd make my way over to cautiously open the front door." ॐ

Using humor is a natural response to living in a world filled with conflict. In many cases, it's the best answer we have for confusion, uncertainty, and ambiguity. For Penny's dad, his experience during the war left him with a serious case of post-traumatic stress disorder, which meant he was easily rattled by sudden sounds, like unexpected doorbells. For him, responding with a joke was the way he could deal with the complex disagreement going on in his brain; otherwise he would fall victim to a panic attack. The disagreement being: *I am in danger. I am safe. Where am I?* To diffuse confusion, other people may break out in laughter during a heated argument with a spouse, after realizing they've forgotten what sparked the argument in the first place. Or, watching a friend take a giant spill on the sidewalk, they can do nothing else but laugh at the friend. It's not necessarily a funny situation, but it is a confusing one—*Is he hurt? Is he kidding? Can I do something?* The brain, in trying to process all of these thoughts, sometimes releases laughter. What does this tell us? Laughter is as natural and hardwired as crying, fighting, fleeing, or freezing.

Professional stand-up comedians follow many rules and approaches to comedy, but one is the reliance on discomfort and unpredictability. Any one of us going through painful experiences will attest that we aren't deficient in this knockout combo. We are pretty much uncomfortable right now and have no idea where we're headed. But in comedy, both can be good things. So I say, let's turn our pain experiences into good things too and put them to use in our lives. Neuroscientist Scott Weems, PhD, explains in his book *HA! The Science of When We Laugh and Why* that our brains use discomfort not only to solve problems but also "to turn our stress and negative emotions into something positive, like laughter." In tragic circumstances, finding humor, it turns out, is not depraved or off-color, inappropriate or uncompassionate, but a natural defense mechanism.

Think of laughter as a language all its own, made up not of words but of an energetic release of truth and honesty. It provides us with a response when we don't have one. It's literally as if the sentiments of humor express what's in our hearts when our own words are drowned by the inexplicable conflict, confusion, uncertainty, or ambiguity we might be experiencing. Laughter helps me address my feelings, often even before I am able to pinpoint what they are. So many times, as a teenager, I'd run from my home in escape to a friend's house, confused but saying to her, "I don't care what we do; I just need to laugh." I also found that humor was a good way for me to express anger, especially when it came to my own family. I'm not saying that's the healthiest way to cope with anger, and it shouldn't be the sole strategy, but there are researchers who would probably say it's not necessarily the worst. There's truth in our anger, and therefore, as essayist George Saunders put it, "Humor is what happens when we're told the truth quicker and more directly than we're used to."

If we think hard, most of the time we are aware that using humor is the only way to react. "All I can do is laugh" we say to connect with others, to express our volatile moods, or to react to social abnormalities and injustices broadcasted by the media. We literally laugh to keep from crying.

Some of the most successful and iconic comedians came from a tragic upbringing.

What does a little boy who grows up in a brothel, the son of a prostitute and a pimp, have to laugh about? Just ask Richard Pryor.

What does the daughter of two alcoholic parents find funny? Just ask Carol Burnett.

What does a victim of rape laugh about? Just ask Margaret Cho.

What does a ten-year-old who loses his father and two brothers in a plane crash do with humor? Just ask Stephen Colbert.

Whatever the problem, if they kept laughing in the midst of it, it must have meant they hadn't been beaten down.

Even with research (and literature) saying it's so, many people assume the advice to laugh more or find humor in crappy situations is insensitive and plain unrealistic. But is it really?

Alex Lickerman, MD, in his *Psychology Today* online post "Why We Laugh," says:

> Some psychologists classify humor as one of the "mature" defense mechanisms we invoke to guard ourselves against overwhelming anxiety (as compared to the "psychotic," "immature," and "neurotic" defense mechanisms). Being able to laugh at traumatic events in our own lives doesn't cause us to ignore them, but instead seems to prepare us to endure them.
>
> Being able to joke about a traumatic loss usually requires the healing distance of time, however. Losing a limb, for example, may make us suicidal when it first occurs, but with the passage of time we adapt to the loss and eventually may even find ourselves able to joke about it. What magic does the passage of time work on us that permits us to laugh at what once made us cry? Perhaps definitive proof that the alarm our loss raised when it first occurred was, in fact, "false." After all, we survived it and became happy again.

Being able to face an old trauma with humor may very well then be considered a reliable signal of psychological recovery. Perhaps also, by extension, being able to laugh at a trauma at the moment it occurs, or soon after, signals both to ourselves and others that we believe in our ability to endure it (which is perhaps what makes laughter such a universally pleasurable experience: it makes us feel that everything will be all right).

The Bridge of Hope

The very least you can do in your life is figure out
what you hope for. And the most you can do is live
inside that hope. Not admire it from a distance
but live right in it, under its roof.

—Barbara Kingsolver

Vito and Deborah's Story

The entire savings account was wiped out. Any college fund that Deborah and Vito had saved for their daughter, Jeanine, was gone as well. The only option to pay for Jeanine's third visit to the recovery center was to sell the house and borrow from Vito's pension. Deborah had had it up to here with family members telling her it was time to give it up, to cut off their only child. In their opinion, Jeanine was twenty years old now and knew what she was doing—the stealing from her own parents, the lying, doing tricks to get her drug of choice, meth. Vito had been putting up with similar unsolicited comments for nearly four years, since their daughter began hanging with a bad crowd in high school. Vito and Deborah, while stressed, turned toward each other in unity because they knew the reality: It isn't *that* easy to turn their backs on their own child, a sick one at that. An addict.

Since she was sixteen years old, Jeanine had been away more than she was home. Cards and letters arrived on a weekly basis, with the return address of the recovery center, and Deborah and Vito would delight in their daughter's eloquence and love and understanding as to why her parents had sent her away. As he read his daughter's words of amends, bittersweet tears of joy and sadness choked up Vito, who still held on to images and hope of one day walking his daughter down the aisle toward a life he had always dreamed for his little girl.

In the meantime, relatives mocked Deborah and Vito, calling them suckers and pushovers, and the family began to tear apart. Jeanine had stolen from everyone she knew, even her godfather. Her much older boyfriend, who had introduced Jeanine to meth, arranged a burglary of her godfather's home. When Vito bailed his daughter out of Rikers, he and his brother no longer spoke. Jeanine had managed to steal much more than the few gold pieces from her godfather; she had stolen trust and respect from two brothers.

Deborah and Vito had some good friends too who were supportive but also quite bewildered by Deborah's bubbly personality. She laughed a lot and volunteered at a homeless shelter. A self-proclaimed people person, she told everyone stories about Jeanine and never hid the fact that she was in south Florida getting treatment.

Deborah and Vito loved to dance. Music was a big part of their life, and had been since Jeanine started playing the piano at the age of four—she had promise. Jeanine's letters often spoke of how she would take up piano again, and she promised to play side by side with her father again. It wasn't rare for Deborah to spontaneously turn up the radio in her own kitchen and have a "dance party" with a friend who dropped by to have a cup of coffee.

When I asked Deborah how she could laugh at a time when she didn't have a penny to her name, was likely to lose her home, and lost the support of her immediate family, she answered, "I laugh because my daughter can't. If she can't be happy, or dance, or laugh, I will do it for her, with the hope that she will one day do all those things again."

Hope. It's a witless-sounding word, one that doesn't get much respect. To their relatives, Deborah and Vito's hope sounded like denial, foolishness, or wishful thinking. To them, it was a reality, a truth, a faith that they knew their daughter's spirit, and she was more than an addict. They knew and loved her spirit.

"I have hope not only in my daughter's full recovery but a belief in the science of the recovery world," Vito told me. "We know our daughter can do it, but we must also trust the people, her cadre, around her to be equipped to do what they do best."

Then Deborah blew me away with this: "We know our daughter was sent to us for a reason. We are learning lessons and being tested every day, as is our daughter. As long as she keeps working as hard as she is, she is showing us how badly she wants to live and that she knows how sick she is and that she has the power to treat and beat her addiction. How could anyone not keep hope knowing that?"

Hope quite literally is saving Jeanine's life. So there's proof right there that it is not some willy-nilly emotion, but a force powerful enough to keep a family intact and a daughter alive and trying as hard as she possibly can. ॐ

Deborah and Vito not only make hope their shelter, they cling to it desperately. Their storm had thrown them mercilessly into the pernicious waters of addiction, leaving them but a solitary buoy of hope that clanged its bell in a wave-swept song when they needed one. When a storm hits and there's zero visibility, a buoy functions as a signal of safety, a marker of location, and a form of communication. Of course it cannot completely save us, as it is not realistic to keep our arms and legs wrapped around the buoy forever. However, it keeps us buoyant so we can catch our breath, and it offers a respite between the painful awareness and acceptance of the circumstances and the moment we take action—sink or swim. Hope functions this way. Hope is a buoy. It floats, and keeps us afloat, until we sense it's time to swim again.

As we move through this transitory space learning to open our mind, hope becomes more critical. We must keep an open mind to be able to benefit from hope's power.

Depression is a complete lack of faith.

—Rabbi David Wolpe

People who have learned to incorporate the power of hope in their journey have usually done so after being exposed to the utter pitifulness of living without it. Hope can alter the trajectory of a person's life. I have felt lucky that I naturally lean toward hope, but I have seen loved ones close to me shrink within themselves once they lost faith and trust in the wisdom of the universe.

After my parents first split and we kids moved with our mom to Spokane, my father promised that he wanted to be with us—and that his mistress was out of his life for good. But when my father left after just two weeks of moving back in with us, I could barely muster the strength to get off my bed and say goodbye. Seeing the boxes hardly unpacked and then repacked didn't hurt as much as watching the sullen looks on the faces of my younger siblings, Jason and Carrie, as they sunk further into despair. Something had switched off inside of them, and I knew what it was— hope. They looked like empty shells of the children they had once been, and their expressions mirrored what I saw in my mother's face. I, too, was sad and disappointed in my dad, but another emotion swept over me—a burning feeling I had never known before. Intense anger and hatred toward Toni, the woman my father was returning to despite his promises. My rage frightened me, but even in that moment I was grateful to be feeling something, whereas the hopeless states my brother and sister had adopted meant they felt pretty much nothing, and I feared what would happen after they shut down.

Only one time did I feel as if any hope for my future had been cut off at the pass. It was not long after my father's conviction. My father's sister drove my brother and me to visit my father at Clark County Jail in Vancouver, Washington, where he was waiting to be sent to prison forever for serial murder. I hadn't yet begun to process that my dad had done those things—raped young women like I had been raped, and then choked the life out of them, as if they were nothing. I would eventually face that reality, but my teenage self had been clinging to the hope that my father would be able to save us from our circumstances: from poverty and our violent stepfather and absent mother. His visits, however infrequent, at least had been a reprieve from a miserable home life. It was the hope of our savior father, of the sprees to the grocery store, of the surprise road trips, that kept us kids going for as long as we had. But as I handed my brother the filthy phone that made it possible to hear my dad on the other side of the glass, all I could think was *There goes my life.* Yes, my father had taken those women's lives—but he'd taken the hope out of mine and my siblings'. With him behind bars, there would be no more child support, no more groceries, and, most bleakly, no protection from the tyranny of Robert.

I began throwing tantrums and eating too much—which became supplements to my ongoing pity party. But then something beautiful happened, something I consider a blend of miracle and biological survival instinct. I began to try to fill my day with gratitude for good things. I can't be sure where this need to see something, anything good in my day came from, but I do suspect it was from prayer. I prayed a lot. I always had talked to God, universe, or source, although I never quite knew what to call it, so I mostly prayed to God, asking for strength to see the lightness in my day, the blessings I knew I was overlooking. I began to appreciate the little moments of grace that were all around me—the gift of being under the same roof as my siblings, the gift of any day when my stepfather didn't lose his temper.

Once you stop taking things for granted, you create space for hope to enter. With hope come freedom and options and trust that you don't have to live life feeling boxed in or trapped in your circumstances. Using hope, you can find more opportunity for power and therefore become more confident in exercising and leveraging it for your growth and repair.

> *Different moments in life bring different*
> *reasons to be grateful. The gift was to capture*
> *what you have when you have it.*
> —Janice Kaplan, *The Gratitude Diaries*

Due to my need for solace, I was thankful for school probably more than most of my peers. Looking back, my gratitude that I had at least the opportunity to attend a decent school with good teachers made me a much better student than I might have been if I had lived a typical life. I listened intently to teachers, believing they had been put in my life for a reason, hopeful that I was crossing paths with them so I could turn out different from the other members of my family.

Dreaming and believing in them made my days better, more bearable, sometimes even happy. I began to feel alive, and hope sprung within me. At first I hoped for my parents to get back together, then it was to live as a family, then it was to have our own home, then it was for me to make something of myself. Some of these thoughts and emotions seemed unrealistic and childish. But it was this hope that kept me going, kept me alive inside. I didn't realize how much of a role these dreams would play in my future. But now that I understand that hope is not something ethereal but an intrinsic part of our personalities and our humanistic abilities—an observation supported by research—I see how it was a force that made my healing and growing and ultimate present-day success and fulfillment a reality.

Why Hope Works

The mind has the power to turn the immune system around.

—Jonas Salk

In the book *Hope in the Age of Anxiety*, Anthony Scioli, PhD, and Henry Biller discuss more than fifty scientific studies illustrating that hope has healing power because it gives a person a sense of purpose and control in one's life. Dr. Scioli, who is professor of clinical psychology at Keene State College, claims that too many of us are giving up on hope's power to heal us physically, emotionally, and spiritually. He calls it a global hope shortage, which is particularly devastating for those dealing with anxiety, depression, or illness. Hope gets a bad rap mostly because the connotation is of people having their heads in the clouds or holding on to magical thinking. A lot of people who cling to hope are accused of being in denial. But hope is about imagining and believing in a positive future filled with purpose, connection, ample degrees of freedom, and a sense of meaning in life. Dr. Scioli's research contends that since the time of Hippocrates, some of the most prominent scientists and physicians have endorsed the idea that thoughts and emotions play a key role both in becoming sick and in the process of recovery. We need to stop overlooking hope as a major healing component, if not the most critical one, when we are faced with painful experiences. In many resilient people, even the ones on their deathbeds, hope can be the last thing to leave, and even then hope stands strong for something better waiting on the other side.

Dr. Scioli's passion for studying and measuring hope in all aspects of our lives is shared by many other prominent researchers and authors who are fighting to improve hope's underrated reputation and garner it more respect. Among the most tireless and preeminent is positive psychologist Charles R. Snyder, PhD, who, along with colleagues in 1991, devised Hope Theory, which hypothesized a correlation between a person's high hopes and her strong will to succeed and clever resourcefulness.

"Having goals is not enough," explains Scott Barry Kaufman, PhD, in his *Psychology Today* online post "The Will and Ways of Hope." "One has to keep getting closer to those goals, amidst all the inevitable twists and turns of life. Hope allows people to approach problems with a mind-set and strategy-set suitable to success, thereby increasing the chances they will actually accomplish their goals."

Everything we have discussed thus far (concepts like vulnerability, fear, forgiveness, self-compassion, and core values) and the things we are yet to explore (like confidence, goal setting, control, and power) all rely on one common factor: how much hope we incorporate in our lives. Hope is less a wishy-washy emotion and more a practical tool—the basis for everything we feel, believe, and do. How can you take a chance on forgiving someone or yourself if you don't hope that doing so will make a difference? How could we bear the risk of being vulnerable if we aren't hoping to gain connection and meaning? As commendable and heroic the motto "Just do it," people don't *just* dive right in without a proper motivator, a meaningful push. The gamut of research includes studies on hopefulness in athletes, students, workers, children, patients, war veterans, dieters, and more. The common finding? The higher the level of hope, the more achievement, growth, healing, and peace a person experiences.

HOPE TRAINING

Hope can get mistaken for a lot of other things, like optimism, wish making, and even denial. While being positive and looking on the bright side are both excellent qualities, they make up only half the hope story and are not synonymous or interchangeable with hope. In 2008, Duane Bidwell, PhD, associate professor of practical theology at Claremont School of Theology, studied hope among chronically ill children. In an article on CNN.com, he clarified the significant difference between hoping and wishing. Wishing encourages passivity, whereas hope signifies an active stance. "Wishing is the fantasy that everything is going to turn out okay. Hoping is actually showing up for the hard work."

So glass-half-full perceptions are helpful, but how do we complete or increase our hope quotient and get ready for the active hard work we want to do?

1. **Come to terms with the unknown.** Accept your past circumstances as things you cannot change, and embrace the knowledge that life is

all about uncharted territory and going with the flow instead of fighting it. None of us have any idea what each day will bring, but we can be determined to do our best in each moment and believe that it means a lot!

2. **Listen to your intuition.** Hope is an important component of a spiritual life, regardless of whether you consider yourself religious. Likewise, intuition is very much a gift from the universe, and it exists with hope in a spiritual realm. To trust that you have been provided an inner compass—one that is guaranteed to be spot on, never faulty or haywire, and that will always send you in the right direction—is nothing but hopeful. When you resolve to trust your intuition, there is no fear, only hope that you will make better decisions with your divine-given guide that will lead you to your destiny.

3. **Challenge yourself.** Mastery tasks are the ones we do because we know we can. What hope can we derive from driving a car when we've been doing it for twenty years? Prove to yourself that you can move out of your comfort zone and you'll find your hope quotient hits fourth gear. The thrill of taking on a challenge—whether you succeed or not—is what will make you better. Growth and improvement do not happen when we cruise in automatic. Once you get out there and try tasks that you aren't good at or have never tried before, you will trust the process more and believe you can improve well beyond your current speed.

4. **Shared community.** We should assume that someone as close as our next-door neighbor is hurting. Seeking out people to talk to or listen to can provide a powerful source of hope because their survival stories are inspirational. They are the proof that you are not alone in your pain, and also that you can pull through. There is also something to be gained by acting as the support system for someone else. We feel useful and hopeful that we are already gaining wisdom from our pain to share with others who need it.

5. **Moderate your news media.** Not only are stories of war, terrorism, economic crashes, abductions, and natural disasters bad for our

moods, they can curtail our hope quotient, bringing us down into a "what's the point?" mode. I'm lucky that while I work on stories that are based on tragic crime, the families I interview are dramatic examples of life after tragedy and act as beacons of hope that inoculate me against anxiety and depression. I cannot recommend the practice of screening your media highly enough.

6. **Believe in a higher order.** There are patterns and opportunities afforded to us by the universe every day. Everything happens for a reason, even the bad stuff. This is called synchronicity, and I believe in it deeply. That everyone who crosses my path has been made to do so in order to implement a grander plan is my greatest source of hope, and we'll discuss how to make synchronicity more available in your life in E: Elevate Your Spirit.

7. **Borrow hope from others.** When you make your goals clear, people tend to rally around you. Gathering practical support from others in the form of cheerleading or advice, doing some pavement pounding, or even just venting to others will help you keep alive the sense that you are on your way to somewhere better. I felt like I told everybody that I was going to take a shot and pitch a show titled *Monster in My Family.* And then one person would mention they knew someone in the business, another led me to meeting people who loved watching television who told me what would make their viewing more pleasurable, and so on. The process of writing the show treatment, pitching it, and negotiating for it became the primary focus of my life for so long, even the people bagging my groceries knew to ask how it all went! And each one somehow increased the quality and relatability of the show itself.

8. **Futurecast.** Shane J. Lopez, PhD, is a senior scientist at Gallup and has been called the world's authority on the psychology of hope. In *Making Hope Happen: Create the Future You Want for Yourself and Others,* Dr. Lopez writes that our capacity to travel back in time and into the future in our minds, or "futurecasting," is *the* fundamental skill for making hope happen. Futurecasting is how well we can preview the future—which is also essentially a measure of our ability to imagine and hope for improvement. He cites using

the tool known as the Cantril ladder as an exercise each of us can do to test our expectations for the future. It goes something like this: Imagine a ladder. The top represents the best possible life for you, the bottom is the worst. Which step of the ladder do you say you're standing on right now? Which step do you think you will be on about five years from now? "No matter where you start, and no matter how far off your best possible life seems," Dr. Lopez writes, "if you expect to be on a higher rung five years from now, you share the first core belief of the hopeful: 'The future will be better than the present.'" We will soon discuss how the practice of visualization can help you further imagine your best expectations for an optimal life.

Each of these eight ideas will be like putting another nail in the floorboards of your house of hope while beginning to shelter you from the constraints of your pain existence. As you insulate the walls with hints of hope, you create progress. Hope and power go hand in hand: When your hope quotient goes up, so does your power. You are about to make miracles happen. It's time to move to L: Leverage Your Power.

What's Inside:

Leverage
Your Power

HEROIC ACTION

*Those who know how to win are much
more numerous than those who know how
to make proper use of their victories.*

—Polybius

"If you play football long enough, I guarantee you're going to get hurt." Football legend Mike Ditka said that in one of his NFL pregame shows. He and his fellow commentators were talking about the increase in knee injuries since stricter rules had been implemented to protect players from vicious neck, spine, and head injuries. Their discussion made me think of Herman Jacobs, an athlete whom my coauthor, Michele, met through her publishing network. Herman's story is the epitome of just how powerful self-imposed guilt and shame can be in someone's life. But it is also a story about the power of friendship, love, self-forgiveness, compassion, and just plain fate.

Herman was indeed hurt while playing college football for East Tennessee State back in October 1985, but it wasn't the kind of hurt you would expect. He was a college senior on a scholarship when he walked off the field without a scratch, his future in the NFL still in play, but emotionally he would be scarred for a good part of his adult life.

"Everyone thought I was destined for the NFL, including me, and the first thing I was going to do with that NFL success was buy my mama a house—a ranch style—with a carport, a pool, and her own orange tree. I was on the way up."

That is, until a player on the opposing team, the Citadel's Marc Buoniconti, rammed right into Herman. "He wasn't in a car, but he was running toward me at a velocity that could be equated to horsepower. The impact sent us both spiraling into the air and flat onto the nine-yard line. I got up. He didn't."

Just in case, like me, you aren't up on your 1980s college football, Marc Buoniconti is the son of Hall of Fame Miami Dolphins linebacker Nick Buoniconti. Marc was following in his father's footsteps, as a linebacker himself, except word was Marc was even better than his dad.

The hit would determine who wanted it the most, but as he turned up the field to make the first down, Herman heard a voice in his head call out to him, "Jump," and he did. Even the cafeteria ladies would later tell Herman that they saw a picture of the hit in the newspaper, describing Herman as doing "a one-handed cartwheel in midair, feet straight in the sky."

"I don't remember flying like that," says Herman. "I just got up without looking back to the field until I got to the sidelines."

Once there, Herman witnessed every player's worst nightmare. Standing next to the head coach of Eastern Tennessee State, for whom he had played running back for four seasons, he watched the Citadel teammates hover around Marc's unmoving body until the medics cleared everyone out. The doctors and trainers didn't let anyone get close while the spine board was brought over. Their sense of urgency and the hush of the crowd were a terrible foreboding of what was to come, and when Herman heard one of his own trainers whisper, "He's probably paralyzed," all he could think to himself was, *That's it. I'm done.*

Marc Buoniconti was a quadriplegic, never to move his arms and legs again. Days later, when Marc was still comatose on a respirator, Herman recalls the darkness of his own state of mind. "I actually found myself wishing the hit had killed him, so then I could kill myself and call it even."

From his mechanized wheelchair, Marc told Bryant Gumbel on HBO's *Real Sports* that when he hit the ground, his right arm flailed, and he knew something was wrong. "I felt a strange sensation of nothingness," he said.

"He took the words right out of my mouth," admits Herman. "From the day that Marc got hurt, and pretty much until I got the guts up to tell my story, I felt that same strange sensation of nothingness."

Playing college ball represented Herman's ambition to create an identity for himself, to be the one child out of twelve to leave the hardships of his home in Tampa, Florida, behind and make a way for his family to have a better life. It wouldn't include his father. Herman saw him gunned down by an older sister's boyfriend during an argument when he was only five. Herman's twin brother had been planning to move in with him to get away from the bad company he was keeping, but the night before he was scheduled to leave, a dispute over drugs ended in his murder.

"That semester, after Marc's injury, I found myself in a hopeless place, one where I felt no connection with anyone, just this sense of isolation and pent-up rage inside I was struggling to control while I got into this weird, self-destructive obsessive behavior." Herman shakes his head at the memory.

Herman's frustrated coaches and teammates tried to drill it into him, "Marc's the one who hit you. He was coming for you!" But Herman didn't care about logic or facts. Somehow Herman made it through that fall semester, but dealing with the guilt of Marc's injury and losing his twin resulted in a double whammy that took away Herman's ability to focus on school— on anything—and he dropped out with just one semester left. With nothing to fall back on, no degree and no job, Herman wound up playing semipro football in the fall of 1987 for the Johnson City, Tennessee, Bears.

It didn't last. Nothing did. He couldn't hold down a job, couldn't function properly in a relationship. Years of his life became like treading quicksand that kept him engulfed in depression, self-hate, barely subdued rage, and denial. Until two decades after that fateful day on a football field, Marc invited Herman to a Citadel football reunion.

"At first all I could see was that damn chair," Herman says, referring to the wheelchair that's operated by a tube Marc breathes into so he can get around without assistance. "I couldn't look Marc square in the face. My bouncing knee took on a life of its own and my knuckles turned white I was clenching them so hard while I just sat there wishing I could beam myself home. I wanted to say how sorry I was then get the hell out, but Marc cut me off at the pass. Out of the blue he asks me, 'What is it you want to do with your life?'"

The question completely threw Herman. "I was hoping for something more along the lines of 'I've hated you for years,' or 'You ruined my life,' or 'If God told me I could move for just thirty seconds, I'd spend that time beating in your face.'"

Instead, Marc wanted to talk about vocation, as if he were aware Herman didn't have one.

With uncertainty, Herman answered, "I guess I always wanted to be . . . a chef?"

"Done."

Herman didn't know what Marc meant by that one word at the time, but unbeknownst to him, it was the beginning of a journey toward Herman's healing that only Marc could see coming. Marc had, by this time, earned his bachelor's degree in psychology and knew that Herman was in way too deep—a place even *Marc* hadn't let himself go.

Marc invited Herman to his home in Miami and set up a tour of the North Miami branch of the renowned culinary school Johnson & Wales.

They met the admissions officers and learned how Herman could apply. But he had to want it enough to take a chance on himself again—something he hadn't done since dropping out of college. A few months later, Herman called Marc with the news: He was enrolled and had a scholarship. There was only one minor issue.

"I have no place to live," Herman said.

"Live with me," Marc replied.

So Herman moved to Miami to begin culinary school, and Marc had a new roommate. As they grew to know one another, Marc asked pointed questions at unexpected moments and allowed Herman, a shy and private person, the time to answer. Then, when Marc's twenty-four-hour nurse had a heart attack, Herman had the opportunity to take over his daily care. Herman remembers, "When Marc was thirsty, it made me feel so good to bring him a drink. It's like Marc understood that I needed to feel like I was 'doing something' to care for him."

In allowing Herman to help him, Marc had given Herman a powerful gift—the gift of offering his own gifts of caregiving, compassion, and friendship that he didn't know he possessed.

Herman not only excelled at Johnson & Wales, he found his passion and would go on to ply his skills in the restaurant biz. Part of Herman's charm is his own lack of pretense, never more apparent than when he thinks back on that auspicious day of graduation in 2011.

"You know, I get choked up just remembering Marc being there to see me graduate, and how I tried to tell him how indebted I was to him, how much I loved him for becoming the best brother and friend any man could have. I wanted him to know that he was my inspiration—he still is, always will be—only Marc hit me with something I didn't see coming. He told me, 'Herman, you're *my* inspiration.'"

PAIN INTO POWER

Pain can be turned into power, as Herman and Marc have proved. Up until this point, you've been reading about concepts, learning some new philosophies that you may or may not have heard of before, and considering different lenses through which pain experiences are viewed. And I humbly thank you for hanging in there with me. I decided to introduce this section with the story of Herman and Marc because I couldn't imagine a better example of two people with very different "debilitations" using their pain to find their power to gain so much—and give so much! I want you to be as inspired as I was when I heard the story. I want you to be motivated to uncover what you're really made of—opening up to your strengths, talents, and uniqueness—and to learn to trust that nothing is bleak in absolute terms. All the mindfulness and emotional acceptance, the forgiveness and hope practices, and the self-compassion discussions have hopefully built an armor around you, one that makes you feel strong and protected. But there comes a time when empowerment moves from a feeling and desire to an action in the form of strength, resourcefulness, responsibility, and self-determination. The word *leverage* comes from "lever," which is a device used to make something easier to move. The trick to knowing which actions we want to take is to explore concepts and ideas that help make it a little easier to find that power and begin to feel confident enough to use it to your advantage—be it professional or personal.

This is the part of the story when the confused, insecure, naive hero emerges from the fortress of solitude—*after* she has done the hard, introspective work of moving on from her past and discovering her uniqueness—and flies high into the sky. Cue the music.

Believe It: You Are Built to Last

What you are, you are by accident of birth;
what I am, I am by myself. There are and will be a
thousand princes; there is only one Beethoven.

—Ludwig van Beethoven

Jenifer Joy Madden's Web site, Durablehuman.com, is a great one to read if you're ever in need of a little self-validation. Jenifer writes of the Bugatti Veyron, said by many to be the most elite street-legal sports car in the world. It can reach the speed of a jumbo jet when it takes off, and a spoiler under the rear window keeps the car *from leaving the ground.* Typically, I don't think twice about machinery and would not be caught dead at a car show, gawking at waxed and buffed automobiles as their metallic bodies bounce halos of light from behind red velvet ropes. But even *I* might consider petting a Bugatti Veyron. Since its inception in 2005, only a few hundred of the vehicles have been built. The most souped-up model will set you back more than three million dollars. Technicians carry parts for the 1,001-horsepower engine in padded cases, as if they were the crown jewels. Jenifer wisely uses the Veyron as a point of reference for our own value, explaining, as only a hard-nosed science writer can, "Veyrons certainly seem extraordinary until you realize—there is only *one* of you. Consider that there are about 10^{80} atoms in the known universe.

$10^{80} =$
1,000,000,000,000,000,000,000,000,000,
000,000,000,000,000,000,000,000,000,
000,000,000,000,000,000,000,000,000,000

"But if you count all the times in human history your ancestors were neither killed nor otherwise prevented from meeting and mating, the odds you were born are 1 in $10^{2,685,000}$."

Thank goodness for Jenifer because there's no way I'd be doing *that* kind of math, nor have I really ever grasped the function of an atom. Elusiveness aside, Jenifer drove her point home by posing to her readers this question:

"Having beaten *those* odds, don't you think you should care for yourself as much as a Veyron owner cares for a car?"

There was something about seeing these odds factored in such an empirical way that made it click for me: *You were no accident.* In fact, none of "it" has been an accident. I looked back on my past, even my most recent past, and acknowledged that despite it all, I'm still lucky enough to be here. Like it or not, I am, as the famous Ford motto goes, "built to last," or as Jenifer Joy Madden coined it—a durable human.

Now what would I do with this trait of durability? How would I use it to go from "built to last" to "built to leverage"? I don't just want to hang on with one hand to a branch on the tree of life, languishing in midair, as Herman did for so long. I want to plant myself firmly into the earth, as he did when Marc came along, so my roots can grow and flourish. I deserve that. And so do you. We all do, because we are all way rarer than the Veyron, and we have the right to be admired (by ourselves and others) and be treated with the prestige we came to this earth to achieve. We need to own who we are, own where we have come from, and use those not-so-accidental facts as leverage for finding our true value, acknowledging our gifts, and making our presence known until, ultimately, we bounce back so hard that our own halos of light finally ricochet as they have been intended. Consider this my little pep talk to you, because throughout your healing process, you will always need to remember how unique and special you are, that you are more than your pain, and that you deserve to keep trying until you succeed. The point is, we can't leverage our power without lifting our confidence and keeping it sky-high. You are a miracle—an empirical miracle. It's time to act like one.

Confidence

*Confidence is that feeling by which the mind embarks in great
and honorable courses with a sure hope and trust in itself.*

—Cicero

When I started to focus on important, life-and-death things—like what I wanted, what our family desperately needed, and the protection my younger half-brothers deserved from their abusive father—and let go of the fear of being judged, I was able to channel my energy toward discovering the resources inside me. I had a brain, and I used it not by imagining what my life would be like if I had been dealt a different hand but by imagining myself researching what I thought my family was eligible for—a house. And then I stopped imagining and did something. I began by taking one step— research—until I wrote one letter and then another and eventually scored an interview with the local directors of Habitat for Humanity. Seeing how my own action begot more action did wonders for my self-esteem and confidence. It was a lesson I was lucky to learn as a high schooler. Finally I wasn't acting like a victim of my circumstances. I would be the victor of them, or at least die trying. I found my voice.

"What are we still doing here?" I asked my mother when we returned to Grandma Frances's. I had never spoken to my mother about the mess our lives had become, but after weeks visiting my aunt's airy home, I could see how living in Grandma's basement was incredibly unhealthy for all of us. It was time to say something, to confront my mother. While Grandma and Uncle Bart lived upstairs, Mom; her husband, Robert; my siblings, Jason and Carrie; Uncle Lewis; my half-brother, Benjamin; and I were all crammed downstairs in the tiny hole of the cellar.

In my aunt Anne's home, my cousins didn't have to worry about how they were going to get clothing; they just had clothes. They didn't have to wonder about being homeless or where they would move next; they had a warm and clean home, food in their cupboards, and even vacations. Where had we gone wrong? I wanted to learn from my aunt. Although it was hard work, she chose to be a daycare provider so she would be available when her children got home from school. Her paycheck paid the bills, and when she struggled at times, she chose to keep moving forward with faith that things would work out. I resented my cousins for having a secure home and family life. But I also realized their example could be a gift; it gave me hope that I too could have a healthy and loving lifestyle. It's okay to be jealous of what other people have; it's okay to acknowledge that it's unfair that some people have more than others. *But it's not okay to do nothing.* You can be resentful and let that resentment be motivation to move ahead, to take steps, to gain momentum toward your goals, which is why our housing situation became priority number one—the ticket to sorting out the rest of our problems. So I began searching for opportunities to make my goal a reality.

Habitat for Humanity was building homes near my grandmother's house. My mother was skeptical when I told her I thought we were candidates, but I had a *feeling* that I didn't just stumble onto the program's literature. It was for a good reason.

At night I would visualize clean, bright walls and new carpeting and appliances. I thought about what it would feel like to not be embarrassed to leave the front door open for fear people would see inside, or to have a care-free relationship with Jason and Carrie again, as we had before my parents' divorce. I thought about what it would be like to feel normal. Decorating my very own room in my mind's eye made me feel light and joyous. The more I pictured and decorated this bright new home, the more I believed it was mine. In my daydreaming, I could smell brand-new carpeting and see the shine of untouched linoleum. I reveled in the freedom to take a shower without stealing hot water from someone else. I convinced my mother to go for it, and after a nail-biting process, we were approved!

One spring day, it was time to move into our Habitat for Humanity home. The kitchen was new and bright white, with shining appliances that still sported yellow Energy Star labels. Every wall was smooth and perfect, not one nail hole. I could not wait for everyone to leave so I could move my stuff in and celebrate our new beginning. A lady handed my mother her key with an enormous smile!

I knew from that moment that whatever I desired could come to be, if I just believed in myself, in my abilities, and in the generosity of the universe. My visionary home now a reality, I was powerful and in control for the first time. I had identified my deepest need, taken all of the actions that were in my power to take, and opened myself and my family up to others to receive help that was available.

> *Telling yourself what matters to you is one thing,*
> *but equally important is taking control of how you*
> *tell your story to yourself and to others.*

—Amy Cuddy, PhD, *Presence: Bringing Your*
Boldest Self to Your Biggest Challenges

It's difficult to be an agent of change, especially if you feel more accustomed to failure than success. As you move forward, certainly there will be roadblocks, setbacks, and times when you need to change course. But there's a difference between a setback and a power puller; setbacks are moments where you need to take a different tack, whereas power pullers attempt to sabotage you on your journey. Whether they come from outside or within, you must be on the lookout for them.

POWER PULLERS

Power pullers are insidious yet hard to spot. Here are a few I have personally dealt with, and I hope that exposing them will help you avoid their sabotage.

Fear of failure: Why is it so easy to preach to children that the only way to learn something is to fail at it, but when it comes to failing in adulthood, we can't see how it's integral to our continual growth? Being afraid of failure myself, I hate being a hypocrite, but it seems in this area that is what I am—with a capital H, cheerleading my son with "If you don't succeed . . . " as he pretends to gag. We gain so much from our failure—experience, perspective, and the knowledge of how to succeed next time. It also shows that what doesn't kill us really does make us stronger. When my father bought me my first bike, the first thing I thought wasn't *What if I fall and scrape my knee?* Instead, I nearly flattened him as I raced to get my hands on the thing. The possibility of failure simply didn't occur to me—and it certainly didn't stop me from getting back on the bike when I inevitably did tip over.

At some point, our motivation to save face causes us to become self-limiting. But it is time to make friends with failure. Doing so means we are building resilience, being persistent, bolstering self-confidence, and keeping our power. Contract a serious case of the "screw-its." Deal with any failure after the fact, and don't let it stop you from pursuing your goals.

The gem cannot be polished without friction,
nor man perfected without trials.

—Confucius

Cup mind: Cup mind refers to perception and how you relate to your fear. How you perceive yourself, and how you choose to tell your story to others, and whether you own the story as yours depend on how open- or close-minded you are to your pain. In his book *Wisdom 2.0: Ancient Secrets for the Creative and Constantly Connected,* Soren Gordhamer sheds light on our inevitable negative thoughts and emotions by saying we need not deny them but "make space for our experience" with them. I love an analogy he created to expand on this idea of space making. It goes like this:

> If you put a couple drops of blue dye in a cup of water, what happens? The water turns blue. However, if you drop that same blue dye in the ocean, what happens? Not much. It has almost no visual impact. The same dye is put in, but the difference is in the amount of space or volume. The volume of the ocean is so great that the impact is almost unnoticeable.

In this case, the blue dye represents our fear-based challenge; when we keep our minds small and give in to our fear, our perceptions are profoundly colored by that fear. The emotion can completely consume us. Gordhamer calls this cup mind. Cup mind is a small space in which mental energy is quickly and easily threatened by the emotion. The smaller the space, the more controlled we are. In contrast, we can possess a mind full of expansive space so that whatever happens can be felt emotionally while not defining us or dictating the rest of our days, weeks, or years. We can feel the emotion, sit with it, then release it. This is what Gordhamer describes as having an ocean mind. It is a mind that has enough space to be able to see ourselves in the larger context of the storm so that the same amount of fear barely changes us. We are all born with ocean minds. We are gifted with the ability to have limitless thoughts. But as we grow older, we become more limited by outside forces. It's why children believe they can fly and aren't afraid of strangers; their expectations and abilities and beliefs are as vast as oceans. When we feel we are pouring ourselves into a cup, we need to remember that it is against our own natures to be too self-limiting. If going from cup to ocean is too big a shift to make in one step, at least aim for a Big Gulp and see where that leads you.

Saying yes when you really mean no: The saying goes, "Doing the same thing over and over again and expecting different results is the definition of insanity." Nothing represents this better than our incessant need to people please. And what a power puller this is! Look, as a reader myself, the advice to stop putting everyone else first, and to say yes to ourselves instead of over-committing for the sole purpose of being liked, is no news to me. In fact, it's the one rule I know to be true yet *consciously* break all the time. I can see a request coming before it leaves the lips of the deliverer, and my mind preempts by murmuring things like *Say no to running the cookie sale; Sam will kill you if you take another weekend away for the show; Don't cancel your pedicure for this—it's been months.* And then, like an automaton, I go ahead and spew, "Of course! That's fine, totally should work. I'd love to." *Idiot.*

After years of falling on my face with this habit, I finally figured out the trick to saying no. Since I seem to have a propensity for yes, I now try to frame my no in a more positive way. (I say *try* because I'm still a work in progress on this one.) I look back and realize that my whole journey of growth began with a *positive no* to my shame. When my daughter was learning about family trees in her kindergarten class and asked me whether I had a father or not, I realized that I had been so shamed that I was denying my daughter the truth about her own mother. My experiences, if shared with my children, could act as guideposts for them, and not something to make them feel shameful about. Shame is contagious, and sooner or later they would hear where I came from and what kind of childhood I had endured. So I took control by saying yes to my daughter's fledgling curiosity about her heritage by first saying "No longer!" to my shame.

A positive no doesn't have to go as deep as my story. It can be saying yes to your health by saying no to a cigarette; yes to your career by saying no to your boss's come-ons; yes to your granddaughter by saying no to alcohol. Again, it's all about perception. For all my fellow yes addicts, you have permission to say yes as many times as you want, as long as you are mindful to whom you are saying it and the way in which it is framed.

The comparison trap: Another power puller is comparing ourselves to others. We all spend way too much time playing the game of How Am I Inferior at This Very Moment. Just as we try to pull ourselves out of this mind-set, there goes another skinny blonde, a smarter executive, a better broadcaster, a more mindful mother, a more selfless soul, a more doting wife, a better athlete, a more successful person . . . Stop the madness!

We must avoid this trap. We must retrain ourselves. If we stop focusing on how others are stronger, faster, smarter, *whatever*, we can strive to leverage our own power. Like a marathon runner intent on beating his best time, the only person worth beating as a measure of excellence is yourself. Just by considering the ways you might compete or compare yourself to others and by imagining opportunities to break the habit, you are more improved than before, which means you have already regained some control over your goals.

Hanging around with haters and shamers: These are the bitches and sons-of-bitches in our lives. We know who they are, and even though their very presence pulls our power, we keep them around. I'm finally at the age where I have eliminated a lot of the negative people in my life. There's something to be said about the few precious hours you have to yourself as an adult and whom you choose to spend them with. You can recognize the vampires by the way they talk to you—always in a passive-aggressive way that passes judgment disguised as inquisitiveness. Notice that I say "passive-aggressive," because the people who straight come out with it are, at least in my opinion, more honest and not really judging. Sure, maybe they don't have the delivery down or the emotional intelligence or couth to offer an unsolicited constructive opinion, but they aren't out to shame you. The haters and the shamers act as judge and jury because of their own insecurities (see "the comparison trap," above) and therefore want to make you feel worse. To a friend who excitedly shows off her new engagement ring, a hater will inquire, "Don't you think you're rushing into this?" To a grown daughter who wants to go back to work, a judgmental mother might inquire, "Do you really think it's a good idea to put your kids in daycare? I mean, those people could be child molesters." To a mediocre student, a mean stepfather might inquire, "Aren't there other colleges more suitable to your intelligence level?" To a mom at the playground, the shamer might say, "Does your child always act that wild?" Shame. Shame. Shame. The messages are not asking you anything but are designed to state: "According to my gauge: You aren't doing it the right way; you aren't a good mother; you aren't smart; your kid is a problem."

We must be careful of the company we keep. Shamers need to be shut down. No longer do I walk away from shame games replaying the conversation in my head, thinking, *What I* should've said *was* . . . I've finally devised the perfect comeback. According to my own informal, unscientific experiments, the following response has been shown to shut down the conversation about 95 percent of the time and put me back into a power position:

Shaming Sheila: "You mean, your kids don't have a bedtime? *Don't* you think they need a little more . . . *structure?*"
Me: "It works. For me *and* my family."

Whenever it feels as if someone is trying to shame you, make you feel less than, or lay down guilt, be loud and clear that the shame game is no longer working. It's important to let the shamers in your life know you are no longer vulnerable to their judgments. They'll keep at it for a while, testing your fortitude, commenting on even the most insignificant things you do or say ("Don't you think ten a.m. is a little early to order a sundae?"). But when they realize you don't need nor do you seek their approval or validation, they will find some other victim to toy with. Talk about taking back your power. It's an awesome feeling! You'll enjoy your ice cream even more!

Imposter syndrome: The syndrome isn't listed in the *Diagnostic and Statistical Manual of Mental Disorders*, but it plagues many of us and totally kills confidence. In fact, Amy Cuddy, PhD, writes in her book, *Presence: Bringing Your Boldest Self to Your Biggest Challenges*, that her teary-eyed admission of her own imposter syndrome during her famous TED talk was unplanned. In my opinion, her spontaneity in that moment is when viewers, including me, fell in love with her—Dr. Cuddy's vulnerability spoke to us all. Here was a brilliant, beautiful, accomplished, influential Harvard professor who at one time believed she was a phony, an inferior, an imposter in her domain. We too have felt like "we're not supposed to be here." If we haven't, then exactly who are the millions of people who have watched Dr. Cuddy's TED talk more than twenty-seven million times, making it the second most-watched talk in TED history?

When you are standing outside the locked door of an elite, clandestine society and don't know the secret knock, what do you do? Keep knocking until they let you in. Some have interpreted this as "Fake it 'til you make it"; Dr. Cuddy says to take it further: "Fake it 'til you become it." It's all in how you visualize your power.

> *If you really trust your heart, you will not be troubled*
> *by the voice inside your head that discourages you, worries*
> *you, or criticizes you. Cut off any questions starting with*
> *the words "but what if?" and send loving-kindness*
> *and heart energy to yourself.*
>
> —Baptist de Pape

Resilience

*The human capacity for burden is like bamboo—far more
flexible than you'd ever believe at first glance.*

—Jodi Picoult, *My Sister's Keeper*

Good things come when we are ready for change. But making changes means entering the unknown, taking bad falls, and failing most of the time. It requires us to make ourselves bigger when we're feeling small, saying yes when we really want to say no, and celebrating small victories instead of waiting around for the big championship that may never come. What does this all boil down to? Building resilience. What I have found is that getting stronger is not really a state of mind but more of an ongoing process that creates emotional conditions that assist my spirit in its resilience.

The American Psychological Association's definition of resilience is as follows: "Resilience is the process of adapting well in the face of adversity, trauma, tragedy, threats, or significant sources of stress." In *The Pursuit of Nobility: Living a Life That Matters*, organizational change specialist Tim Daniel explains that a healthy organism interacts well with its environment. It is nimble, responsive, and adaptive. "When its environment starts to change, it quickly generates new adaptive measures and means in order to face any threats or to seize any opportunities for its growth," Daniel writes. "In complex living systems, organisms live by these rules. Long-lived species already have ways of preparing themselves for a changing future. Vitality is the ability to do this; pathology is the inability to do this. Sick and dying organisms slowly lose this adaptive capacity."

The way I interpret this is that living without resilience is dying. I don't want to be sick and dying. Do you? Or will we face threats and seize opportunities for our growth, as Daniel describes in the following excerpt? That's what leveraging our power is all about.

> A decadent forest is one in which there are so many dead
> and rotting trees on the ground that there is little prime
> space in which new trees can take root. The dead and

fallen trees have long since ended their life cycle, and now they block the life-giving sun from reaching the ground, where all nature's miracles start. At the same time the living trees are reaching the end of their life cycle, and there are not enough young trees to take their place. Even the few young trees are compromised, clinging to small pieces of subprime real estate. The forest is dying. It is winding down instead of surging up in an orgy of new growth. Entropy reigns.

Nature meets this crisis with fire. Fire clears the ground; it breaks down the rotting trees rapidly so their nutrients are available for the next generation, and it opens prime, sunbathed space that is ready to unleash seeds of new life. The ground is blackened, but soon brilliant green buds will spring up all over the forest. Fifty years from now there will be a vibrant, productive ecosystem supporting countless species. The forest has overcome its own entropy and has left its decadent phase behind.

We are all born with the genes of resilience, but it's a muscle we need to exercise and strengthen, and certainly some people are better at this than others. If we recognize in ourselves even a spark of the desire to bounce back, then we can begin to realize that the fear we have held on to is not as powerful as our constitution for resiliency. Etched deep inside our DNA are the words *never give up*.

According to Robert Anthony, PhD, "We were born with only two fears: the fear of falling and the fear of loud noises. The rest we developed ourselves." What we have created, we can also destroy, and that is especially true for our fears.

Learning resilience makes putting ourselves out there a little easier. Resilience is leverage for our power because resilience helps protect us from emotional harm and humiliation. There is a school of thought that claims people are actually afraid of the good things that might happen when they exercise their resilience and spring forward into their future. We might be afraid that we will actually be successful, happy, and healthy. When I had to decide whether to enter into an arrangement to produce my own show, I almost didn't do it. My husband asked me why I was afraid. Why wouldn't I jump on this opportunity? In my mind, I feared falling flat on my face and letting down the very people I dreamed about helping, people just like me, who have relatives who are monsters, or others who have been victims of crimes. "What if I fail? What if the show sucks? What if everyone thinks I'm a fraud?" My mind was made up. I wasn't going to do it.

"Melissa," Sam said. His voice was stern, and I knew he was ready to drop a bomb. "Be honest. You're not afraid of failing. You're afraid you'll succeed. Afraid that the show will get picked up and aired. And then what? What are you really afraid of?"

He was right. Success meant vulnerability, putting myself out there for public scrutiny, taking on the responsibility of helping others who hurt deeply and never have the freedom to go back to being the same person they had always been. All that equals something more dramatic and upsetting than failure—change. There is a lot to gain from change but a lot to lose as well, and our fear tends to focus only on what we have to lose. It's known as a negativity bias. Our brains are wired to fear, respond to, and remember danger rather than the rainbows that enter our lives. It's a survival thing, another one of our biological components left over from our hunter-gatherer days when we needed to remember which plant was edible and which would kill us on the spot.

We have to understand our negativity bias for what it is—evolutionary leftovers that on many occasions are no longer necessary for our survival. In fact, these leftovers could actually stink up the place if we are not careful to toss them out.

To stay resilient, we need to fight our natural urges and regulate our emotions more mindfully. Dr. Anthony puts it this way: "Overcoming fear and worry can be accomplished by living one day at a time, or better yet, one moment at a time. Forget about the future beyond that. If you live life a moment at a time, your worries will be cut down to nothing."

We need to write down the good things that will come out of bouncing back. I heeded my husband's advice and wrote down the good changes that could come from producing *Monster in My Family*. I am so glad I did.

Exercise: Finding Reason in Resilience

When heading into uncharted waters, no doubt you'll be tempted to turn your kayak around and paddle home. When that happens, build up your resilience by asking yourself the following questions:

1. If I fail, will it be for forever?

   Failure is fleeting. Just because you lost your banking job doesn't make you a failure as a banker. Kid bit another kid at daycare? Don't hang up your parenting gloves just yet. Losing the race for town councilperson doesn't mean half the city has it out for you. Ask yourself what the true implications of failing are. Does someone get hurt? Will it go against one of your core values? Is the threat toward your ego more than anything else? When I first sat in front of television cameras and made myself look like a stuttering fool, my initial reaction was to go to that place that said I am a failure as a career woman and should head back to my bed where I could live out the rest of my days cheering on other people. But after the humiliation subsided, I saw that the world didn't end, and strangely enough, neither did my career. Ultimately, it really is about asking yourself, "If I fail, what is the worst thing that could happen?" If you can live with the answer, then pick up your oar and paddle faster.

2. What will I do after I fail?

   Having a plan B doesn't necessarily mean you will fail at plan A. For many people, it's helpful and reassuring to have strategies ready to face the worst-case scenario of failure. For instance, one of my friends in the entertainment business filed a small-claims suit against someone for allegedly stealing her intellectual property. She was taking a big chance that she might inadvertently create a reputation as a troublemaker, and she had to prepare for her hearing on her own because attorney fees were beyond her means. "I couldn't afford this professionally or financially," she said. "But I also knew I couldn't live with myself if I didn't stand up to the bully, just like I preach to my kids. That would make me a hypocrite, and my reputation to myself and my kids means a lot more than what any strangers in the industry think of me."

   But she did need a backup plan. "I am taking a major risk that a judge won't come down in my favor. I had a real estate license, and I'm already talking to some people about getting it reinstated and working for them. I think I am resourceful enough to make a living doing other things. My sister-in-law is also having a baby, so the option for becoming her nanny is there as well."

It's like the movie *Planes, Trains, and Automobiles*. If the airport shuts down, there is always another mode of transportation to get you where you need to go. The point is that you keep moving even if your first plan doesn't work out.

3. Is your decision time-sensitive?

Pay attention to whether the clock is ticking while you ruminate. If it is, mark your calendar so that you know how much time you have. We can give ourselves paralysis by analysis, thinking way too much about the reasons we shouldn't do something. In the business world, the phrase "fail fast" has made failure a posh thing. So consider how fabulous you'll be as a big fat failure and stop wasting precious time. Windows of opportunity open, but they can always close. Don't let one slam down on your fingers. Then you'll really have something to stop and think about.

Visualize Your Power

*The harder you work . . . and visualize
something, the luckier you get.*

—Seal

I think it was difficult on my mother when I reached the point around my freshman year of college when I no longer considered discussing our family issues as off-limits. She still did, especially when I spoke openly to her of the abuse she was suffering at Robert's hands. My vocal rebukes put Robert on notice, and for a little while he stayed away. People don't like it when you exhibit power. Too bad for them.

Growing up watching my mother working so hard outside our home, only to come home and be treated like a piece of garbage by her unemployed husband, led to my desire to help others escape or recover from similar lifestyles. What was worse than hearing people recount the physical and emotional abuse they endured was witnessing how little self-worth they had. With each strike, a piece of their value had been stricken as well. I know how hopeless things can seem and how simply reading a section of a book pontificating "find your value, use your voice" can be frustrating, maybe even insulting, especially if you are living under fear and duress. But if you find yourself in such situations, I implore you to get help, seek counseling, find a shelter, or call the National Domestic Violence Hotline at (800) 799-7233 (SAFE). If simply asking for help seems daunting, can you begin by visualizing your power? If you find you are not ready to stand up to the bully, whether it's a person, place, or thing, visualizing is empowering. Visualization is a form of self-communication that has been found to influence hormone levels in the brain and change a person's perception of themselves from a weakling to a warrior. If nothing else, you can escape to this power place until you feel you are ready to go public with your pain experience.

Earlier I mentioned Dr. Amy Cuddy and her book, *Presence*. After her TED talk unveiled her research in how nonverbal behavior affected people's perceptions, Dr. Cuddy became an Internet sensation. She made famous the idea of "power posing," which is when a person either physically positions her body or mentally imagines positioning her body in a way that communicates power and confidence rather than fear, insecurity, and weakness. Dr. Cuddy encourages people to make tiny tweaks, such as changing how they stand or sit for two minutes, to create leverage in high-stake situations. Her TED talk and book offer pictures of people displaying different power poses, from putting one's feet up on a desk to leaning over a boardroom table to what has become the most talked about image, the Wonder Woman pose—standing with legs wide, hands on hips, shoulders down and back, head held high. You can practically see a cape flapping in the wind. I love this pose myself, and while I don't literally stand in it, I tend to visualize it, especially when I'm in new terrain, like the television world, where I'm still a novice working with people who have tons more experience than I have. When you think people know more than you, it's hard not to experience the imposter syndrome, where you're thinking, *I'm not supposed to be here; my ignorance will out me soon enough!* Power posing helps with that. I took an informal poll to get ideas of what kinds of power poses other people would choose to visualize. Some of them wound up going beyond Dr. Cuddy's definition of power posing; some ideas represented states of minds and attitudes people associated with certain actions, music, and dialogue. Here's a fun sample:

Michele: Rey in *Star Wars: The Force Awakens*. When she lifts the light saber against Kylo Ren for the very first time, it's as if she is familiar with its force, despite never having controlled it before.

Sabrina: The Travolta pose from *Saturday Night Fever*.

Rob: Rhett Butler walking out on Scarlett, saying, "Frankly, my dear, I don't give a damn."

Nora: Katniss from *The Hunger Games*.

Barry: Axl Rose swaggering with his microphone doing "Sweet Child of Mine."

Scott: Muhammad Ali throwing his hands up after a knockout victory.

Bobby: I pose like the Heisman trophy.

Mike: Definitely Babe Ruth calling his home run with a finger point.

Stephanie: I like to "bend and snap" like Elle Woods.

Behold Your Power Points

*When the whole world is silent, even
one voice becomes powerful.*

—Malala Yousafzai

Power doesn't have to come in grandiose packages of caped crusaders, parades, or invasions. *All or nothing* is not how power works. *Either/or* is not an option—you are not either standing at the end of the boardroom table *or* sitting in the corner taking notes. Power is achieved throughout the points of your uneventful day. Little points of power, like any other small steps, add up to pivotal moments. Not that I am having tea lately with any politicians, but I would bet that if you asked them where their power came from, they would tell stories about small victories and little moments that added up to a feeling of wholeness, competency, and power until they, as Dr. Amy Cuddy has so famously put it, "faked it until they became it."

In reality, small power points created every day are much more substantial than a few lucky strikes that flare up here and there, because the commitment to produce daily power points forges a good habit. Soon enough, your day will seem empty without a power point, which ensures that you keep at it, one day at a time, until the habit elicits a positive change in behavior or a healthy shift in perspective. We've all heard by now the term *brain elasticity* to describe the brain's ability to alter, to fire and rewire over time, by means of various techniques—from positive thinking to power posing to gratitude practices to meditation to exercise. A few good things every few months don't build up the mental muscle required to change our brains, but power points, like a thousand points of light, can spread like stars and illuminate our lives.

These power points were inspired by a pep talk I recently gave a young friend of mine. Eliza is a few months from turning thirty, and boy, is her decade ending with a major storm. Right before the holidays, Eliza was escorted out of the daycare center where she had worked since she was eighteen. Her passion had always been in caregiving, especially to young children. In fact, so many people, her parents included, were frustrated with her for "not doing anything with her life." Eliza saw it much differently. "I didn't care about the money or lack of money I was making. I love children, infants all the way to the pre-K kids I helped teach. It is why I was put on this earth; it's how I feel most myself and successful."

Her life came crashing down when a new child was enrolled in the daycare. A late walker, little Joshua finally got on his feet, and Eliza couldn't wait to tell his mom about his first steps. It was a Friday, and Eliza excitedly shared the video she had taken of him walking. The mom was grateful she had the weekend to spend with Joshua to see him walk some more.

But on Monday, Eliza didn't get the exciting report of Joshua's new skill; instead she was called into the office of her director, who told her that a claim had been filed against her by Joshua's mom for an alleged bruise on Joshua's leg.

"The letter they handed to me said I was being investigated by the state for 'child neglect and abuse.' I felt faint, I heard a weird ringing in my ears, and heat flushed my face." She doesn't remember much after that, except the director apologizing profusely as he informed Eliza that if the investigation didn't go in her favor, the policy required him to suspend her without pay and have her "officially walked out" of the daycare center.

"'Why wouldn't it go in my favor?' is what I wanted to ask him," Eliza said. "The threat of the public humiliation of being escorted out of work, past my colleagues and all the children I had cared for and watched grow over the years, keeps me up at night. I can't tell you how incredibly low it feels to be called something that is so obscene and so completely false."

Eliza continued to go to work with her head held high, and thankfully her colleagues and the parents rallied behind her through Facebook and wrote letters of support to her director. The community's belief in her good name was enough to help her get up in the morning.

Until it got worse. Letters from the state sent to her employer informed Eliza that there was supposed "evidence" that proved she hurt Joshua. What that evidence was, Eliza and her employer didn't know, as it wasn't disclosed to them. As promised, Eliza was escorted out of the daycare center where she had grown up alongside so many of the boys and girls surrounding her.

A month later, Eliza is still out of a job, her credit cards have gone unpaid, and her fear of the unknown has melted any hope she held that the "truth would come out and she would be cleared." The daycare doesn't return her calls; her letters to the state are unanswered. "Why are they treating me like a criminal?"

On the phone, Eliza sounded desperate. All I heard in her voice was powerlessness, and for good reason. All we have in life are our health and good name. When one of them is taken from us, it feels as if our precious personal boundaries have been shat on. Eliza's identity had been stolen from her, and she needed to get it back—fast—or else, I feared, she would make matters worse for herself. I told Eliza she had given away her power to the daycare center and to the state as well as to this mother, whom she hardly had time to get to know. I suggested that she start to work on small things she could do to get her power back. The situation wasn't going to be cleared up in a day or a week or even a month. Too many players were involved, and she couldn't control all the paper pushing that was keeping due process at a standstill. I asked Eliza, "What can you do *today*, something minor that will help you remember you are in control, that you are capable of exuding power? Like power points of light."

We actually had some fun brainstorming; it was definitely a lighter moment in our conversation. Here are the ideas we came up with for the day and the week.

- Contact her network to see about picking up part-time work. Right now she needs to make cash with jobs she has done before. Being proactive, regardless of the result, will make Eliza feel she is helping herself rather than waiting around for other people to get moving on her case.

- Research as much as she can about her rights as an accused person and the rights of the daycare center. Knowledge is power, and hitting the library or the Internet, or talking to some experts, is a surefire way to ensure Eliza understands the language used in formal correspondence with the state, as well as the proper response, when the time comes.

- Do some cleanup around her apartment. What does she have of value that she doesn't need or use that she can sell online and apply toward her latest credit card statement? Keeping current with her debt is important, and there are things of value she can sell without much personal sacrifice.

- Use the newfound hours in her day for healthy activities she usually doesn't have the time for, such as running, going to church to pray, and mailing a card (the old-fashioned way) to a friend or relative for no reason other than to say "I love you."

- Asking her network for help—financial, emotional, and spiritual. This is not the time to let ego stand in the way or allow her life to get messier with debt and back rent. She will always be able to return the favor, with interest.

Will these little power points alone save Eliza's career and good name? Not necessarily. But she agreed they could at the very least be pivotal in helping her remember that every day is an invitation for action, response, and forward momentum and prove that she is competent and capable. Nobody feels good at the mercy of a storm. What we can control, we can control well and leverage to our advantage. These power points *will* keep Eliza afloat, day by day, adhering patches to the holes that have been poked in her raft. The day will come when Eliza gets her chance to formally defend herself, and when she does, she will be ready, feeling competent and sailing off in the breeze of her own power.

I suppose that is all I hoped to prompt Eliza to do with her daily power points—to approach life day in and day out, and not avoid it. In turn, she can retain some personal power and keep her boundaries fenced off from the system that is seemingly out to get her.

Now, with her power points accumulating, Eliza has become more optimistic and willing to take risks, which means she purposefully keeps her eyes open for new opportunities and pursues them to shape her future for the better.

What have you hidden away because you feel shameful? What are the things about yourself, your past, your guilt, your marriage, your disease, your so-called crime that you want to better understand? Have you hidden parts of yourself for so long you're afraid to answer this question, or have you lost a sense of self to the point you don't know how to begin answering it? Leveraging my gifts organically happened once I realized that the heart of my shame—being raised by a man who was serving consecutive life sentences—was my actual gift. It partly makes me who I am. Not the serial killer father part, but the way I choose to deal with the darkness—that is the

If the Shoe Fits, Wear It!

I feel righteous indignation when I think of Eliza; I hate it when bad things happen to good people, and there is a core part of me that empathizes with Eliza's shame. Unfortunately, she slipped into the dark place where being shamed led to feeling shameful for something that she didn't do. For a long time, I was in that dark place, also feeling shameful about circumstances that had nothing to do with me. What I hope happens for Eliza is that her power points help her take back her story, a story that is rightfully hers. Back in O: Open Your Mind, we discussed how our lives are stories and we are the heroes of them. When a crisis happens and our core values are challenged, pieces of us break off and drift away, and we feel powerless in our story. It's the equivalent of handing the pen to someone less equipped and saying, resigned and defeated, "Here, *you* finish the story." That is the opposite of power, the antithesis of self-confidence. Eliza knows who she really is, and she is leveraging whatever power she can to take back her story as best she can with the resources she has available.

There is no better way to disarm a crisis than by accepting it. When I was deciding whether to go public about who my dad was, one of my driving reasons to do so was to be in control of my story instead of having other people control it. By sharing my life the way I experienced it, I could prevent my reality from becoming a rumor—an exaggeration or an untruth. I'd be the director and take my tale where I'd like it to go, so that it could not be used against me. The adage "If the shoes fits, wear it" applies here. I put on the old scuffed-up boot and paraded around in it unapologetically. *Happy Face Killer? Yup, that's my dad. What's it to ya?*

greatest evidence of who I truly am. Whether you leverage your strengths or lose them will also tell the world and yourself who you truly are. That's why your story, whether it's the stuff of fairy tales or Greek tragedies, *must* be told by you. Don't you want to be the one who decides how it ends or where it leads? That is the beginning of regaining your self-confidence and being self-aware.

Most likely, whatever you have hidden away keeps your gifts locked up too. So unlocking those unseen parts will naturally lead you to great benefits—discovering the good stuff. You can't dig for gold without first delving in the mud. During our formative years, far too many of us lacked the people who pointed out what we are good at or who noticed where our interests seem to lie and offered us more opportunities to experience them. As I grew older, I shut down and didn't get to know myself well. I knew I liked aesthetic things, but I didn't think that made me different from other girls or women who liked to look pretty, do their hair, and experiment with makeup. After I became a professional makeup artist, I never considered my occupation as a gift or strength. Instead, what resonated with me was feedback from my book *Shattered Silence*. I was fueled by e-mails from strangers telling me I struck a chord, that I was brave, or that I should consider getting "out there" to help others in a larger way.

My friend Tina also needed positive feedback to finally make her realize that her calling was more than being a caregiver to her ailing mother-in-law. Married in her late teens, Tina was a stay-at-home mom for most of her adult life. With her kids away at college, she volunteered to take in her husband's terminally ill mother, an undertaking not for the faint of heart. Tina bathed and fed Marie, took her to doctors' appointments, administered her medication, and monitored her health as it began to deteriorate.

"Tina," Marie said, looking up in her face with grateful eyes. "I am dying, but yet you make me so happy. You take better care of me than any nurse or doctor can. You should go to medical school."

Tina laughed. She had only a high school diploma, and while she did understand much of the research she had read about her mother-in-law's heart disease, medical school seemed like a ludicrous idea.

"I truly thought the meds I was giving her kicked in *too* much," Tina recalled with a laugh.

After Marie passed away, Tina's days became mundane once more, and those empty spaces were filled with her researching healthcare jobs. She enrolled in community college and worked toward her associate's degree. When her children returned home from college for good, it was a full house again, and Marie was torn between helping her children with their own résumés and job hunts and her own. Her whole family urged Marie to focus on herself, and soon she enrolled as a premed student at the University of Texas.

Today my friend Tina is a board-certified medical internist at the age of forty-three!

Whether someone takes notice of a talent for you or you discover your skills on your own, there are ways to figure out where your strengths lie and make them a part of your power. For example, does a hobby have to be *just* a hobby? Whether you love to decorate, write poetry, read, or tell jokes, can you make a living with your skill or teach others your gift so they can use it to leverage their own power? Who says you can't start a decorating blog and gain advertising dollars through it, or create a line of greeting cards with your rhyming acumen? Why can't you tutor people or teach them to read? Or take a stab at writing a comedic script? Your hobby can be transformative to you and others.

Do you notice when you are complimented? Sometimes we don't see ourselves as clearly as others do. Tina didn't notice that her caregiving was an actual skill until Marie told her repeatedly what a natural she was. If more than one person is giving you the same kudos on different occasions, shouldn't you take that as a hint?

How to Set Goals When You Don't Know What You Want

*Sometimes in life you don't know how to
make the change. But the very fact that you are
committed to making it, that you are clear that it
is necessary, opens up new possibilities.*

—Marianne Williamson

Charon didn't know precisely what she wanted, but she knew what she could no longer stand.

"I used to think it was a gross exaggeration when people said they look in the mirror and don't recognize themselves. I mean, how could that be? But I kid you not, it's exactly what happened to me. I didn't expect to be scared of the unidentified reflection. It wasn't prompted; there was no particular trigger or catalyst or special occasion. It was a typical Groundhog's Day at my mother-in-law's house, where I had been living for years, raising my three children as a single mother. It was sometime around November, because the holidays were coming and stressing me out. *How would I make this Christmas happy for the kids?* I didn't have a job, a high school diploma, a driver's license, or a credit score. Their father was long gone, estranged from us and his parents, probably in jail or getting high somewhere.

"The anxious dialogue of 'what-ifs' and 'how-will-I' had been a run-on sentence in my mind on most days, but today was different. The dialogue wasn't just mindless rambling and worrying; it made an actual impact. I was in the bathroom, putting on a fresh pair of pajamas because I showered in the morning and put new ones on ritualistically. (No need to put actual clothes on as, for the most part, I was an undiagnosed agoraphobic.) But in the bathroom mirror, *she* appeared to me. All I had to do was notice her. She was a vision, all right. A slob. A thirty-four-year-old woman who looked fifty. Cue the music, just like in the movies. I got a little closer to the rusty medicine cabinet, thinking maybe that would help the ugliness—the baggy eyes and extra belly fat—vanish. But as close as I got before my nose touched the glass, all I could get was a clearer glimpse of the deadness of some stranger's dilated pupils. I looked closer into those eyes, desperately thinking that doing so would reveal a soul, a friendly reminder that Charon was still in there somewhere. It was no use. The best way I can describe it is, it was like there was a coat of shellac where my baby browns used to be."

Somewhere among all the abuses and neglect of her alcoholic father, the narcissistic and criminal behavior of her children's father, and the general worthlessness she had come to identify with, Charon had ceased to exist.

"It was the first time I had admitted and processed the hard reality that Charon was no longer here, her body had left the building to make room for a body snatched by victimhood," she continued. "The soul that I had been taught was present inside each and every one of us had gone elsewhere, or I had killed her; I'm not sure if she had left my body or I had left her behind. It didn't matter. So I did what came naturally. I mourned her."

I related to Charon's tears for her lost self. That is what can happen when your pain makes you feel small, when you shrink your existence to the size of a cup and let the blue dye pour in. But in that moment when she saw herself in the mirror, Charon acknowledged her storm and watched it. As low a moment as it may have seemed, it was the first step on her journey up through her pain, because only after that acknowledgment could she begin to flex her resilience muscle.

"On New Year's Eve," Charon said, "I made six declarations to my children, my mother- and father-in-law, and, most important, to myself: Before 2015 was over, I would (1) lose weight to lower my skyrocketing blood pressure; (2) receive my high school diploma—not a GED, but the real thing; (3) get my driver's license; (4) find a job; (5) raise my credit score; (6) start college.

"Pretty ballsy for a person who had zero self-confidence or resources, I know, but they were the things that *had to be* done for me to discover who the real Charon was—to invite back in the spirit that had gone or I had abandoned. I became less afraid of putting myself out there in such major ways because I had finally become more afraid that I would screw up my children by showing them an example of such victimhood and powerlessness. The poltergeist needed to be expelled, and I finally got the message that I was the only one who had the power to do it."

The pain of remaining in the situation became greater than the pain of making a change.

—Chris Guillebeau, *The Art of Non-Conformity: Set Your Own Rules, Live the Life You Want, and Change the World*

When Charon shared this with me, it brought to life everything Thom Rutledge had told me about fear. Charon had become aware of her circumstances and also aware of her role in creating them. Rutledge said, "We humans naturally are not big fans of awareness when it is about tuning in to thoughts and emotions that make us uncomfortable." But it is with this awareness that we can begin to move past fear.

It took Charon a long time, but she was able to stop identifying with the storm and cease being a victim. She began to own her story and look to it for clues about who she has become and where she wants to head next. Realizing that she was not the "I" of the storm around her helped her set ground rules about how she needed to be treated by others and how she would begin to treat herself. And as she took these steps, Charon became empowered. The six declarations she made to her family became the challenges that she focused her energy on. She created an active hope practice that helped her change the way she saw herself and her place. Gradually, she began to feel empowered rather than hopeless.

"The biggest difference in me, aside from being thinner, more educated, independent, and employed (thank you very much!), is now I choose to make myself happy first, *before* anyone else."

Charon is taking occasional spoonfuls of "positive selfishness," as Thom Rutledge called it, and tending to everyone else only *after* her own needs are met.

"The craziest thing happened, the opposite of what I thought would happen if I took care of myself before one of the kids, or a friend, or a relative— my kids became happier as I became happier," she told me. "Now, I *know* when my fifteen-year-old pushes back against a bad grade or a bitchy classmate, it's because she learned from her mother not to give up and that it is never too late, as long as you scare off the victim in the mirror.

"I lost twenty years of my life to victimhood and self-deprecation. What I take away from that reality is the most critical lesson I hope to pass on to my children. All those years that I lived as 'less than' were not their father's fault, and it wasn't my dad's either. It was mine. When you allow things to happen *to* you, it's no longer the other person's fault. All I had (aside from bad taste in men) were excuses. I had chronic depression, a bad upbringing, no family support, three children, no education. *Poor, poor Charon*. No! Poor Charon went on medication for her depression, found an eager support system in her mother-in-law, went on public assistance to help with the children, and looked for grants to get her diploma and college tuition. I dug myself into a deep ditch, and I dug myself out. But I take full responsibility for every mistake and failure I have made. It's all on me. If I didn't, I wouldn't be able to take full credit for the life I have created and where I am headed next. And nobody is going to take that glory away from me, especially not *me*."

Charon says next year she will get on an airplane for the first time in her life and visit a new friend, and she's planning to enjoy herself. Self-limitation is not an option anymore. She's proved that even after twenty years, a person has the capacity to bounce back, to be resilient. It is never too late.

"The most ironic thing about all of this is now that I have found some of my power, my children's father is on a kick that he wants us all back. Karma is kicking him in the ass. If this were last year, I'd probably open the door wearing my raggedy pajamas and invite him back in to treat me like a doormat. I'm strong enough and trusting enough in myself now to be able to say, 'It's not going to happen . . . it's *never* going to happen. Ding-dong! That crone is dead.'"

❧

One of the hardest questions for me to answer is "What do you want?" I mean, I know what I want on a very high level: I want to be happy, I want my kids to be healthy, I want to leave a mark on the world. But when you go micro on me and ask me what I want, I can only muster "I'll know it when I see it." Therefore, my philosophy leans toward "I don't know what I want, but I can tell you what I *don't* want." Interestingly enough, knowing what I don't want usually leads me to figure out what I do. It's a little dyslexic, but it works for me.

It's one thing to learn what your gifts are, or to have rediscovered them, but what to do with them is a loftier decision. Now that you've been lifted from the inaction of your pain experience, what do you want to achieve? Where do you want to go? How have you been changed? And what *don't* you want? Where do you *not* want to be or go? How haven't you changed?

Remember negativity bias? I think because we tend to remember the junk in our lives, taking this approach feels kind of natural. Blogger Chris Guillebeau's book *The Art of Non-Conformity: Set Your Own Rules, Live the Life You Want, and Change the World* opened my eyes to the necessity of "not to-dos." He suggests that instead of giving so much credence to our to-do lists, we should practice writing what he calls *to-stop-doing* lists. When you stop focusing on the things that suck your energy, detract from your personal value system, or just plain make you unhappy, you free up mental and spiritual space to invite fulfilling, productive stuff back into your life.

I know a man named Barry who is in the process of figuring out how to leverage his power to do something he wants. This is not always a straightforward road. A high school teacher for nearly twenty-five years, Barry had become weary of the daily grind of managing teenagers and dealing with increasing bureaucratic and political nonsense that detracted from his ability to engage with students, as well as the monotony of teaching the same curriculum year after year, with no control over how he could inspire the children. Forlorn, he came home tired and cranky after working extra hours morning and evening on endless paperwork and grading. He found he wasn't patient with his teenage son and fought with him over homework. A teacher with nothing left to teach his own child, Barry felt the shame of knowing he could do better but was frankly too exhausted to deal with it.

The only good thing coming around the bend was tax season. He got excited about tax season, not because he enjoyed paying his taxes but because he loved helping people with their finances. His second job in accounting allowed him to play with numbers and exercise his underutilized left brain. Learning tax law and how different codes applied to diverse situations opened up a new, exhilarating world.

It turned out, however, that the tax preparation company Barry worked for was not a good fit. With a house to maintain, young children to raise, a career that had become a grind, and a second job that was expecting way too much for little pay, Barry was the definition of burned out.

When I asked Barry what he wanted to do to make his life work for him, he spaced out. "I have no idea." He was in so deep, he couldn't fathom how to swim toward the surface.

"What *don't* you want to do?" I asked him.

"What do you mean?" he asked.

I told Barry about *The Art of Non-Conformity*, which was based on Guillebeau's viral manifesto *A Brief Guide to World Domination*. In his book, Guillebeau suggests completing a to-stop-doing exercise: "Name three things you hate doing, feel enslaved to do, suck your energy, anything . . . "

"Paperwork," Barry replied without hesitation. "I am tired of paperwork. I am up to my ears in paperwork. I can't catch up." The six classes Barry taught were demanding. One hundred fifty essays a week needed to be read, corrected, and graded.

I asked him about the next item on his to-stop-doing list. "I dread going to work at the tax company tonight."

Now he was in the groove and continued: "The last thing I would want to do today is lawn maintenance. I feel like if I have an hour to myself, it has to be spent bagging up leaves, plowing snow, planting seeds, or cutting the lawn."

Now Barry had action points to work with. How could he lessen his paperwork load? What can he do about the tax firm? The lawn? Suddenly Barry's to-stop-doing list gave way to a proactive to-do list.

To-do number one: "I have to change my course load," Barry admitted. "I'll talk to my advisor to give away those classes and take different classes with less paperwork."

Next Barry decided to quit working for the tax company on weekends. "All I need is ten of my own clients to start up on my own. I know that's doable; I've just been afraid. Once I get those clients, I'll quit the tax company for good." His wife by his side, they designed a logo and filed to become a limited liability company (LLC). Within one week, Barry became a business owner!

Last, with the influx of income from private clients, he and his wife happily planned to hire a landscaping company so Barry could spend the reclaimed hours on meditation, exercise, and fun family time.

This is how change can happen, how momentum begins. Even the smallest things like lawn care, once taken control of, can create the space in your brain (ocean mind) for you to consider the bigger things, until, like Barry, you make your day work for you instead of succumbing to unreasonable demands on your time.

The to-stop-doing list can be a great tool to assist you as you identify and separate negative motivations from positive ones.

Exercise: Discover Your Gifts, Set Your Goal

No wind blows fair for a ship without a destination.
—Nautical proverb

Here are curiosity conversation starters to explore your goals when it's time for you to make a move.

1. Is this job/task something I deeply want, or am I doing this as an obligation or to fulfill an expectation someone else has of me?
2. Does this support my core values?
3. Is it feasible?
4. Will I become better as a result?
5. When I see it in my mind's eye, does it feel authentic and good in my gut?
6. Do I have the support system in place—internal and external—to create conditions for reaching this goal?
7. Am I jumping the gun? Are there smaller steps I need to take before this one?

To make plans:

- Write a mission statement for your goal.
- Set an exact date to begin. For instance, when Barry filed his LLC, he made the induction date the same as his upcoming fiftieth birthday.
- Have an exact date by which you want to achieve your goal. Barry promised himself that his course load would be different effective September. In his book *Making Hope Happen: Create the Future You Want for Yourself and Others,* Shane J. Lopez, PhD, calls this a *when/ where plan.* Being specific by stating when and where you will start your plan "uses the power of cues to prompt us to work on the long-term projects that matter most to us . . . keeps us on track, guards us

against our tendency to procrastinate, and keeps us from getting over-whelmed by competing demands." People who have a specific date and time achieve their agenda item or goal more often than people who don't set timelines.

- Create a written plan. Barry thought about the people in his commu-nity with whom he could network to gain clients. He leveraged the practical experience gained during his tenure at the tax company, and he began using social media for the first time in his life.

- Plan for a thirty-, sixty-, and ninety-day review. Checking in with yourself is essential to achieve any goal. Reassess conditions, evaluate small successes and setbacks, and shift plans accordingly.

- Keep a symbol of your goal with you in a wallet or purse or in your car. It serves as a reminder and a pick-me-up every day. Barry keeps a photo of him and his family from their only vacation together to remind him of how much he wants to preserve what he and his wife built. Additionally, he kept a color copy of his new company's logo in the glove box of his car to remind him of how he created something that just a few weeks earlier didn't exist. That fact continues to be a huge positive motivator and confidence builder that will no doubt stay with Barry as he tends to other parts of his life.

- Compartmentalize your goals according to the aspects of your life. For instance, Barry kept his family life goals separate and thus not depen-dent on his achievement of unrelated goals.

- Resist becoming overambitious. One thing at a time. We know what happens when we come out of the gate on New Year's Day with a mil-lion resolutions like losing weight, saving money, getting a new job, being a more mindful parent, reconnecting with old friends, or training for a marathon. Just like Barry, we'd burn out fast and wind up with nothing to show for it.

- Look for goal contagions. Dr. Lopez's book cites research that identi-fies goal setting as contagious. We are more likely to follow through with something or pursue a goal if we see others doing it. We should look for goal contagions because they are all around us. Through Dr. Lopez's writings, I read about Henk Aarts, PhD, of Utrecht Univer-sity in the Netherlands, who studies the way people form goals. His research reveals how much "our conscious sense of wanting and doing things depends on an unconscious foundation of habits, social cues, and environmental triggers." He has shown that simply reading stories about adopting and acting on goals compels people to follow suit. Anyone who was inspired to take ballroom dancing lessons after watching Marie Osmond shed pounds on *Dancing with the Stars,* or who signed up their children for swimming lessons after the 2008 Olympic swim team riveted the nation, knows how contagious goals can be. People even tend to recycle more when a hotel or restaurant posts signs saying the facility's patrons and workers take recycling seriously.

- Plan for the unexpected. When people train for a marathon, they train in different situations, all devised to prepare them for the unknown. They learn the course beforehand. They train in the rain, in the dark, in smaller crowded races, in the cold, in the heat, when they are dehydrated or in physical pain. Because they have no idea or control over what the big day will bring, they plan for the what-ifs. Similarly for us, the proverb "Man plans and God laughs" is often true, so in our own goal setting, we should be creative about gathering as many coping strategies as possible. With plan A, B, C, and so on, "we are more likely to escape a bad situation quicker or tolerate an inescapable situation better," advises Dr. Lopez. This is like staying on a diet by planning for possible derailments: "What if they serve my favorite dessert? What if they don't have a gluten-free menu? I will send back the breadbasket, fill up on water, stay away from saucy items, etc."

- Stay enthusiastic about your plans, what you are trying to do, and the prospects you are creating. Your power is something to be proud of but also excited about. Don't deny yourself the pleasure of what you deserve: enjoying what you are doing and making your work fun!

Be Loud and Proud

*I am not someone who is ashamed of my past.
I'm actually really proud. I know I made a lot of mistakes,
but they, in turn, were my life lessons.*

—Drew Barrymore

I remember when my son put together his first Lego set. He was six years old, and it was a huge deal. I don't know who was happier, my son or my exhausted husband, who for at least two years was the delegated Lego Master—begrudgingly fiddling around with specks of plastic the size of dust that would stick in the deep lines of his palms. My son would stare at the instructions and then look to his dad to figure them out, until one day my son decided he could read and follow the instructions himself.

Of course, we had been too busy to notice that our son had been out of sight for so long and uncharacteristically quiet in his room. I had chores, Sam had chores; our family of four was busy being separate together in our home, and we hadn't been the wiser! That is, until the house was electrified by the beaming eyes of my six-year-old.

"Mommy, Mommy! You'll never believe this!" Jake panted as he ran to the kitchen sink, where I was beating up a pot with a pad of steel wool. "I did it! I did! I did it myself! I built a Lego police station *by myself*!"

In one of my phony enthusiastic tones I had developed for those times when my brain didn't register what my kids were telling me, I mustered, "That's . . . great."

He was too smart to let me off the hook. "Come see it. Now."

Guilty of inattentiveness, my phony enthusiasm and I moseyed down to his room, where there it stood—the Lego police station—an exact replica of the picture on the box, if I do say so myself. I really was impressed and quite pleased with my smarty-pants six-year-old. And then my son turned to me and said something I will never forget.

"I am soooooo proud of myself!"

I will never forget it for two reasons: The first is he didn't stop saying it all day long. The second is because I couldn't remember the last time I had said such a thing aloud about myself, or heard my husband—or any other adult, for that matter—say it, even when at one time or another we had accomplished a super feat that deserved to be praised!

What the heck is that about?

The cliché goes that we run on the treadmill of life toward our goals but, once there, don't give ourselves permission to bask in the glory. We have a lot to learn from children, and my son taught me a lesson that day with his innocent proclamation. *Be proud and say it out loud.*

We must stop and recognize our accomplishments, praise ourselves, and use each victory as momentum to leverage our power today and tomorrow. Giving ourselves this blessing is just one of the many ways we can elevate our spirit and keep it raised.

What's Inside:

Elevate Your Spirit

MOTIVATION IS ALL AROUND

Instead of asking, "what do I want from life?" a more powerful question is, "what does life want from me?"
—Eckhart Tolle

Spirit is the force within us that is believed to give our bodies life, energy, and power. But just as energy is subject to depletion or elevation, spirit fluctuates based on our attention or inattention toward it. Our spirits are threatened on a daily basis. Our nonphysical selves can hurt in ways we can't see, until we begin to feel hollow and no longer whole. We know about the mind-body connection, which experts have revised as the mind-body-spirit connection, contending that it is this third component, this force of spirit, that is integral to "knowing thyself," to quote the ancient Greeks. The previous parts of this book, I hope, have helped you inch toward knowing yourself. Now think of E: Elevate Your Spirit as the maintenance plan: the part where we discuss what it means to live in spirit and with spirit, and how without spirit, the body and mind are as incomplete as a certain snowman without his black silk top hat. That hat is the magical detail that brings a few piles of snow to life and enables him to dance around.

A MODERN-DAY PHOENIX

When I spoke to Allison about my silk-hat spirit metaphor, she laughed in a gentle way that moved her dirty blonde bob over her black-framed glasses. She had her own silk hat, one that had been propped on her head by the most unlikely source—cancer.

Allison's breast cancer diagnosis hit home. She was only a year older than I am now when she received her news. At thirty-seven, Allison was a busy mom of a daughter and son, five and four respectively. She had been diligent about receiving routine mammograms for her "dense" breasts since she turned thirty-five. "Thirty-five is the new forty, at least that's what my doctor told me," Allison said. "And I am so glad he believes that." Just five months after her last clean mammogram, Allison's nipple inverted, sending her doctor into high alert. Tests revealed Allison had invasive ductal carcinoma, or stage 3A breast cancer. She was ordered to stop work immediately and begin chemotherapy the very next day.

"I didn't panic or cry. I figured, aside from this cancer, I am young, am in relatively good health, have science on my side, and that was that," said Allison.

Once a week for five months, she had chemo treatments. Two weeks after her double mastectomy, she received more bad news. The chemotherapy hadn't been effective. In fact, her tumor had grown to eight centimeters and was said to be estrogen induced. "Up until I got that pathology report, I pretty much considered the bright side of the disease. I'd finally get the thirty pounds off that I have been gaining and losing since I was twelve thanks to closet eating, and I would get new boobs!

"But once I realized the chemo didn't work, that this breast cancer wasn't just about poisonous boobies you get replaced, I was forced to accept my new reality: This disease is a part of me now, something that will be with me for the rest of my life—because it dictates everything from the food I eat to the way I deal with stress to the vitamins I take. I need to take better care of myself, inside and out, from head to toe. That alone was new territory."

Within a year and a half, Allison would have a double mastectomy, four lymph nodes removed, a hysterectomy and an oophorectomy, radiation, and several rounds of breast reconstruction. She would enter a surgically induced menopause a few decades too early.

In my imagination, I pictured a woman in a nightshirt hovering over a toilet bowl in the dead of night with two babies crying from their toddler beds and a husband not knowing what to do to help ease his young wife's pain. I soon learned how wrong I was. Allison was so jovial and strong, it made me wonder where her spirit came from. "How did you manage it all, Allison? How did you keep hope?" I asked.

"I didn't have to," she explained. "Being sick, I felt super-empowered."

Allison had her bouts of self-blame, she admitted, speculating that her cancer was due to her two rounds of in vitro fertilization and the doses of oral fertility drugs she took to become pregnant. She wondered if a lifetime of unhealthy closet eating contributed. And she found it painfully ironic that for so long she and her husband had put so much emphasis on her reproductive system to conceive children and then to nurse them, only to wind up void of all of her female parts—from her breasts to her uterus and ovaries to her hair.

"It wasn't too long ago that I was pregnant, so the fact that I was in menopause was a lot to make sense of, but then I felt okay with it because of course it's natural to feel a loss. We all feel entitled to things in our life, in certain times of our lives. At one time, I felt like I was entitled to have children, and I took charge of a dire situation and got the results I wanted. Sure, I thought I was entitled to hold on to my uterus for a few more years, but then I realized life is not about entitlement."

Allison found herself transforming in ways she hadn't expected. "First of all, my husband and I were on each other's last nerve, just going through the motions, before I got sick. And now we're stronger than ever. I also discovered I had my very own army of generous, loving, compassionate supporters—from acquaintances at the school yard to colleagues and students to close family members to strangers in waiting rooms. Friends I hadn't seen from grade school would show up on my doorstep with hot meals for my family. My brothers and father bonded with me in ways I never thought possible. All of it, the love everywhere . . . it brought me to my knees.

"I've concluded that people are like little misunderstood piles of love. They want to do something, but rarely do they know what, when, or how. But if you guide them, they can help you achieve miracles."

One of those miracles was Allison's ability to be vulnerable, to share her story with others, and to not feel ashamed of her baldness or her mutilated chest. The more she opened up about the scary "C" word, the more she disarmed people's fears of being around her or of saying the wrong thing. She connected better, something we know from back in O: Open Your Mind that vulnerability offers.

If you evaluated Allison by her physical appearance, you'd see a woman who, thanks to cancer, gained sixty pounds, went bald, and started menopause. Not quite "pretty." But in her opinion, this was Allison's purest and loveliest form.

"I have never felt as beautiful in my life as when I was bald. I felt like I was attracting love and sending love everywhere I went, and it made me feel like this fucking warrior—all that *love*. I was a rockin' mom and fighting the fight, and I felt more feminine than I should've felt. I thought, *This is what* woman *means, this is how I was meant to feel*. I believe I was enlightened. I can't explain it.

"Every woman has a plight she must face. Are you going to lie down and cry, or are you going to stand up and fight this? For me, it wasn't a choice. I am not living in denial. There is a 50 percent chance my cancer can come back, likely at stage 4. Then I'd be dealing with metastatic cancer, and it's possible I will die. It is possible I won't be here to see my children get married. That is a truth that affects every decision I make."

Those decisions included finding stuff that fills her silk hat with magic; it's what elevates her spirit. Allison began volunteering as a helper at a cancer center, acting as a resource for women recently diagnosed with breast cancer; taking a holistic approach to her health, including monthly Reiki sessions, nightly meditation, and acupuncture, in addition to studying up on better nutrition; and assuring that her children grow up feeling secure in their mother's love.

Since her remission, Allison has been sought out by several cancer support groups because of her unique view on her experience. "I have been told I have been my best in *this* role. But really, all I truly believe is that everyone wants to leave a mark on this world. I'm lucky that I am already doing that, as a teacher teaching wonderful kids in a terrific high school. I get to be creative every day and share with others what I have learned about life thus far. The most important is being authentic.

"Each night in order to fall asleep, my meditation is to imagine a golden light getting brighter and brighter, stronger and stronger, starting at the crown of my head and moving all the way down to my toes. The scan is such that it lights up my insides with vibrancy and health, an infinite glow of peace. I fall fast asleep."

Allison might not know it, but she is not the only one who feels her light. So many others can see it too. She radiates realness, vulnerability, and self-awareness. "I can't wait to show the women at the support group my tattooed nipples. It's as real as I can be with them, because I am compelled to connect with people in more and deeper ways. This disease has connected and reconnected me with community, family, and friendship and underscored my purpose. I know now that life is driven by connection—deep connection. It's my number one goal."

And that, I realized, is what an elevated spirit is.

Trust and Intuition

Listen. Listen. That is what we are asked to do.

—Pat Longo

My stepfather, Robert, had fled the house after beating up my mother just a few hours earlier, so why would he be back skulking around and peering through our windows?

I saw his shadow in the night, and then his eyes through the living room window. Frantic, I told my mother, "I should call the police."

"No, we'll be fine," she said, walking out of the living room, still holding her shoulder. The fear of her husband had victimized her for far too long. Now all she was capable of was cowering toward the kitchen.

Call anyway.

It was "the voice"—a voice in my head I had heard often as a child, that gave me chills and accompanied pangs of nausea. It was a voice I didn't want to tell anyone about, that I didn't want to share, yet I never feared it. The voice was sometimes soft and gentle, other times loud and urgent. It had been a year or so since I last heard it, when the voice warned me not to go back with Sean to his house, to continue avoiding him after he raped me. I didn't listen, and when we got to Sean's basement, he beat my belly and tossed me to the floor in a desperate attempt to kill the baby I was carrying.

By now I had spent enough time listening to *and* ignoring the voice that I had historical evidence in its accuracy. The voice was never wrong. I dialed 911 just as Robert broke through our door and charged at me, ripping the phone off the cord. I had no idea if I had gotten through to the dispatcher. Robert headed toward the back of the house, hunting for my mom. When I got up from where he had knocked me, Robert was attacking my mother in the hallway. I flew at him, hitting him on the back, but he was unaffected as he continued his rampage against my mother. I was afraid she was going to die, and that I and my siblings would be next. I grabbed the three of them and ran across the street to a neighbor's house. I banged desperately but nobody would answer.

Sirens sounded around the corner, and police cars screamed to a stop, surrounding our home. I was standing on the sidewalk in my pajama top and underwear, watching as four police officers tried to pull Robert from our home. Out of his mind, Robert attacked the officers, and they did what they had to do to contain him. Once I saw Robert escorted to the police car in handcuffs, I was deathly afraid of what I might find inside. But there she was, my mother, crying in the arms of an officer, who rocked her consolingly as her face was beginning to swell beyond recognition. The voice had saved her life.

The root of the word *intuition* comes from the Latin *tueri*, meaning "to guard, to protect." We all are born with intuition and can learn to develop it, just like playing a musical instrument. It is said that the more intuitive you are, the closer you are to the higher realm, which I have interpreted to mean that if I want to elevate higher and higher, where I feel most powerful, peaceful, and safe, I must constantly sharpen and develop my intuition. Researchers have been studying telepathy, intuition, and psychic matters since the early 1800s. According to Sophy Burnham, author of *The Art of Intuition: Cultivating Your Inner Wisdom*, hundreds of thousands of laboratory studies have now been carried out in such acclaimed institutions as Harvard, Princeton, and Stanford, all substantiating the reality of intuition. This isn't about woo-woo parlor tricks. Burnham explained it best when she wrote, "Intuition is intended for our spiritual, not psychic, development."

Intuition is sometimes referred to as gut instinct or listening to your gut, and there are fascinating reasons why this might be truer than we thought. Paul Pearsall, PhD, wrote a bold and brave book titled *Awe: The Delights and Dangers of Our Eleventh Emotion*, in which he said gut feeling is physiologically connected to our brains. As Dr. Pearsall explains, modern medicine has recently learned that our gut and our brain develop from the same clump of fetal tissue. One part ends up in the brain and the other in the intestines; they become what are called the central and enteric nervous systems. Our intestines are lined with more than one hundred million neurotransmitters, about the same number as found in the brain, and these two nervous systems are connected by the longest nerve in the body, the vagus. Writes Dr. Pearsall, "When one of the systems is responding, the other always does too. That's why indigestion produces nightmares and why antidepressants that calm the brain are sometimes used to soothe the stomach."

I'll never forget one of my earliest experiences of intuition, when I was in kindergarten. The symptoms of nausea and head spinning could easily have been written off as a virus or flu. My symptoms began before I boarded the bus home at the end of the school day, but I ignored them. My father had been away on a long haul, and it wasn't unusual for me to miss him while he was gone. I thought that I had butterflies because our house would be so empty without him and I didn't know when he'd be getting home. *Don't go home,* a voice inside me said. *Stay at school. Call Mom to pick me up. Don't go home on the bus.* I wanted the voice to stop. I was scared. It made me feel like something bad was about to happen. And then I remembered I had heard this voice once before—*how could I forget?*—when my father hung my kittens from a clothesline and left them there to suffer and die. He waited for me to discover them and watched me scream bloodcurdling cries as I ran to rescue their lifeless bodies. I squinted the image away, pretending the voice was not speaking, and made my way to the back of the bus.

As the bus made its way along winding roads, I started feeling sicker. The bus was hot, even with the windows down, and I began dripping sweat. Looking frantically around, I saw my friends noticed the heat too. Then we saw flames darting out of the back of the bus. Twenty-five of us howled for help as thick black smoke formed and flames enveloped us. My seat was on fire!

As the bus ignited, I recalled the time that a stray cat got stuck in our burn barrel at home. I couldn't get her out, and its frightened moans had alerted my brother Jason and my father. Instead of setting her loose, however, as my brother Jason and I thought he would, Dad poured gasoline on the pile of debris in the barrel and set it on fire in front of us. The cat's agonized screaming blended with Jason's and my own.

I thought I was going to die like the cat. As everything was going black, I was whisked up and out of the bus.

The force within us that is our spirit speaks to us all the time, especially to guide us toward what is right for us and away from what is detrimental and dangerous. We refer to it as intuition, defined as the ability to know something instantly, without conscious reasoning. Sophy Burnham writes in *The Art of Intuition*: "We recognize it most often in times of crisis and danger, those moments, rare and dramatic, when it saves your life or offers prescience you cannot understand. By definition intuition involves information not available to the intellect, and it is always to be trusted."

In L: Leverage Your Power, you met Herman Jacobs and Marc Buoniconti, athletes who collided in midair during a college football game. How did they get so high and land so hard? Herman said he "heard this voice, one I never heard before, and out of nowhere it ordered me to 'Jump.'" Herman had regretted listening to the voice, because he thought it was responsible for the impact that paralyzed Marc. But when specialists reviewed the tape, they concluded that without Herman's jump, the resulting direct collision would have killed them both. If Herman hadn't listened to that voice, the outcome could have been even more tragic.

Rick Hanson, PhD, coauthor of *Buddha's Brain: The Practical Neuroscience of Happiness, Love, and Wisdom,* also describes being moved by what felt like outside forces that gave him guidance at a bleak moment. He wrote about a time when he was a college student facing insurmountable forces and was overtaken by extraordinary strength and the will to live. Lost in the Yosemite high country in late afternoon as temperatures were getting chilly, and with the nearest people miles away, young Rick was faced with spending the night at six thousand feet in a short-sleeved shirt and jeans. "Then an unprecedented and powerful sense came over me," he writes. "I felt like a feral animal, like a hawk that would do whatever it takes to survive. I felt a fierce determination to live through the day and, if need be, the night."

Revitalized, Rick circled the area and scurried through bush and wilderness in search of the trail back to his campsite. He found the trail and his group later that night. "I've never forgotten the intense feelings of that day, and have drawn on them for strength many times since."

> *[Intuition is] what your higher Self knows*
> *that your mind can't see yet.*
>
> —Sophy Burnham, *The Act of Intuition*

The way in which our intuition communicates with us is as unique as we are as individuals and varies from person to person. For me, intuition mostly spoke to me, literally in the form of a voice, using words I understood and that I myself would use throughout each stage of my life. The voice was never over my head or patronizing, and it met me exactly where I was mentally, intellectually, and emotionally. Other people experience intuition as physical feelings—a sensation "from their gut," shivers and goose bumps, or an intense desire to flee, among other things. People with more developed intuitive powers can see things that will happen, movies that play in their minds as warning signs of what's ahead if they don't listen. That's why there are people like Pat Longo. If you have ever heard of Theresa Caputo, also known as the Long Island Medium, then you know Pat, whom Theresa has publicly credited with curing her anxiety and opening her up to her spiritual gifts. From her modest home in Hicksville, New York, the same town from which Theresa hails, Pat Longo works tirelessly as a one-on-one spiritual healer for people around the world. She also provides workshop series and training for mediums, healers, and intuitives. She began teaching her first class with a medium and friend, Kim Russo, star of the Lifetime Movie Network series *The Haunting of . . .* and author of *The Happy Medium: Life Lessons from the Other Side.* Serendipitously, one evening Pat and Kim met Laura Lynne Jackson, medium and author of *The Light between Us: Stories from Heaven,* and the three became fast friends. One of the most recent mediums to have emerged from Pat's classes is MaryAnn DiMarco, author of *Believe, Ask, Act.* Interestingly enough, many of the mediums Pat trains don't know they're mediums when they first visit; they are initially there for their own physical or emotional healing.

Pat Longo sees her fair share of skeptics too. "It's healthy to be a skeptic," she says. "It's counterintuitive not to question things. When I first started this, people thought I had horns and a tail and waved around dead chickens. I let people feel me out until they are comfortable. It is important not to deny your own sense of intuition, your gut feelings, and then make your own free will choice."

My coauthor, Michele, had the opportunity to sit with Pat Longo in her living room to learn more about intuition, trust, and spirit, all of which keep us balanced and centered and connected deeply with our life purpose. We cannot be whole without spirit, and intuition and trust guide and elevate the spirit in ways our minds and bodies cannot.

"Everyone has a gift. We all came here with gifts. Everybody. No one is exempt," said Longo. "We all came with guides as well. From the moment we were conceived, these guides were assigned. Your guides speak to you in *your* voice in *your* head in *your* thoughts. So a random thought that infiltrates your mind, seemingly coming from nowhere? It's your guides. It's a thought sometimes so unexpected and unrelated to what you are doing that it gives you pause and makes you ask, 'Why would I just think that? Why did that person's face just pop into my head? Why did I just have that vision? Why am I suddenly feeling this way?' It's your guides trying to get your attention.

"Have you ever argued with your own thoughts, engaging in a ping-pong dialogue of 'I'm going to say this or do that,' and then your 'logical' voice comes in and says, 'No, you're *not*, you'll say *this* or do *that*'? But then the original thought persists. Well, that is when your guides are really being persistent. When you have an argument with yourself, pay extra attention."

I remember when the voice spoke to me at age sixteen. I was home alone, and it said, *Don't open the door. Stay very still.* The voice was gentle, like a mother's knowledge. *Do not make one single move. You are in danger. Lock the door.*

I peeked through the curtain and saw it was only my father, who had come for an unexpected visit. I had no idea why I was suddenly afraid. But I listened. I didn't let my father in, although he came back later and slept next to my brother and sister. With him breathing the very same air in my room that night, I sensed he was dangerous, and I couldn't fall asleep. Later I would discover that it wasn't long before this visit that he was in his girlfriend Toni's home, cleaning up her blood that had splattered on the walls and dumping her body near our favorite family picnic spot in Oregon.

Understanding our intuition, our guides, the knowing, or whatever we want to call it, is a necessary component in elevating our spirit and ensuring all the hard work we do every day to live well, to be WHOLE, is sustained.

Among other things to do to elevate the spirit, Longo says, is to use your own healing powers to forgive, take accountability for your part in something, let go of fear, empathize with the stories of the people who have hurt you, believe that thoughts become things, pay attention to synchronicity, stay unattached to emotions and thoughts, and listen to your wise inner voice.

One of Longo's tools is to have her clients write a forgiveness letter. "The concept of a forgiveness letter isn't unique, but where many people go wrong is they write their letters and *reread* them! Don't make this mistake! When you reread your thoughts, you download them right back into your hard drive. Don't even keep them on your computer. When you put it out in cyberspace, it goes out there. So I like the writing to be a physical exercise, and afterward, the letter can be burned or shredded safely, releasing the thoughts once and for all.

"And as you end your letter, write, 'I thank you, I bless you, and I release you.'"

The idea of thanking the person who might have hurt us the most can be a bitter pill to swallow. After all, who would want to thank their rapist, their alcoholic parent, their cheating partner, their cancer, their bankruptcy, their drug addict child? Why would I ever thank my serial killer father?

"Because they are teachers," Longo suggests. "Anyone with whom you have strong interaction *is* a teacher, who teaches you how to figure out what to do and what not to do. If you become a better person, choose a certain career path, become an advocate, a volunteer, a role model, a better partner, you have that teacher to thank. Forgiveness is for you, not for them."

Allison is grateful for the lessons her breast cancer bestowed. She is wise enough to be humble and open enough to pay attention to the wisdom in her experiences, and she has deep gratitude and appreciation for the abundance of love and support in her life. We can all be open, even in the harshest of times, and learn to say thank-you for all of the experiences in our lives, beautiful and painful: "I thank you because I have become better and more whole in the face of _____."

Pat Longo explains that all she can do is hand people the tools they need to bring balance and wholeness into their lives. It is up to each of us whether we choose to use those tools or not. She generously shared the following tools that can be used to elevate our spirits to achieve that sense of balance:

Watch your words. Be positive with each other and yourself. "I get letters and e-mails from people every day who feel anxious, sad, and desperate. One tool is for people to be mindful of the thoughts they are sending out into the universe and work to change the negative into positive. I ask my clients to start by monitoring their thoughts and words for two weeks, noticing how many negative things they are thinking and saying. When they say or hear something negative, I advise them to say, 'Cancel, cancel.' Soon they will catch how negative they are and how negative others around them can be." Longo uses the example of a person in late-stage cancer. "Someone will tell me her story about how she 'has' breast cancer, and then I say, 'Thank you for sharing, and now I don't want you to ever say those words again.' When you say, 'I have it,' you cement it to the ground. When you instead say, 'I am diagnosed with it,' you put the onus on the person who diagnosed you. By saying 'I am feeling better every day,' you take the cancer out of your energy field, or by saying 'I used to have,' you put it in the past. Thoughts become things. The better the thought, the higher the elevation."

Use balance to connect to God, source, or universe. "To be balanced, we need to simultaneously be connected to the light above us and grounded to the earth beneath us," explains Longo. "Light helps protect us from negativity and connects us to God and the universe." The more we envelop ourselves in light by using meditation and visualization, the stronger that light becomes each day. Then we need to plant our feet firmly on the ground, envisioning the soles of our feet and our tailbone anchoring to the deep soil of the earth. "We are spiritual beings, and if you're not grounded, you're not balanced. Most people are not grounded. The light (high) and the grounding (below) create balance."

If you want something, tell someone. Have you ever crossed paths with someone by accident and found yourself saying, "That's weird, I was just telling my husband we need a plumber." Something like this happened to my coauthor, Michele, after she and I brainstormed experts to interview for this chapter. At a birthday party, Michele was talking about her work on *WHOLE* when Tricia, a fellow mom, said, "My mother is a spiritual healer. She worked with Theresa Caputo."

"That's so crazy!" exclaimed Michele excitedly. "Melissa and I were *just* saying we needed to speak to a healer."

Enter Pat Longo! Turns out Longo was *just* picking up the pace in writing *You're Not Sick, You're Psychic,* a book that connects anxiety to spiritual gifts and provides the tools to eliminate anxiety for good. This is synchronicity at its best. You will be amazed at what you can attract when you are open about what you are seeking.

Raise your vibration. Human bodies are made of electromagnetic energy, which means we vibrate at a certain frequency. Spirit vibrates at a higher level, whereas we on earth are much denser. We want to raise our vibration because we manifest positive things when we operate at a higher level. "When you're depressed, going through trauma, experiencing a loss, dealing with an addiction, or just feeling sad, your vibration is low, it's on the floor," explains Longo. "Any negative vibration around you will act as a magnet. Negative attracts negative. If you're on the floor, only floorlike things will stick to you, so you manifest things that are low in vibration. When you're up on the ceiling, vibrating at high frequencies, the positive manifest more in your life because that is what is attracted to you."

"Good vibrations" is more than the title of a killer Marky Mark song; good vibrations can be manifested through music, love, gratitude, laughter, prayer, meditation, and anything you are passionate about, according to Longo.

Sophy Burnham puts it this way: "As you raise your vibration by prayer and purity of heart, you become more sensitive and you 'hear' without the static of your surroundings or the chatter of your own racketing monkey-mind."

A teaspoon of sugar helps the messages go down. Longo loves to talk about the Disney production of *Mary Poppins* as a metaphor for what it means to raise our vibrations and how much impact vibrations have in our lives and on one another.

When strict, business-as-usual Mary Poppins, her friend Bert, and the children, Jane and Michael, visit Uncle Albert, they find him unusually sad. Once Bert tells a few jokes, Uncle Albert begins to laugh and floats to the ceiling, levitating from laughter. He opens into the song, "I Love to Laugh," and before long Bert chimes in, laughing and floating above Mary and the children. Against Mary's orders, infectious laughter sends the children soaring as well, while Mary Poppins watches and winces. When Mary looks at her watch and says, "It's time to go, children," they all frown and unwillingly descend to the floor.

Longo explains, "When we engage in something we love, or incorporate one of the vibration raisers mentioned earlier, laughter being one, we send our souls to the ceiling. We are operating on a higher level, one that attracts only positivity and one that is closer to our authentic selves. It is a space we feel very, very good in. Nobody wants to be on the low vibrations.

"When you are in your emotional basement, I want you to be on the ceiling," says Longo. "To get from here to there, you need to choose something—a person, place, or thing—that brings joy to your heart and a smile to your face." These include thoughts of pets, a funny movie, something a child did or said, or an accomplishment or experience.

SYNCHRONICITY

I opened my mind to develop the faith that things happen for a reason and that it is no coincidence I keep hope alive through dark times. What I am talking about is known as synchronicity—a word coined by Carl Jung. It describes the times in your life when a coincidence occurs but you recognize it as something more, something of meaning and significance, and something of power. You can't necessarily justify why you need to talk to a homeless person or why you don't want to answer the doorbell or why you have a hunch that something is going on with your kid at school. You can't articulate it because it's a knowing, and that is usually enough. That knowing alerted me that the young man who smiled at me at a dance would one day be my husband. It alerted me when I noticed a flyer on a pole about Habitat for Humanity, which led to my mother finding housing for her large family. I felt that knowing when I met my best friend in high school, who became my confidante and savior through the turmoil of my teen years. My knowing was telling me that these were all synchronistic events, small miracles that were leading me where I needed to go.

Years later I would be able to consider my rape and abortion of the child that was conceived as synchronistic in positioning me to help other women in similar circumstances. Complete faith and trust in the universe gives me immense hope—hope that I didn't do something wrong to deserve all the crap, hope that I have handled myself the best I could, and hope that there is still more good to result as I live my life with intention and openness to the synchronicity that is the universe.

According to Baptist de Pape, who wrote a book based on his movie *The Power of the Heart,* "Synchronicities seem like small miracles, anonymous gifts from the universe. They come as a pleasant surprise, a marvelous connection that can transform your life from one moment to the next, opening an exciting path with the possibility of growth or insight. These events are highly unlikely—and yet they happen." Just this morning, Michele texted her very close friend Jessie from journalism school, whom she hadn't heard from in a few months. Jessie was always dealing with a lot: a daughter with cerebral palsy, a tough work schedule, money concerns, and constant battles with her health insurance provider. Then three feet of snow shut down her business and the schools for a week. Then her daughter's full-time nurse put in her notice. Michele had no idea that Jessie was at her wit's end, feeling "unbalanced" and generally not in a happy place, because Jessie is one of those people who keeps laughing when the sky is falling. But today, after Michele sent an impulsive text asking Jessie for some writerly advice, the floodgates opened. Jessie vented the only way a person who loves words knows how, by writing and pressing Send. In turn, Michele suggested it wasn't a coincidence that she contacted Jessie when she did.

> *Aren't we angels at times, acting on behalf of others and being moved occasionally (to our surprise) in mysterious ways—and always (how curious) to help another, even when we don't know the other person is in need of help?*
>
> —Sophy Burnham, *The Art of Intuition*

Michele obviously couldn't do much to help her friend, who lives a life filled with challenges most of us couldn't begin to relate to. But Michele did wonder if reaching out with friendship and general concern was enough to show Jessie that she is loved and supported by her college bud and enough to help Jes keep up her hope that this week of wreckage would soon pass. *Why this day?* Michele wondered. *How come I didn't text her yesterday or tomorrow, but on the day the nurse quit, stranding Jessie like that?* It brought to mind a line from de Pape's book: "When improbabilities appear to multiply, one after another, and the usual laws of cause and effect are suspended, that is synchronicity."

Even if you are just beginning to explore the synchronicity mentality, you can develop and grow your awareness of it right away! Every single day something uncanny happens that looks like a coincidence. It's stopping and acknowledging this event that takes mindful awareness. Is it a fluke that your friend's face popped into your head only for her to text you that very hour? Or what about the new person in your office? Why are your paths supposed to cross? What is it your child has been sent to teach you, or why did plans for a cruise fall through? Being curious about the seemingly insignificant things we take for granted and giving credence to them will attract more synchronicity.

Modest Meditation

*Allow yourself to dream. Your Higher Consciousness
will point out where you ought to go.*

—Sophy Burnham, *The Art of Intuition*

Sophy Burnham says we can invite intuition through being relaxed and easy; "to not be afraid to be with ourselves, in solitude with nothing to do but daydream and be in nature." She gives us permission to "space out" and not fill all our moments with busywork. "You'll be amazed how much is revealed to you by merely opening yourself to your environment, observing with attention and without judgment."

You don't need gongs and crystals, a bench, or a guide to meditate. Meditating can be done anywhere in any way, as long as you focus on turning inward and listening until you can honestly hear what your guides are saying. When we listen, we give ourselves the gift of becoming at one with ourselves.

Meditation is simply "me time," a private space you carve out as a spiritual practice, however you define spiritual. That could be as simple as getting together with a soul-mate best friend who makes you gleam and with whom you feel most like yourself, or it could be something that requires more commitment, such as joining a sangha.

In *Buddha's Brain*, Drs. Hanson and Mendius explore the issue of figuring out where a sweet spot of refuge is in the event we aren't quite sure. It's not unusual in our harried lives to have no idea where we might head to let go and calm down. I've discovered that my go-to refuge is nature, but I have also been known to peruse the aisles of a bookstore or head to a yoga studio. To come up with your own options, complete the following sentences.

I find refuge in _____.
I take refuge in _____.
I go for refuge in order to _____.
There is _____ here.
When I go here, I feel _____.

I am one with _____.

I come from _____.

And on and on.

When I use this method, I come up with surprisingly unique answers that I wouldn't have arrived at if I had simply asked the same old "Where do I like to go to feel better?"

As I mentioned, nature is my sacred place. Canadian peaks and serene valleys, the breathtaking Cascades in Washington State, and rivers meandering wherever I look: Such locales provide limitless inspirations for dreaming, visualizing, clearing the mind, and talking to God. I meditate best while walking in the lush terrain of the Pacific Northwest, where I grew up. My formative years were spent in nature, in mountain valleys. I could see them, and feel them, as if I were a part of them. I remember pushing my way out of my trailer door and having the horizon at my beck and call. I felt safe.

Grandma Lucy's house and our trailer sat on miles of orchard-covered hills in the Yakima Valley, nestled by the Naches Pass. We played for hours in row upon row of fragrant blossoms and red-speckled apple trees. No matter the season, we would think it a punishment to be called inside.

> *Philosophically considered, the universe is composed of Nature and the Soul.*
>
> —Ralph Waldo Emerson

Personalizing your meditation preferences moves beyond selecting the location. The style of practice is highly personal as well. Some people like to download apps and be guided at nighttime by a soothing, steady voice from their smartphone. Others find they meditate while being creative, tapping into a side of their brains that helps them clear the static by means of art, music, writing, acting, and so on.

Some people meditate best through movement—runners, walkers, yoga and Pilates practitioners, martial artists, and gardeners. They'll put on Nikes or exercise garb or grab a pair of shears to go think.

On the flip side is meditation through pleasing repetition, things such as watching a newborn sleep, listening to a cat purr, or walking a dog. Some people zone out while vacuuming; others find they clear their head by playing strings on a violin or doing vocal exercises.

Meditation—in all of its forms—helps us process our thoughts and our days and gives us clues to what fulfills us and what doesn't. When we process, we become clear enough to see which aspects of our lives make us feel good and which ones don't. We intuitively start to lean toward what serves us and away from what no longer does. In this way, we lift ourselves above the fray.

Melissa Harris is a psychic and teaches psychic development to students. She explains how she listens to her intuition: "Intuition speaks to me from my solar plexus (the area about two fingers above the belly button). If I have a yes to something, I feel as if I want to physically move in a forward direction. If I receive a no, I feel as if I am shrinking backward. If I don't listen to my intuitive guidance, I sometimes experience a slight sense of dread, sometimes a slight feeling of guilt. I know that I am being spoken to from my core, and in not listening I am betraying myself. Other people I know experience sadness or fear when they don't listen to their inner guidance."

When we listen to our intuition, we truly feel as if we have come home, because in our intuition we enjoy the luxuries a home offers—familiarity, comfort, security, love, consistency, balance.

How else do we develop our intuition and let it guide us?

Harris says to simply ask and listen. "Have you found yourself asking spirit for guidance on a situation and found yourself watching for 'signs' that may be your answer?"

I had a powerful experience with the ask/listen approach myself when I was in my "emotional basement." I had come to the point where I knew I had screwed up basically everything. The house in Spokane was foreclosed on; both my husband and I were out of work; bill collectors and my son's teachers were calling every other day. I succumbed. Alone in my house, I just let my spiritual guides have it, and I yelled to the air, "Okay, you got my attention. I am screwing up here. I have no clue what to do now, and I have apparently not listened to you." I could have sworn my guides were mad at me, or else they swiped the rug out from under me to jolt me to attention. Like Pat Longo said, I had the free will to listen or ignore them, but I had ignored them enough, and they had let me know. "I need help, guys. I can't do this alone!"

I instantly felt a sense of relief just by voicing my feeling of helplessness. Change took longer to come, and it certainly didn't occur all at once. The house still foreclosed, but my husband did find a job, and my television show got picked up. We eventually moved to California. While this may all have happened in due time, I truly believe it was the sense of not being alone in all the crap that helped me spur forward momentum. The less senseless I felt, and the more I spoke to my guides, the stronger my inspiration grew to figure out how to get out of the messes that afflicted my life. Once I reached out, as angry and frustrated as I was, and as crazy as I might have looked screaming at the walls of an empty house, I immediately felt less alone, less abandoned. And I swear that made all the difference.

Exercise: Quick, Cost-Efficient Creative Ways to Calm the Mind

Automatic writing: Automatic writing, as defined by Melissa Harris, is to write without thinking. It's a way to let our analytic mind take a lunch break and open up channels we wouldn't have predicted. It can be a brain dump in the morning or at any other time; it can be done with pen and paper or on a computer. As Harris wisely points out, there is nothing to do to prepare, as the act of writing itself clears the mind and makes room for discovery.

Sensory grounding: For the meditation impaired, like me, a mindful meditation known as 5-4-3-2-1 can be a sensational primer. I learned it from psychiatrist and meditation teacher Charlene Richard. The purpose of a sensory-grounding exercise is to use all the senses to engage in the present moment to avoid anxious ideas, worst-case-scenario thoughts, and negative self-talk. Richard says to:

- Look around the room and name five things you can see.
- Move your focus into your body and explain four things you can feel.
- Bring your attention to your hearing and name three things you can hear.
- Pay attention to your sense of smell and name two things you can smell—or imagine two things you like the smell of.
- Name one thing you can taste or like the taste of.

DAYDREAM

Melissa Harris contends that "our fantasies create our realities," so if you have ever been accused of having your head in the clouds or of being a daydreamer, you might be very lucky. Remember, we are trying to tap inspiration in order to elevate ourselves from weighty circumstances, and what can be more creative than a good daydream?

For me, daydreaming was an escape from a dismal reality but also a practice of self-efficacy—not a waste of time at all. In my early twenties, I learned a lot about my desires and insecurities through imagining myself in different careers and born to different circumstances. My most vivid memory of daydreaming was when I worked in the fragrance department of Victoria's Secret. All day long, thin, beautiful girls wrapped in designer clothes would take their time pampering themselves, spritzing different scents on their bedazzled wrists and necks, feeling the fabrics of silk peignoirs with their manicured hands, and dabbing different eye shadows on their already made-up faces. I was envious that they had the means and resources to *really* take care of themselves and be so selfish or narcissistic, at least in my presence. *How great would it be if I could pamper myself like that?* I daydreamed. In my world, pampering myself was inconceivable and would have been irresponsible. Yet this job made me consider my skill with hair and makeup and remember when, even as a little girl, I was told I was great with aesthetics.

Day after day, I drafted different career paths I could take in cosmetology. I started doing makeovers and consultations at Victoria's Secret and gained enough confidence to apply to cosmetology college. After graduation, I worked at high-end salons, which led me to decide to pursue a real dream—heading to Hollywood to work in the studios. I told people my dreams, and they would let me do their hair and makeup. The more people I told, the more connections I made. I ultimately realized that people want to support other people, but if you don't vocalize your dreams, people won't know how to help you.

I discovered that even though I wasn't focusing on myself in the same way as those women who came to Victoria's Secret, I was pampering myself in a different way. They took moments to visit tanning salons or get a makeover, and I daydreamed my way to listening to my intuition directing me to my career path. With deeper knowledge of myself, I plotted out my life, charted a new course, and considered cool, outlandish possibilities.

Choose the Creative Mode

*The essential ingredients for creativity remain exactly
the same for everybody: courage, enchantment, permission,
persistence, trust—and those elements are universally
accessible. Creative living is not easy, but it's possible.*

—Elizabeth Gilbert, *Big Magic*

Up until about six months ago, I had been walking around blissfully ignorant of a video game that has swept the entire world. That is, until my son
got his hands on my smartphone and began building his "worlds" with just
a touch on the screen. Maybe you have heard of it . . . Minecraft. Taking a
quick peek, I determined it was a benign enough hobby, like playing with
blocks or Legos. And then my son started muttering something about being
killed, starving, or trying to slaughter a pig for food, and I decided I needed
to research a bit on how my child (along with millions of other children,
teens, *and* adults) has chosen to spend his time. Here is the gist of what I
learned before determining I'd seen enough. There are different modes players can play in. My son chose between survival mode (which challenges
players to find and use resources in their world, lest they die) and creative
mode. A line struck me as I read the paragraph-long description of creative
mode on the Minecraft wiki: "Players are given an infinite number of blocks
to build with and no health or hunger bar *thus rendering the player immune
to all damage.*" [italics mine]

It struck me: *For those of us living in the real world, operating in creative mode can keep us immune to all damage.* That's really all it takes to
elevate our spirit—creativity. To think creatively, act creatively, love creatively, we need to switch to creative mode.

Knowing I was going to write about the human-only ability of creativity
and its usefulness in elevating our spirit, I gathered wisdom from other
authors and researchers, including Brené Brown, PhD, and Elizabeth Gilbert. But of all things I've read, nothing has hit home the way that one line
on the Minecraft wiki has. No matter what you think of yourself, whether

you can't draw a stick figure to save your life or would never choreograph a dance or direct a play, *everything* we do has a spice of creativity to it, if we choose. When we are creative in our thoughts and actions, in our approach to life and healing, and in our relationships, we begin to develop immunity to things that poke holes in our souls. Being creative keeps us intact; it keeps us in a mode of wholeness.

In her book *On Looking: Eleven Walks with Expert Eyes*, Alexandra Horowitz explains that the idea for the book came from her sense that she was "missing it all." So she posited the experiment of simply walking the New York City block on which she lived to prove how devastatingly right her hunch was. "We are walking around like zombies, missing it all," Horowitz writes. "Even when we are mindful, and pay attention to things, we are missing it all—the events unfolding in your body, in the distance, and right in front of you."

Creativity is required to live and grow and heal. We are turning our backs on an instinct that is necessary for us to exist, and when we do that, something feels off. We can't put our finger on it, but life just isn't right. It's our spirit crying out, *You're killing me.*

Fleshing out details of your pain experience (the who, what, where, why, and how), dissecting your emotions, accepting accountability, finding ways through fear, forgiving transgressions, strengthening hope, deepening motivation, defending core values, setting goals, hearing the divine being inside you—all of it, the hard work you are doing to become WHOLE again, is dependent on—and all the while deepening—your unique creativity.

There are simple tools and resources around us every day that beg for us to utilize them in creative ways to keep us healthy and whole. It is so simple that we take our ability to see them for granted, just as Horowitz proved as she recounted eleven walks she took around the city with various "experts," including her toddler son, to experience their unique lens of the world and to "knock herself awake."

Horowitz writes, "After taking the walks described in this book, I would find myself at once alarmed, delighted, and humbled at the limitations of my ordinary looking. My consolation is that this deviancy of mind is quite human. We see, but we do not see: We use our eyes, but our gaze is glancing, frivolously considering its object. We see signs, but not their meanings. We are not blinded, but have blinders."

The following spirit elevators are suggested to assist you as you take your second look at the resources that are as readily available to you as the clock on the kitchen wall. The more creative we are about how we use these resources, the more we enhance them and see how multifaceted they can be, like using a potato for food but also fuel. All we have to do is stop our ordinary looking to increase our immunity to damage.

NATURE

Nature heals. Study after study shows that being in nature is a stress reducer, lowers blood pressure, and promotes heart health. In my humble opinion, there is no better proof that nature heals than the fact that our bodies are incapable of creating an essential vitamin—vitamin D—without physical exposure to the sun. By the way, here is a cool fact about vitamin D: It's actually not a vitamin, but a hormone produced by the body after the skin is directly penetrated by sunlight. You can fortify milk as much as you want, but the body requires being outside to live. Author Richard Louv coined a phrase that sums it up nicely: We have "nature-deficit disorder." A famous study proves that just a picture of nature hung on a hospital room or an office wall can have beneficial mind-body healing effects. Anecdotally speaking, being in nature also obviously helps us get the exercise we need to stay healthy (walking, hiking, running, mowing the lawn, chopping wood), and nature is the place most people retreat to when they need a break or a vacation, be it the mountains of Vail or the beaches of Montauk or the vineyards of Napa. It's a mood lifter; anyone with seasonal affective disorder can attest to that. And being in and experiencing nature reconnects people by disconnecting them from their gadgets. Being in nature also improves self-esteem, lowers depression, and reduces anxiety. So when we need to improve our physical and emotional health, we need to get ourselves some ecotherapy!

Nature provides answers. Over billions of years, Mother Nature has evolved solutions to its own engineering and design challenges. Therefore, nature is teeming with ideas for solutions to our own human challenges. An example I read about explained how termites in the African savanna manage to keep their buildings, called mounds, at a consistent temperature while temperatures outside drastically fluctuate. Their wisdom might help an industry known as heating and cooling. When engineers go to nature to mimic its wisdom, by the way, what they are doing is called biomimicry.

Even Jesus was known to seek out nature to think things out. Luke 5:16: "He often withdrew into the wilderness, and prayed." Two thousand years later, our beings are still hardwired for connection to nature.

Nature provides inspiration for ideas to work out our troubles in relationships and for staying motivated. To this day, no matter how often I see it, I am always stunned to watch an ant carry food on its back. I have such respect for the ant colonies that live around my home; what they do is admirable, and I imagine how they are engaged in the present moment when they are just doing their work. We are brought to tears by Facebook videos capturing a cat and dog grooming one another, a reminder that maybe we should try to better understand those who are not like us—and love them anyway. I could go on with the way nature provides us answers. It's just how creative you are in looking at it.

Nature is humbling. As my plane made its descent into the Los Angeles International Airport for my first trip there in too long, I lifted the shade to watch the landing. The earth below was darkening, with lengthening shadows on the city skyline, and the stars glittered above me in clear, magical view. I was reminded how I take for granted the beauty and natural wonder of my surroundings. All day long, like you, I'm rushing off to complete one task or begin another, rarely seeing what is right in front of me. One of those facts is that we exist by a fluke on a humongous rock floating in infinite space. That's remarkable! My daily concerns suddenly seem petty when I go cosmic.

Another time I was humbled when I was drawn to dirt. I spotted rocks and a stick and felt this overwhelming urge to sketch in the earth. I popped a squat and meditated in the dirt, scraping circles around rocks, relaxed as a child on the beach. My years of playing with cars in the dirt were long gone, and now, as a grown woman, I found the simple joy was much missed. And not completely outgrown.

Nature loves unconditionally. Our senses are drawn to nature, yet nature renders only service to us. This is one of the reasons Shel Silverstein's tragic tale *The Giving Tree* never fails to bring tears to my eyes and to puzzle my wide-eyed children, who wonder (but intuitively know) why the tree had evolved into a stump. Nature is also our source, and it loves us no matter what we do because we are one with it. As astronomer Carl Sagan stated, we are star stuff: "The nitrogen in our DNA, the calcium in our teeth, the iron in our blood, the carbon in our apple pies were made in the interiors of collapsing stars. We are made of star stuff."

> *The man who can forget his worries by means of a*
> *genuine interest in say . . . the history of stars, will find*
> *that, when he returns from his excursion into the impersonal*
> *world, he has acquired a poise and calm that enable*
> *him to deal with his worries in the best way.*
>
> —Bertrand Russell, *The Conquest of Happiness*

LIFTING YOUR SPIRIT BY LIFTING THE SPIRITS OF OTHERS

We all know that to grow a thriving plant, we need to water it and give it sunlight. But we also have scientific evidence that talking nicely and positively to the plant, even praising it, will help it thrive and grow. The same holds true with the power we have over others. I recently heard a story about a lonely man in a nursing home who told one of the aides that he would give his one good knee just to hear the giggle of a child. So she arranged with her granddaughter's nursery school to organize a class trip to visit the residents and lift their spirits. The man wept with happiness.

Camille, a waitress at a diner, is a single mother on government assistance. After her old beater of a car broke down, she was two hundred dollars short of getting it back on the road. So Camille walked to work every day and delivered food with a smile on her face, sometimes to come home after an eight-hour shift with only thirty bucks in her pocket. Then one of her regulars, a widower in his sixties, left Camille a two-hundred-dollar tip, saying comically, "Here's a tip for ya, Cammy—go get your car fixed."

We eat up stories like this because they remind us that people are kind and that, most of the time, we are good to each other, even strangers. We are all connected, and acts of kindness and generosity and giving of ourselves in some way, large or small, put healthy, vibrant energy back into the universe. We all benefit when the universe feels good; that's when we receive abundance.

We get things done when we help others accomplish things. I know this because I have been the recipient of a lot of generosity. If it weren't for the kindness of strangers building houses with Habitat for Humanity, I probably wouldn't be where I am now. If those generous volunteers had instead thought my family should fend for ourselves, would we have wound up on the street? But our being homeless and hungry wouldn't help other people in any way. We would pull resources from the system and be five more uneducated kids to grow up as ignorant adults. Instead, the Habitat folks gave my siblings and me a chance to stay in school and get our education and have heat in the wintertime and a place to gather for dinner.

According to Dr. Robert Anthony, "Giving help is one of the little-known secrets of success. . . . If you are a supervisor, manager, or boss, by assisting those under you to become successful, you become more successful yourself. If you are a teacher, success comes in direct proportion to your success in helping your students succeed; it comes by showing them how they can get what they want, not what you want. Any relationship can grow and prosper when we learn to assist others."

We don't have to hand out cash or volunteer at a charity to be charitable. Just by our actions, we can support people. Recently I was embarrassingly late for a meeting. As I frantically rushed into the restaurant for a meeting scheduled almost an hour earlier, I apologized profusely to my associate. I was horrified by how long I had kept him waiting. "It's fine; stay calm, Melissa," he said in his chill manner. "It was meant to be that we meet later. I ate something, read an article I've been meaning to read; it's all good." He eased my guilt so convincingly that I thought maybe he should thank *me*. "Just one caveat," he said. "Pay it forward. Next time someone screws up with you, ease their pain."

When we act kindly, we lift the spirits of others, and we make them feel important, alive, and capable of growing and improving. We remind them and ourselves that we are all flawed and imperfectly perfect and nobody is above reproach or deserving of judgment.

A compliment can go a long way too. Doling out compliments is probably one of my favorite pastimes. You don't know what kinds of hardships a person may have endured that day or that week, and a compliment points out the person's positive traits. "One of the greatest gifts we can give to other people is to open their eyes to their own greatness; to the potential they never realized existed," writes Dr. Anthony.

To be selfless in giving ourselves, we are being wonderfully selfish. We increase our self-confidence when we help raise others'. By giving encouragement and underscoring the strengths of others, we satisfy our own need for love. A positive action begets a positive action until it generates so much positive response, it creates an incredible feedback loop in the brain. According to acclaimed neuroscientist Richard J. Davidson, PhD, founder of the

Get Your Generosity Juices Flowing

It feels so good to give back or to help out a friend or family member, and that doesn't just mean in their down times. Generosity could be networking for a friend who is trying to start her own natural beauty line, or introducing two people who have the same struggles with their special needs children. I find that even acting as a connector of people helps me feel like I have shown my friends and family that I notice them and care about them, even if I am being swallowed by my own schedule, because it doesn't take but a minute to send an e-mail or share a contact card from my phone.

You can really flex your creativity muscle by figuring out ways to make other people feel special. I've been known to give a pep talk to a stranger in a nail salon or a hug to the bartender who just told me about her child's run-in with the law. I can't help it sometimes. Give hand-me-downs to your needy sister-in-law. Or go "spooking" or "elfing" by dropping off anonymous goodie bags on the doorsteps of friends during Halloween and Christmas. You'll feel as good as if your own mailbox were filling up with chocolate!

This is not the most unique idea in the world, but maybe nowadays with technology ubiquitous in our lives, it can really surprise someone: Send a card in the mail. Like, with real postage. Who doesn't love getting mail that isn't from the credit card company? And it's a nice way to keep the men and women at the post office employed. Journeying through our pain experience, we have likely rounded up some great people who have supported us and whom we know we can never repay. But little things like cards and elfing, an extra hug or a text message, tell our personal army we love them and still need them in our happy times, not just the bad ones. We should all be like Stevie Wonder and just call to say "I love you." No strings attached.

Center for Healthy Minds at the University of Wisconsin–Madison, "The most effective strategy for changing specific circuits in the brain associated with well-being is generosity."

I decided to test this for myself. After hearing about a movement and book, both titled *29 Gifts*, I picked up the book and read it in one plane ride. Author Cami Walker is an absolute miracle and inspiration. After being diagnosed with multiple sclerosis just one month after her wedding at age thirty-three, Cami found herself battling her neurological condition in and out of Los Angeles hospitals. She was barely able to walk and experienced enormous stress on her marriage. Each day her negative thoughts persisted:

I'm going to end up in a wheelchair. My life is over.

Why did this have to happen to me?

Confiding in her friend, a South African medicine woman named Mbali Creazzo, Cami received the prescription of her life: *Give away twenty-nine gifts in twenty-nine days.*

"By giving," Mbali told her, "you are focusing on what you have to offer others, inviting more abundance into your life."

The gifts could be anything—an act, a phrase, an actual present—but their giving had to be purposeful and authentic. At least one gift needed to be something Cami believed was scarce in her own life.

And that's exactly what Cami did. When she had no money in her checking account, she donated spare change. When she felt depressed and despondent about her disease, she comforted a friend who also had MS. Her other acts were as simple as making a phone call and offering a tissue, yet they were transformative as Cami embraced the natural process of giving and receiving. By day twenty-nine, Cami had more strength to walk, was solicited for consulting jobs spontaneously, had better communication with her husband, and was generally happier and healthier. Her journey reminded me of Pat Longo's discussion of raising vibrations. Do good deeds and find yourself lifting to the ceiling to attract more of what's waiting for you there.

Cami was so affected by her newfound remedy for living, she began an online movement (29gifts.org). In my journal, I record some of the kind things I do or say purposely during the day. It helps me take stock of how I am living according to my values and trying to mindfully bring joy to others and feel connected to them. Certainly check out the Web site for ideas on how to get your own calendar—and your heart—filled with good vibrations.

> *When I do good, I feel good. When I do bad,*
> *I feel bad. That's my religion.*
>
> —Abraham Lincoln

SENSE-ATIONAL

Touch

Ken Wilbur wrote in *The Spectrum of Consciousness,* "For every mental 'problem' or 'knot,' there is a corresponding bodily 'knot,' and vice versa since, in fact, the body and the mind are not two." So your shame, guilt, grief, or stress can get stuck in your body as what Karen Farber, PhD, describes as "body memories." When the site of the emotional difficulty is effectively touched through massage, it not only can release the physical pain but may make the emotional pain reachable.

> *If you feel something, let people know that you feel it. Don't*
> *you get tired of these stoic faces that don't show you anything?*
> *If you feel like laughing, laugh. If you like what somebody*
> *says, go up and give them a hug. If it is right, it will be right.*
>
> —Leo Buscaglia, PhD

"Massage therapy is a mechanism for me to guide people and introduce them to their own power to heal," explains Daniel Rios, a healing therapist at the famed Gurney's Montauk Resort and Saltwater Spa, who also is in private practice. Touch is a universal form of communication and care. In the wild, a primate that hurts himself will immediately grab his aching part. The same nonhuman primates spend 10 to 20 percent of their waking day grooming each other. We're not so lucky. Western culture is quite "touch-deprived," to quote Dacher Keltner, PhD, the founding faculty director of the Greater Good Science Center and a professor of psychology at the University of California, Berkeley. In Eastern medicine, however, touch is one of the pathways to healing, with the transfer of energy emphasized.

Put away the thoughts that massage is a feel-good spoiling session reserved for people with too much money and/or too much time on their hands. To the contrary, contend experts at the Mayo Clinic, massage can be a powerful tool to help you take charge of your health and well-being, whether you have a specific health condition or are just looking for a stress reliever. Self-massage at home or with a partner is also an option. People additionally can scratch their itch for touch by seeking out chiropractors, physical therapists, Gestalt therapists, Rolfers, Alexander technique and Feldenkrais practitioners, massage therapists, martial arts teachers, and tai chi instructors.

"Proper uses of touch truly have the potential to transform the practice of medicine," explains Dr. Keltner. Studies show that touching patients with Alzheimer's disease can have large effects on helping them relax, make emotional connections with other people, and reduce symptoms of depression.

In his article "Hands On Research: The Science of Touch," Dr. Keltner cites Tiffany Field, a leader in researching touch, who found that massage therapy reduces pain in pregnant women and alleviates prenatal depression—in the women and their spouses alike. "Research here at UC Berkeley's School of Public Health has found that getting eye contact and a pat on the back from a doctor may boost survival rates of patients with complex diseases," writes Dr. Keltner.

Field also found that premature infants who received fifteen-minute sessions of touch therapy each day for five to ten days gained 47 percent more weight than premature infants who'd received standard medical treatment.

According to Dr. Keltner, "Touch can even be a therapeutic way to reach some of the most challenging children: Some research by Tiffany Field suggests that children with autism, widely believed to hate being touched, actually love being massaged by a parent or therapist."

Touch is important, and our dependency on touching those we love and have compassion for as well as being touched is nothing to be ashamed of or embarrassed about. When we stop turning our back on our most biological need, we can be sure we elevate our spirit.

Sound

Do you hum when you're happy, whistle while you work, or listen to Barbra Streisand when you're sad? Perhaps you like the sounds of meditation bells or gongs or even the sound of a white noise machine. To try to soothe my screaming newborn back to sleep in the wee hours of the night, exhausted and desperate, I began a two-note repetitive hum. Now, even though he's all grown up, if I hum it, he falls right asleep (accompanied by a back rub, of course—see "Touch," above). He has no recollection of hearing the hum as a baby, but it never fails. And you know what, I think it's just as soothing to me to hum it. It's sound healing, and that's nothing new.

In an article in *Today's OR Nurse*, Carol L. Cirina wrote about the remarkable effects music has on preoperative patients. Patients' anxiety, fueled by loss of control, pain, mutilation, and the unknown, surprisingly is unrelated to the seriousness of the surgery. But going into surgery accompanied by the side effects of anxiety—including raised blood pressure, shortness of breath, trembling, restlessness, muscular tension, and fatigue—could have negative efficacy on the surgery and recovery. Cirina reports that music

Ways to Elevate Your Spirit Using Touch and Smell

Stroke your pet.

Smell your child's skin.

Hug.

Buy your grandmother's perfume and smell her again.

Bake cookies.

Light scented candles or incense and diffuse essential oil.

Take note of how the fireplace smells or how the air smells right before a snowstorm.

Invest in high-thread-count sheets that make your skin tingle when you slip into them.

Grab someone's shoulder while you shake their hand.

Take up ballroom or Latin dancing.

Have more sex.

Splurge an extra ten bucks once in a while and add a foot massage to your pedicure.

therapy, as a relaxation technique used for patients before, during, and after surgery, can manage, reduce, and prevent undesired outcomes.

But not all music is created equal. "The response to music is a function of the music and the listener," reports Cirina. "The individual's personal preference and past experience with music play a major role." Tempo also plays a more objective part in music therapy, according to Cirina. "The effect of the music depends on pitch (the number of vibrations from sound waves) and tempo (the number of beats per minute)."

It isn't surprising that high pitches act as a psychological stressor while low pitches promote relaxation by stimulating the parasympathetic nervous system, resulting in decreased heart rate, blood pressure, and respiration.

But it's not just music that soothes our sense of hearing. Ambient noise, crinkling, low steady voices, the slice of scissors over a strand of hair at the salon, the smooth sounds of cursive writing with a pencil, even the tapping of a woman's fingernails on a box: These can create what people have described as a head tingle or a sensation of complete and total relaxation. It hits like a wave. One time it happened to me at the bank as the account manager was rustling papers gently in a file cabinet. It was like a wave of thick static washed over me, and I drifted into a calm sea of air. I felt weird because I was hoping she would never stop. Now I know, thank goodness, that this experience is something that happens to millions of people. The technical name is autonomous sensory meridian response, or ASMR, and proponents say it can lead to a number of therapeutic, albeit scientifically unproven, benefits. Not limited to the sense of hearing, ASMR is said to be a response to visual, auditory, tactile, olfactory (sense of smell), or cognitive stimuli.

All you have to do is google ASMR and tons of videos are available, from pouring and drinking a cold soda to people going on doctor's visits. I felt out of the loop on what is now an emerging subculture of everyday people using video and audio to trigger the head tingles for millions of strangers worldwide. Viewers and listeners report an ASMR effect that relieves insomnia, anxiety, or panic attacks. I watched some of the YouTube videos, and they work! On his blog *NeuroLogica*, Steven Novella, MD, a prominent neuroscientist and assistant professor at Yale University School of Medicine, wrote briefly on the topic of ASMRs. He believes that ASMRs are most likely real, and their neurological causes could range from mini seizures to hardwired evolutionary reactions.

Sight

A great mindfulness practice is repetitive viewing. Psychic Melissa Harris describes it as visiting the same scene at different times of the day as well as different times of the year. Michele told me she practices repetitive viewing during vacations spent with family at her in-laws' summer home.

"On the top of the hill sits our house overlooking Peconic Bay," she explained. "We sit and watch the sunset every evening in the summertime. The ritual is so sacrosanct, even the four- and five-year-olds announce when it's time to head to the deck, which is raised a hundred feet above the beach. My husband and I got engaged there during the winter, and I'll never forget where the sun was positioned in the sky as he got down on bended knee.

"The repetitive viewing not only keeps us in tune with the beauty and wonders of our planet and the real power player in our solar system, it's something we as a family come together to enjoy each and every time. So in a way, we are repetitively viewing each other. It is something you just never get tired of the way you do a television series or a played-out song. Each time, it's different, like a snowflake, and we are so lucky to have had this home passed down to us through generations."

Repetitive viewing makes your vision expansive, and it trains you to make a habit of viewing repetitively other things you take for granted, like a sleeping infant, a grandmother rocking in her chair, or a football team running onto the field before a big game. Each time, the players are bigger, different, more confident, more fired up. They are ever changing, and that is a humbling idea the soul needs to remember.

ART THERAPY

Writing to Heal

Writing is simply another path to meditation, to making space for a healthier emotional life by observing and then letting go. When we process, we see clues as to what we find comfortable in our lives and what we don't. As renowned meditation guide Davidji explains, in meditation, connections and themes arise. I have found this to be true of writing. In his hypnotic voice, Davidji explains, "By being a silent witness, by being that observer of all your behavior, day after day, you get clues to what truly nourishes you and what doesn't. You get insights to what direction it makes sense for you to lean, and which direction it makes sense for you to lean away from. You are given the answer to what is comfortable and what is not comfortable, and at the most innocent and cellular level, you begin to lean closer to what serves you and lean a bit further away from what doesn't serve you. You'll become more connected and closer to those things in your life that are nourishing, nurturing, and supportive."

In a study by psychologists, another common theme is the idea of manifestation in writing that is similar to manifestation meditations. For instance, Sonja Lyubomirsky, PhD, and Kennon M. Sheldon, PhD, discovered in their research that subjects who wrote about their best possible future selves experienced health benefits and had a higher aptitude to set and achieve goals. There's a meditation for that as well.

No matter where you find yourself in your pain experience, writing will help you maintain and sustain your spirit.

As you write, don't write as if anyone else is reading your prose. This is not the time to try to impress anyone. There should be no other purpose than reviewing and exploring your thoughts and feelings by recording them. Include conversations with others or reflections you want to make about a session with a therapist. If something becomes too difficult to write, just jot down a laundry list of things that happened. But don't stop. Like all practices, writing to heal must be done every day. Writing, in general, if it is for creative or publishing pursuits, should be done daily. Don't skip because you had a rough day or you're too spent. Write that fact down, and then turn out the light.

Healing Poetry

Diane Morrow is a former medical doctor turned English teacher who through her own pain experience used writing as a pathway to healing. She now runs the Web site writingandhealing.org. It's a cool site that invites readers to, over a year's time, engage in Diane's suggestions and prompts to write their way to healing. Not much of a poet myself—or a poetry fan, for that matter—I was awakened to amazing prose by some of the suggestions Diane included on her site for poems that inspire healing and solace. Here is a list that resonated well with her personally. Perhaps they will encourage you to seek out your own favorites or try your hand at writing poetry yourself.

POEMS THAT CONJURE A HEALING PLACE

"Last Night As I Was Sleeping" by Antonio Machado

"The Peace of Wild Things" by Wendell Berry

"The Lake Isle of Innisfree" by W. B. Yeats

"Island of the Raped Women" by Frances Driscoll

"Keeping Quiet" by Pablo Neruda

"What I Want" by Alicia Ostriker

POEMS THAT MIGHT OFFER COMPANY DURING A DIFFICULT TIME

"The Guest House" by Rumi

"A Ritual to Read to Each Other" by William Stafford

"Satellite Call" by Sara Bareilles

"The Armful" by Robert Frost

"The Spell" by Marie Howe

"Talking to Grief" by Denise Levertov

"Sweetness" by Stephen Dunn

POEMS FOR LOOKING AT THE WORLD IN NEW WAYS

"Wild Geese" by Mary Oliver

"Thirteen Ways of Looking at a Blackbird" by Wallace Stevens

"who knows if the moon's" by e.e. cummings

"The Snow Man" by Wallace Stevens

"His Bathrobe Pockets Stuffed with Notes" by Raymond Carver

"The Summer Day" by Mary Oliver

"MEDICISE" = MEDITATION PLUS EXERCISE

"I don't think I ever really understood the importance of stretching until I started Pilates," Michele told me. We knew we couldn't avoid the discussion of exercise in this chapter, as it is a scientific fact that exercise is good for us in every possible way, and Michele's enthusiasm for Pilates made me want to learn more about how it has elevated her spirit. From physical health to brain health to disease prevention, exercise is key. But in certain forms, or if approached in certain ways, physical exertion can also be your choice of meditation. Meditation meets exercise, or "medicise," is how Michele defines Pilates. "Because it incorporates the strengthening of the core with an emphasis on lengthening the body, it is the single most important form of exercise I do. With each session, I know I have inoculated my body against injury, and as I grow older, I have begun to put more emphasis on aging well and being strong than on the numbers on the scale."

Michele told me that during some of her own trying times, the repetitive motions on the reformer—a machine on which practitioners perform movements with resistance—coupled with the hormone release from the exercise itself have helped her feel more balanced. "Aside from the obvious benefits of the exercise, it's more meaningful that this is the only exercise I have done every single day for more than three years. I haven't broken that appointment with myself, and that is what is really elevating my spirit. Elizabeth Gilbert in her book *Big Magic* says we should have affairs with ourselves. Going to my Pilates classes is exactly that. I go out of my way to get there because when I leave, I know I am going to feel high."

Marisa Minutoli, founder and owner of the Pilates Studio Inc., in Glen Cove, New York, has witnessed emotional, physical, and spiritual transformations in her clients for going on a decade. "I have had clients who have had terrible things happen to them and use Pilates as a form of meditation, which is only one component. Because the exercises are repetitive, the repetition itself soothes stress," explained Minutoli. "The second benefit is the exertion and sweat, which obviously increases endorphins, making you happy."

Minutoli became an instructor because of her personal experience with serious back problems at the age of sixteen. Three herniated disks had led the young Marisa to be medicated with dangerous (now off the market) anti-inflammatories. She was prescribed twelve Advil a day and ordered to bed rest. While her peers were out doing what teens do, Marisa was preparing for dangerous surgery and a long recovery. Her uncle suggested Pilates. She gave it a whirl, despite the fact that nobody was really talking about Pilates at the time, and three months later was off all her meds. A year later, she was pain-free, flexible, mobile, and strong. She never had the surgery.

While a discussion of back pain might not seem to fit this book, it is important to note that emotional pain experiences are known to affect the back. The pioneering book *Healing Back Pain: The Mind-Body Connection* by John E. Sarno, MD, is a prime example of this idea. The most common physical complaints of people who are stressed are backache and headache. When you work the back through Pilates, you help shield your central nervous system from responding to the psychological or emotional trauma you are facing. Neurosurgeon Patrick Roth, MD, author of *The End of Back Pain*, pays the bills by performing spine surgery, yet in his book he urges back-pain sufferers to try to commit to a host of other therapies before visiting him; one of his suggested therapies is Pilates.

"When I am stressed, my back begins to bother me, so I go work out, and my stress goes away and so does my back pain," said Minutoli. "And when you're in pain, you get depressed. But Pilates creates space in your disk, so it's not all mental, but even a little physical relief you might achieve after a class mitigates your depression."

The stretching component of Pilates is critical. In fact, a recent finding has shown that a predictor of life span is the ability to get oneself off the floor without pushing off with the arms or leaning on the knees. "That's all core, flexibility, and strength," Minutoli posited. "Stretching has a lot to do with people's muscles being tight every single day and that tightness pulling on your body, so being limber will help you feel lighter. There is an oxygenation process that happens through stretching. For me, I feel like my brain opens up. I am breathing repetitively, deeply. To work the core properly, you must breathe and engage the core simultaneously."

Minutoli knows firsthand that exercise "1 million percent can help you get through painful experiences." She told me that after her mother passed away, her studio was her only retreat to feel free. "I get the best workouts when I'm a little bit sad."

While Pilates or any other kind of exercise is a subjective choice, the takeaway here is to elevate the spirit by choosing a practice that allows you to breathe and stretch and focus on flexibility; sweat and work the core; connect with others; and enjoy it immensely. Through acts of caring for yourself, you build an inner sanctuary that will be there when you need to retreat to it most.

We Will No Longer Languish:
The Real Secret

*The most beautiful and most profound emotion we
can experience is the sensation of the mystical. He to whom
this emotion is a stranger, who can no longer wonder
and stand rapt in awe, is as good as dead.*

—Albert Einstein

Close writer friend, novelist, and overall super-talent Olivia Rupprecht and I were talking about my friend Allison's extraordinary experience with and view of her cancer. Even as much as Allison's strength and optimism were contagious, I still wasn't quite sure what she had that so many of us don't.

"I know the feeling," Olivia told me. "My sister-in-law is one of those special souls who have soared in the face of one of her life's greatest challenges." With that, Olivia told me Chris's story, one that so many caregivers know all too well. The following is an e-mail Olivia wrote that she graciously allowed us to include here.

Chris's Story

When my sister-in-law, Chris, said these words to me, I had to reconsider what had seemed like a cruel trick of nature that has visited too many families with aging parents: Alzheimer's disease and other forms of advanced dementia.

My mother-in-law, LaVerne, is ninety-three, and while physically in amazing health, her once-sharp mind has been deteriorating for some time. She and my sister-in-law have always been birds of a feather, but it wasn't until LaVerne really started to struggle that they became close in the way that Chris told me about when she uttered those words.

Over time, Chris watched as LaVerne segued from having almost virtual recall of dates, even birthdays of people she met only once, to not knowing the day, the month, or that being fully dressed and waiting for breakfast at four a.m. at her nice assisted-living apartment was a wee bit early. Painting, knitting, all the crafts she so enjoyed became too challenging to attempt . . . or remember how to. Basic skills such as cooking, reading, even signing her name little by little diminished until it became apparent to the three children their mother needed hands-on caretaking around the clock, either by one of them, or at a full-time dementia care facility.

Chris had recently retired as a teacher, unlike her two younger siblings who had another five or ten years to go before retiring themselves. With her sons now grown and on their own, she was able to enjoy the payback of her own hard work with the occasional cruise and travels abroad with her friends. She'd just bought a little condo in Florida for the winters when decision time came. Without hesitation Chris said, "I'll take care of Mom." Simple as that. And yet it was not at all that simple. Many sacrifices and changes to her own lifestyle had to be made—such as giving up her new condo, her independence, and any travel plans beyond trips to a daycare provider while caring for a mother who had not lived outside the state of Wisconsin for nearly ninety years and had to be moved to Colorado.

The trajectory of this disease is unpredictable, and watching its leeching progress is an awful thing to witness, even from a distance. But Chris did not complain while she washed Mom's hair, bathed her, instigated a routine to keep her as stabilized as possible, changed her clothes, took her for drives in the mountains, went over old pictures, and recalled old memories again and again and again. Chris told me, "I have asked myself, *Why couldn't I have been this person when dealing with a troubled marriage? Why couldn't I have been this patient with my children, or found the wherewithal to handle things better when I was younger?* I don't know, but I do know this. I am the best version of myself that I have ever been as a caretaker for Mom. And crazy as it might sound, as much as I hate seeing Mom deteriorate like this, I feel a sense of gratitude for an experience that has allowed me to become a better me."

It was like I'd climbed up Mount Everest and received a gift of insight from some great Zen master.

A few months ago, LaVerne had to be moved to a memory care home where nurses and staff members are able to provide the assistance she needs and Chris is not professionally qualified to give. I think the move was harder for Chris than for LaVerne, who no longer recognizes the daughter who gave up three years of her own life for 24/7 care. Chris has had a little time for some restorative self-care she needed and damn well deserves, but she goes to see her mother nearly every day. It is an act of devotion and love that I'm not sure I would have the internal depth or wherewithal to emulate but is something I aspire to. And I have to believe we can all take hope in knowing that if there is any purpose to be had from any disease that seems senseless, inhumane, and without merit—some event that could happen to any of us or our loved ones, be it Alzheimer's, cancer, or a debilitating illness that could strike at a young age—perhaps there is still something to be gained if we can find the best part of ourselves as a result of the unthinkable. ❦

Reading Olivia's e-mail sparked something of an epiphany. Allison and Chris, while experiencing completely different storms, were experiencing a delightful and dangerous emotion known as awe.

In 2007, Dr. Paul Pearsall, a renowned neuropsychologist and author of nineteen books, wrote his final work, a book based on his lifetime of research on awe, what he called the most intense, wonderful, upsetting, and transcendently terrible of all human emotions. He also said that we are lucky to have the natural propensity to experience awe.

Oh yeah, sign me up for some of that terrible and tragic sensation! Sounds kind of nuts, especially since we're attempting to be WHOLE here. But if you think about it, the emotions we usually accept as normal—love, fear, sadness, embarrassment, curiosity, pride, enjoyment, despair, guilt, and anger—skew toward the negative, and they don't necessarily lead us to the meaning of life. Dr. Pearsall was sending us an urgent call that he knew the secret to finding purpose and meaning, and it was in our choice to experience our life, every part of it, through the mysterious emotion of awe.

"Unlike all the other emotions," he writes, awe is "all of our feelings rolled up into one intense one. You can't peg it as just happy, sad, afraid, angry, or hopeful. Instead, it's a matter of experiencing all of these feelings and yet, paradoxically, experiencing no clearly identifiable, or at least any easily describable, emotion. Awe overwhelms and drains the power out of any other singular emotion we may have had before it took hold, and the best description I've been able to give it so far is that—no matter how good or bad our brain considers whatever is happening to be—it is feeling more totally and completely alive than we thought possible before we were in awe."

The way I make sense of it, awe is like mindful awareness, except you are encouraged to think, and think hard and a lot. When you are in awe, whether it is like Dr. Pearsall's first experience of awe when he held his tiny newborn son, who was afflicted with cerebral palsy and was fighting for his life, or like the butterfly that landed on your arm and stayed there for a remarkably long time, awe wants you to remember the incident and the insurmountable wonder and fear that accompany this miracle that is touching you. Then, awe helps you focus on that moment so intensely that it imprints itself on your soul, and you forever contemplate the event and consider what it means to your being, your trajectory, and your choices moving forward.

We usually neglect our awe response, says Dr. Pearsall, because we are afraid of how uncomfortable it makes us. Instead, we choose to be happy or sad, and both emotions pass and therefore the experience with it. But by its nature, awe demands to be reflected upon, or else it will no longer bestow its messages of why we are here and how we should live. "Awe is an emotion designed to help us experience and learn from the paradox that life is as dreadful as it is divine, better than we can imagine and worse than we fear, and as short as it is meaningful."

This part of the book has been devoted to elevating the spirit, and each discussion of this topic turns on our senses: our ability to listen to our intuition, to stop ordinary looking, to see nature as an extension of us, and to use our physical senses more adeptly while nurturing our souls with the gifts art and exercise bestow. If we can take all these elements to a higher level by choosing to live with more "open-ture" than closure, to contemplate our meaning to the point that it makes us feel uncertain, strange, and excited, then we will spend less energy trying to move past our pain and instead move into life itself.

In W: Watch the Storm, we spoke of the necessity of accepting our emotions, even soaking them in, before doing anything else. Philosopher Immanuel Kant believed that without our full perception and processing and understanding of what happens to us, even if the occurrence upsets us and we are meant to not excel or succeed, life becomes "less than even a dream."

Awareness, however, is not the end goal. Awareness becomes the pathway to the real goal—the real secret: Awareness leads to awe.

"Awe is an emotion we seem able to tolerate only in short, small doses, but thinking about what awed us can take a lifetime," writes Dr. Pearsall. As Allison experienced, awe is one emotion that feels wonderful, beautiful, ugly, dreadful, scary, empowering, invigorating, and frightening all at the same time—but it is the miracle that carried her through and no doubt sustains her to this day. Awe intensifies the need to connect not only with what inspired our awe but to, in Dr. Pearsall's words, "make a commitment to more loving, caring, protective relationships with others and the world in general." That is what elevation is about—not just the fleeting experience of awe, but committing to the act of pursuing it.

When I visited my father in jail for the first time after his conviction, accompanied by the harsh realization that I was now fatherless and the realities still sinking in regarding what he actually did, I believe the whole experience awed me. The event remains in my mind as a turning point and a terrifying feeling that I am one degree of separation from so many families because of his murderous nature. We often say that we are all connected, but I know that I am connected to these women because their blood was shed at the hands of my father. That is awe-full and it speaks to me now, so many years later.

Deciding to live a life filled with awe is choosing a difficult life, but choosing awe allowed me to realize that now I was officially in charge and alone without a father. My father would be out of my life forever and could not provide for me. He would and could no longer shield me from my fears and my problems or be a protector. It was liberating as much as frightening, the paradox that awe brings. To know life was on my terms now. I was alone, but I could determine my own life. Awe helped me to grieve, to let go. Had it been a subtle emotion, I would have languished in the middle space of hope. Hope for things to change, hope that would have been delusional.

Emotion means "energy in motion." How we feel is an engine of energy chugging forward or backward. Whether your awe is triggered by something like Dr. Pearsall experienced when he held the body of his thirty-five-year-old son after he committed suicide to escape the pain of his cerebral palsy, or whether it is brought on by a comet sighting that connects you to your own star stuff, awe is the only emotion—the only true power you have—that will unlock the lessons of terrible loss.

The awe response is one of the most powerful ways in which we go from languishing to flourishing—a state psychologists define as living at the optimum range of human functioning *no matter what is happening to us.*

When we get there, we are truly WHOLE.

ACKNOWLEDGMENTS

My deepest heartfelt thanks go to my brilliant coauthor, Michele Matrisciani, whose talent and wisdom is shared on every page. It's been wonderful to have gotten to know you over all these years of research and Skype calls. This would not have been possible without your dedication and partnership!

To my book family at Rodale. I feel very lucky to have worked with these extraordinary people who shared Michele's and my passion for *WHOLE*. Thank you, Leah Miller, who gave invaluable editorial guidance; Jennifer Levesque; Gail Gonzales; Hope Clarke; Carol Angstadt, for the beautiful cover design; Susan Turner; Sindy Berner; Angie Giammarino; and the Macmillan team.

To Marilyn Allen, my literary agent. They say people will remember you by how you treat them, and Marilyn is the embodiment of that statement with her unconditional affirmations of love and support.

To my beloved family: my children, Aspen and Jake Moore. And to the wonderful women in our lives: my mother, Rose; my sister, Carrie Jesperson; my mother-in-law, Linda Moore; and my sister-in-law, Lori Ruckhaber. To my husband, Sam, who was my consistent cheerleader and a fierce believer in all I do. God bless him for thinking I am so wonderful, but I'm glad I have him duped. To Dan and the Moore family. To the Jesperson family: Betty, Les, Sharon, Brad, Bruce, Jill, and Jason, who are brave examples of dignity in times of crisis.

To my tribe of friends who supported me and my family through the process of creating *WHOLE*; Shalise Cox, Andrea Rothstein, Jen Antonelli,

Tania Allen, and Amber Harris. Thank you for reading my drafts, providing moral support as I put my work into the world, and for building my faith in my true purpose.

To my supporters at A&E network: Laura Fleury, Jennifer Wagman, who allowed me to forge a path for all families affected by serial violence and to dissolve the stigma and silence that surrounds perpetrators' families. Some of those families' stories are shared within these pages.

To Warner Brothers, Lisa Gregorisch, Jeremey Spiegel, and Scott Eldridge. Thank you for making it possible to travel to meet families around the United States who were seeking to share their story in the aftermath of crime. Pat LaLama and Andrea Isom, you have been wonderful mentors and examples to me.

A special thank-you to Lisa Soloway, Joseph Diaz, JuJu Chang, Eric Strauss from ABC. Many thanks go to Stacy Ann, Katya Golberg, and Dr. Mehmet Oz.

Finally, thank you to all the brave families who shared their stories.

—*Melissa Moore*

First and foremost, I send my heartfelt gratitude and appreciation to my coauthor, Melissa Moore, who has made my job so inspiring and fulfilling. There have been many tears, much laughter, and numerous aha moments shared via Skype over the last three years, and they are imprinted on these pages. Melissa, I truly cannot thank you enough for the joy you have brought to my personal and professional life. A million hugs for all you contribute to this world.

I want to thank all the folks at the Glen Cove Library in Glen Cove, New York, who not only made me feel at home as I set up shop there, but ordered me countless books for research and assisted me at the reference desk. Marissa Lee Damiano and Amy Mondello were particularly helpful, enthusiastic, and cheerful. Libraries rock!

To our agent, Marilyn Allen, of Allen O'Shea Literary Agency. I loved her when I answered her calls at publishing houses years ago, and I love her now in *my* corner! Marilyn, thank you for being so genuine, supportive, and fun!

To all the amazingly talented and dedicated people at our publisher,

Rodale, especially my longtime buddy and former cubicle mate, Mark Weinstein, who made sure our proposal got into the right hands, and boy did it! He delivered it to Leah Miller, who shared our vision for this book and championed it all the way through on our behalf. Thank you for believing in this book and in us!

Thank you to the rest of the Rodale team: Editorial Assistant, Anna Cooperberg; Editorial Director, Jennifer Levesque; Publisher, Gail Gonzales; our tireless and meticulous Senior Project Editor, Hope Clarke; Susan Turner in public relations; Sindy Berner and Angie Giammarino in marketing: and the Macmillan sales team. And a special shout-out to Carol Angstadt, who brought tears to our eyes with her magnificent cover and interior design. What a talent!

I begin every single workday with a phone call to my colleague and one of my best friends, the brilliant editor and writer Carol Rosenberg, who always listens to me and who acted as my closest confidante throughout the writing of this book.

To my mentor, the talented novelist Olivia Rupprecht, who made me press "send" on the proposal when it was time to find an agent, who helped me through insecurity, and who is always there for me. Thank you for teaching me about writing.

Thank you to the last of my virtual water-cooler triad, writer Julie McCarron. You saved me so many times by burning up the phone lines with me. I am forever indebted.

When a project this important comes along, sacrifices need to be made, and my family, nuclear and extended, was there to help me make sense of it all. Thank you to the Matrisciani family, especially Robert and Sabrina Matrisciani and my cousin Sheri; the Rottino family; Piazza family; and Christina and Bobby Wahlig, who were with me when I committed to *WHOLE*. Thank you for helping me stay true to my goal.

A working mom isn't worth her salt without a great caregiver. Thank you to our babysitter, Liz Lottes. You made my life work! And thank you, Steven Yellin.

To all my friends, old and new, from those who played with me in the schoolyard when we were wee bitty to the ones who stand with me now to watch our kids run around the playground, thank you for being so open about your own experiences in becoming WHOLE.

My grandfather, Alex Matrisciani, was the one who handed me his antique Remington and told me I would one day work with words, but it was my parents, Margie and Dan Matrisciani, who told me that I actually *could* do it. My parents have not only emotionally supported me my entire life, but worried about me, loved me, and believed in me only as a mother and father could. It is because of their cheerleading, unrelenting faith, and gentle nudging that I got into this line of work in the first place.

My grandfather's prescient statement along with my parents' support weren't enough to push me in the direction I now live. My husband, Matthew Rottino, is the one who told me I *should* do it—take the leap, face the fear, and see what happens. I don't know who gets more excited about my work—Matthew or me. Actually I do know, which is why I am the luckiest woman in the world. You can't accomplish much without a partner who is picking up the slack, taking the brunt, and sitting in the backseat of the narcissist ride otherwise known as writing. Matthew, you have stepped up in the name of my happiness in more ways than I can count, and I will never forget that I am nothing without you.

Finally, to my sunshine, my sons, Daniel and Julian Rottino. When I was much younger, I saw you both in a dream. Now, I am living the dream.

—*Michele Matrisciani*

RESOURCES

W: Watch the Storm

1. Rabbi David Wolpe, *Making Loss Matter: Creating Meaning in Difficult Times* (New York: Riverhead Books, 2000).
2. Daniel J. Siegel, MD, on the fight, flight, and freeze response, see http://www.stressstop.com/stress-tips/articles/fight-flight-or-freeze-response-to-stress.php, accessed May 11, 2016.
3. Richard Levine lecture about evolution of trauma response, see https://www.youtube.com/watch?v=nmJDkzDMllc&index=18&list=PL_eozynnqyAUCK JrT-3K9sQbOFcAWghfg, accessed May 11, 2016.
4. Richard Blonner, EdD, *Stress Less, Live More: How Acceptance & Commitment Therapy Can Help You Live a Busy Yet Balanced Life* (Oakland: New Harbinger Publications, 2010).
5. 4 Swords Tarot card meaning, see http://www.aeclectic.net/tarot/learn/meanings/four-of-swords.shtml, accessed May 11, 2016.
6. The Chopra Center, "Rewire your brain for happiness," chopra.com, http://www.chopra.com/ccl/rewire-your-brain-for-happiness, accessed May 11, 2016.
7. James W. Pennebaker, PhD, *Opening Up: The Healing Power of Expressing Emotions* (New York: The Guilford Press, 1990).
8. Art Markman, PhD, "Trauma and the Benefits of Writing about It," *Psychology Today,* October 20, 2009, https://www.psychologytoday.com/blog/ulterior-motives/200910/trauma-and-the-benefits-writing-about-it, accessed May 11, 2016.
9. Marci Shimoff, *Happy for No Reason: 7 Steps to Being Happy from the Inside Out* (New York: Free Press, 2009).
10. Yvonne Boggs, interviewed by Melissa Moore, July 3, 2015.
11. Thich Nhat Hanh, *You Are Here: Discovering the Magic of the Present Moment.* Translated from the French by Sherab Chodzin Kohn. Edited by Melvin McLeod (Boston & London: Shambala, 2012).

H: Heal Your Heart

1. The Chopra Center, "The Health Benefits of Practicing Compassion," chopra.com, http://www.chopra.com/ccl/the-health-benefits-of-practicing-compassion, accessed May 11, 2016.

2. Amy Morin, "6 Reasons to Treat Yourself Better," *Psychology Today,* October 2, 2015, https://www.psychologytoday.com/blog/what-mentally-strong-people-dont-do/201510/6-reasons-treat-yourself-better, accessed May 11, 2016.

3. Marcia Cannon, PhD, *The Gift of Anger: Seven Steps to Uncover the Meaning of Anger and Gain Awareness, True Strength, and Peace* (Oakland: New Harbinger Publications, 2011).

4. Kristin Neff, "Why Self-Compassion Trumps Self-Esteem," University of California, Berkeley, Greater Good, May 22, 2011, http://greatergood.berkeley.edu/article/item/try_selfcompassion/, accessed May 11, 2016.

5. Amy Morin, "Science Explains the Link Between Self-Compassion and Success," *Forbes,* 2015: http://www.forbes.com/sites/amymorin/2015/10/01/science-explains-the-link-between-self-compassion-and-success/#2097322532b0

6. Angus MacBeth and Andrew Gumley, "Exploring Compassion: A Meta-analysis of the Association between Self-Compassion and Psychopathology," *Clinical Psychology Review,* 32, no. 6, August 2012.

7. Dr. Robert Anthony, *Ultimate Secrets of Total Self-Confidence,* 2nd revised edition (New York: The Berkley Publishing Group, 2008).

8. David Knighton, MD, *The Wisdom of the Healing Wound: A New View on Why We Hurt & How We Can Cure Even the Deepest Physical and Emotional Wounds* (Deerfield Beach: HCI Books, 2011).

9. Thom Rutledge, *Embracing Fear: How to Turn What Scares Us into Our Greatest Gift* (New York: HarperCollins, 2005).

10. Thom Rutledge, *The Self-Forgiveness Handbook* (Footlocker.com, Inc., 2015).

11. Dr. Fred Luskin, *Forgive for Good,* revised edition (San Francisco: HarperOne, 2005).

12. Rick Hansen, PhD, *Buddha's Brain: The Practical Neuroscience of Happiness, Love, and Wisdom* (Oakland: New Harbinger Publications, 2009).

13. Shasta Groene, interviewed by Melissa Moore, October 25–26, 2015.

14. Desmond Tutu and Mpho Tutu, *The Book of Forgiving: The Fourfold Path for Healing Ourselves and Our World* (San Francisco: HarperOne, 2015).

15. Anneli Rufus, *Unworthy: How to Stop Hating Yourself* (New York: Tarcher Perigee, 2015).

16. Martin Seligman, PhD, *Learned Optimism: How to Change Your Mind and Your Life,* revised paperback edition (New York: Vintage, 2006).

17. Kristin Neff, PhD, *Self-Compassion: The Proven Power of Being Kind to Yourself*, reprint edition (New York: William Morrow Paperbacks, 2015).

O: Open Your Mind

1. Christopher Vogler, *The Writer's Journey: Mythical Structure for Writers,* third edition (Studio City, CA: Michael Wiese Productions, 2007).

2. Peter Buffet, *Life Is What You Make It: Find Your Own Path to Fulfillment* (New York: Three Rivers Press, 2011).

3. Peter Gray, Free to Learn: *Why Unleashing the Instinct to Play Will Make Our Children Happier, More Self-Reliant, and Better Students for Life* (New York: Basic Books, 2013)

4. Elizabeth Gilbert, *Big Magic: Creative Living Beyond Fear* (New York: Riverhead Books, 2015).

5. Brian Grazer and Charles Fishman, *A Curious Mind: A Secret to a Bigger Life* (New York: Simon & Schuster, 2015).

6. Martin E. P. Seligman, PhD, *Learned Optimism: How to Change Your Mind and Your Life* (New York: Vintage Books, 2006).

7. Scott Weems, *HA! The Science of When We Laugh and Why* (New York: Basic Books, 2014).

8. Alex Lickerman MD., "Why We Laugh: How Laughter Can Build Resilience," *Psychology Today*, January 23, 2011, https://www.psychologytoday.com/blog/happiness-in-world/201101/why-we-laugh, accessed May 11, 2016.

9. Janice Kaplan, *The Gratitude Diaries: How a Year Looking on the Bright Side Can Transform Your Life* (New York: Dutton, 2015).

10. Anthony Scioli, PhD, and Henry Biller, PhD, *Hope in the Age of Anxiety: A Guide to Understanding and Strengthening Our Most Important Virtue* (New York: Oxford University Press, 2009).

11. Scott Barry Kaufman, PhD, "The Will and Ways of Hope," *Psychology Today*, December 26, 2011, https://www.psychologytoday.com/blog/beautiful-minds/201112/the-will-and-ways-hope, accessed May 11, 2016.

12. Shane J. Lopez, PhD, *Making Hope Happen: Create the Future You Want for Yourself and Others* (New York: Atria Books, 2014).

13. Baptist De Pape, *The Power of the Heart: Finding Your True Purpose in Life* (New York: Atria Books, 2014).

14. Sophy Burnham, *The Art of Intuition: Cultivating Your Inner Wisdom* (New York: Jeremy P. Tarcher/Penguin, 2011).

15. Deepak Chopra, *Synchrondestiny: Harnessing the Infinite Power of Coincidence to Create Miracles* (London: Rider & Co., 2004).

16. Nicole Force, "The Way of the Comedian," PsychCentral.com, http://psychcentral.com/lib/the-way-of-the-comedian/, accessed May 11, 2011.

17. Amanda Enayati, "How Hope Can Help You Heal," CNN online, April 11, 2013, http://www.cnn.com/2013/04/11/health/hope-healing-enayati/ (accessed May 11, 2016.

18. Toni Scioli, PhD, *New Hope: For Anxiety, Depression, and Mind-Body Healing,* unpublished manuscript.

19. C. R. Snyder. *The Psychology of Hope: You Can Get There from Here* (New York: Free Press, 1994).

L: Leverage Your Power

1. Herman Jacobs, interview with Michele Matrisciani, July 21, 2011.

2. Linda Robinson, "Life-Changing Football Tackle Led to 'Best Friends' Buoniconti and Jacobs," *Miami Herald*, October 24, 2015, http://www.miamiherald.com/sports/nfl/article41319459.html, accessed May 11, 2016.

3. For more information on the Miami Project, see http://www.themiamiproject.org/.

4. Merriam Webster dictionary definition of resilience can be found at http://www.merriam-webster.com/dictionary/resilience.

5. Dr. Robert Anthony, *The Ultimate Secrets of Self-Confidence,* second Berkeley trade edition (New York: The Berkley Publishing Group, 2008).

6. Jenifer Joy Madden, *How to Be a Durable Human: Revive and Thrive in the Digital Age Through the Power of Self-Design* (Vienna, VA: Austral Arc, 2016).

7. The American Psychological Association's definition of resilience can be found at http://www.apa.org/helpcenter/road-resilience.aspx, accessed on May 11, 2016.

8. Tim Daniel, *The Pursuit of Nobility: Living a Life That Matters* (Deerfield Beach, FL: HCI Books, 2010).

9. Sorem Gordhamer, *Wisdom 2.0: The New Movement Toward Purposeful Engagement in Business and in Life* (San Francisco: HarperOne, 2013).

10. Amy Cuddy, *Presence: Bringing Your Boldest Self to Your Biggest Challenges* (New York: Little Brown, 2015).

11. Chris Guillebeau, *The Art of Nonconformity: Set Your Own Rules, Live the Life You Want, and Change the World* (New York: Perigee, 2010).

12. William Ury, *The Power of a Positive No: How to Say No and Still Get to Yes* (New York: Bantam Books, 2007).

13. Pat Love and Jon Carlson, *Never Be Lonely Again: The Way Out of Emptiness, Isolation, and a Life Unfulfilled* (Deerfield Beach, FL: HCI Books, 2011).

E: Elevate Your Spirit

1. Sophy Burnham, *The Art of Intuition: Cultivating Your Inner Wisdom* (New York: Jeremy P. Tarcher/Penguin, 2011).

2. Rick Hanson, PhD, *Buddha's Brain: The Practical Neuroscience of Happiness, Love & Wisdom* (Oakland: New Harbinger Publications, 2009).

3. Paul Pearsall, PhD, *Awe: The Delights and Dangers of Our Eleventh Emotion* (Deerfield Beach: HCI Books, 2007).

4. Melissa Harris, *99 Keys to a Creative Life: Spiritual, Intuitive, and Awareness Practices for Personal Fulfillment* (Woodbury, MN: Llewellyn Publications, 2015).

5. Sensory grounding exercises by Charlene Richard, http://www.charlenerichardrsw.com/2014/02/quick-tip-stress-management-28-days-self-care/, accessed May 11, 2016.

6. Alexandra Horowitz, *On Looking: Eleven Walks with Expert Eyes* (New York: Scribner, 2013).

7. Richard Louv, *Last Child in the Woods: Saving Our Children from Nature-Deficit Disorder* (Chapel Hill, NC: Algonquin Books 2005, 2008).

8. Dr. Robert Anthony, *Ultimate Secrets of Total Self-Confidence,* 2nd revised edition (New York: The Berkley Publishing Group, 2008).

9. James W. Pennebaker, PhD, *Opening Up: The Healing Power of Expressing Emotions* (New York: The Guilford Press, 1990).

10. Linda Joy Myers, PhD, *The Power of Memoir: How to Write Your Healing Story* (San Francisco, Jossey-Bass, 2010).

11. Patrick Roth, MD, *The End of Back Pain* (San Francisco: HarperOne, 2013).

12. Pat Longo, interview with Michele Matrisciani, December 14, 2015.

13. Charlene Richard, "I Went on 6 Interviews & Got 5 Job Offers. Here's How," Mindbodygreen.com, September 8, 2014, http://www.mindbodygreen.com /0-15180/i-went-on-6-interviews-got-5-job-offers-heres-how.html, accessed May 11, 2016.

14. King James Bible online, https://www.kingjamesbibleonline.org/Luke-5-16/, accessed May 11, 2016.

15. Definition of creative mode on Minecraft, http://minecraft.gamepedia.com /creative, accessed May 11, 2016.

16. For a fun and informational video on nature-deficit disorder, visit Atlantic.com, http://www.theatlantic.com/video/index/383642/nature-deficit-disorder/, accessed May 11, 2016.

17. Lindsay Holmes, "'Nature Deficit Disorder' Might Be Made Up, But the Health Benefits of Being Outside Are Real," *Huffington Post*, December 11, 2014, http://www.huffingtonpost.com/2014/12/11/benefits-of-outdoors-jame_n _6310672.html, accessed May 11, 2016.

18. Laura M. Holson, "We're All Artists Now," *New York Times*, September 4, 2015.

19. Cathy Malchiodi, PhD, "The Ten Coolest Art Therapy Interventions," *Psychology Today*, February 11, 2010, https://www.psychologytoday.com/blog/arts-and -health/201002/the-ten-coolest-art-therapy-interventions, accessed May 11, 2016.

20. "Healing Poetry," Writingandhealing.org., http://writingandhealing.org/healing -poetry, accessed May 11, 2016.

21. Amanda Knapp, "Writing for Mental Health," *PsychCentral*, http://blogs.psych central.com/anxiety-depression/2015/06/writing-for-mental-health/, accessed May 11, 2016.

22. Carol L. Cirina, RN, MSN, CNOR, "Effects of Sedative Music on Patient Pre- operative Anxiety," *Today's O.R. Nurse*.

23. Randi Kreger, "Heal by Writing about Your Trauma," *Psychology Today*, November 21, 2012, https://www.psychologytoday.com/blog/stop-walking -eggshells/201211/heal-writing-about-your-trauma, accessed May 11, 2016.

24. Megan Othersen Gorman, "What Being Able to Sit on the Floor without Using Your Hands Says about Your Life Span," *Prevention*, January 12, 2015.

25. Adam Piore, "When Brain Damage Unlocks the Genius Within," *Popular Science*, February 19, 2013, http://www.popsci.com/science/article/2013-02 /when-brain-damage-unlocks-genius-within, accessed May 11, 2016.

26. Mayo Clinic, "What You Can Expect from a Massage," http://www.mayoclinic .org/healthy-lifestyle/stress-management/in-depth/massage/art-20045743?pg=2, accessed May 11, 2016.

27. Dacher Keltner, "Hands On Research: The Science of Touch," University of California, Berkeley, Greater Good, September 29, 2010, http://greatergood .berkeley.edu/article/item/hands_on_research, accessed May 11, 2016.

28. Sharon K. Farber, PhD, "The Mind Body Connection: Why We All Need to Be Touched," *Psychology Today*, December 26, 2013, https://www.psychologytoday .com/blog/the-mind-body-connection/201312/the-mind-body-connection, accessed May 11, 2016.

29. E-mail from Olivia Rupprecht to Michele Matrisciani, February 1, 2016.

30. Betsy Isaacson, "These YouTube Videos Supposedly Induce Insomnia-Curing 'Brain Orgasms,'" *Huffington Post,* updated March 13, 2014, http://www .huffingtonpost.com/2014/03/11/autonomous-sensory-meridian-response -brain-orgasms-sleeplessness_n_4913080.html, accessed May 11, 2016.

31. Steven Novella, "ASMR," Neurologica Blog, March 12, 2012, http://theness .com/neurologicablog/index.php/asmr/, accessed May 11, 2016.

INDEX

Underscored page references indicate sidebars and tables.

Brain *(cont.)*
  generosity and, 207
  negativity bias of, 50–51, 155
  pleasure centers of, <u>80</u>
Brain elasticity, 160
Brief Guide to World Domination, A,
  172
Brooks, David, 88–89
Brown, Brené, 200
Buddha's Brain, 34, 36, 59, 66, 187,
  195
Buddhism, 26, 33, 34
Buddhist meditation, 23
Buffett, Peter, 101, 102
Buffett, Warren, 101
Bugatti Veyron, 143, 144
Buoniconti, Marc, 138, 139, 140–41,
  144, 187
Buoniconti, Nick, 138
Burnett, Carol, 123
Burnham, Sophy, 185, 186, 187, 192,
  194, 195

C

Campbell, Joseph, 88, 93
Cannon, Marcia, 71
Cantril ladder, 135
Caputo, Theresa, 188, 191
Challenges, for increasing hope quotient,
  133
Change
  building resilience for, 153
  certainty of, 55
Child self, talking to, 12
Cho, Margaret, 123
Cirina, Carol L., 210–11
Clarity, from doing nothing, 13–15
Colbert, Stephen, 123
Comedians, 122, 123
Common humanity, needed for
  self-compassion, 79–80
Comparison trap, as power puller, 150
Compassion, 21, 78. *See also*
  Self-compassion
Compliments, 205
Contagions, goal, 174–75
Conversations
  curiosity, 107–9, 173
  starters for, <u>108</u>
Coping mechanisms, 2, 49, 106, 112

Core values, 111–13
  exercise for defining, 113–14
  finding humor in most situations, 119,
    121–24
  habits and obstacles affecting, 119,
    <u>120</u>
  how to identify, 116–17
  identifying source of, 117, <u>118</u>
  qualities of, 115
  types of, 116
Courage, for facing fear, 54, 58
Creativity, 200–202
Creazzo, Mbali, 207
Crime Watch Daily, 40, 60, 107
Cuddy, Amy, 4, 147, 151, 152, 158–59,
  160
Cup mind, as power puller, 148, 149
Curiosity
  for connecting with values, 111
  for defining core values, 113–14
  importance of, 104–5
  learning from, 103–4
Curiosity conversations, 107–9, 173
Curiosity Is Just a Click Away exercise,
  109–10
Curious Mind, A, 103, 104

D

Dalai Lama, 33
Daniel, Tim, 153–54
Davidji, 212–13
Davidson, Richard J., 206–7
Daydreaming, 198–99
Day in Review exercise, 26
de Becker, Gavin, 9, 28
Decision making, core values assisting,
  111, 112
Deep looking, in Buddhist meditation,
  23
Denial
  effects of, 9–10, 28
  hope vs., 126, 131, 132
de Pape, Baptist, 152, 193, 194
Depression
  from anger turned inward, 48, 49
  self-compassion decreasing, <u>80</u>
DiMarco, MaryAnn, 188
Discover Your Gifts, Set Your Goal
  exercise, 173–75
Ditka, Mike, 138

Doing nothing
  clarity from, 13–15
  creating conditions for, 18–19
  difficulty of, 3
  value of, 11–12
  wisdom of, 2, 4–5
Durable humans, 144

E

E: Elevate Your Spirit, 178–79
  Allison's story, 180–82, 190, 217, 221
  methods of
    for achieving balance, 190–92
    awe response, 217–22
    creativity, 200–202
    daydreaming, 198–99
    exercise, 214–16
    healing poetry, 213–14
    kindness and generosity, 204–8
    meditation, 195–97, 198
    nature, 202–4
    paying attention to synchronicity, 193–94
    repetitive viewing, 212
    smell, 210
    sound, 209–11
    spiritual guidance, 197–98
    touch, 208–9, 210
    understanding intuition, 184–89
    writing forgiveness letter, 189–90
    writing to heal, 212–13
Embracing Fear, 55
Emerson, Ralph Waldo, 38, 196
Emotional storage boxes, 42–44
Emotional wounds, wisdom of, for healing, 52–53
Emotions
  as guideposts, 24–32
  healing from expressing, 28–32
  inhibition of, 26–28
End of Back Pain, The, 216
Exercise (physical), importance of, 214–16
Exercises (mental)
  Curiosity Is Just a Click Away, 109–10
  The Day in Review, 26
  Discover Your Gifts, Set Your Goal, 173–75
  Feeling the Fear, 59
  Finding Reason in Resilience, 155–57

Go "Lite" on Your Life, 97
How Does Your Storm Make You Feel?, 32
Meditation, 18–19
Prepare Your Own Playbook, 113–14
Quick, Cost-Efficient Creative Ways to Calm the Mind, 198
Silence Your Inner Bully, 81–82
Tune Your Humility Key, 66–67
What's Your Return on Suffering (ROS)?, 76–77
Exposure therapy, 26, 32

F

Failure, fear of
  exercise for managing, 156–57
  as power puller, 147–48
Farber, Karen, 208
Fear, 54–56, 58
  Alecia's story, 56–58, 76
  awareness for moving past, 169
  of exercising resilience, 154–55
  of failure
    exercise for managing, 156–57
    as power puller, 147–48
  feeling, exercise for, 59
  self-created, 154
  of uncertainty, 55
Feeling the Fear exercise, 59
Field, Tiffany, 208, 209
Fight, flight, or freeze response, 11
Fight-or-flight stress response, 3, 11, 48
Finding Reason in Resilience exercise, 155–57
Fishman, Charles, 103
5-4-3-2-1 meditation, 198
Five T's, for self-forgiveness, 72
Flaws, finding value in, 96
Forgive for Good, 62–63
Forgiveness. *See also* Self-forgiveness
  absolution vs., 63
  benefits of, 62, 63–65, 68
  difficulty of, 63–64
  meaning of, 61–62, 63, 65, 68
  models of, 65–66
  self-forgiveness vs., 76
  Shasta's story, 60–61, 62
Forgiveness letter, 189–90
Free to Learn, 103–4
Freeze response, for survival, 11–12

Friendly universe, happy people's view of, 15
Futurecasting, 134–35

G

Generosity
   examples of, <u>206</u>
   as spirit elevator, 206–8
Gift of Anger, The, 71
Gift of Fear, The, 9
Gilbert, Elizabeth, 104, 200, 215
Giving Tree, The, 203
Goals
   hope and, 131–32
   setting
      Barry's story, 171–72, 173, 174
      Charon's story, 167–70
      exercise for, 173–75
Goldman, William, 39
Goldstein, Elisha, 19
Go "Lite" on Your Life exercise, 97
Gordhamer, Soren, 18–19, 148
Gratitude, 129
Gray, Peter, 103
Grazer, Brian, 103, 104, 105, 107
Grounding, for achieving balance, 191
Guides, spiritual, 188–89, 197–98
Guillebeau, Chris, 169, 171, 172
Guilt, 50, 73, 74–76

H

Habitat for Humanity, 145, 146, 193, 205
Habits, affecting core values, 119, <u>120</u>
"Hands On Research: The Science of Touch," 209
Hanson, Rick, 34, 36, 59, 66, 93, 187, 195
Happy for No Reason, 15
Happy Medium, The, 188
Harris, Melissa, 197, 198, 212
Haters, as power pullers, 150
HA! The Science of When We Laugh and Why, 122
Haunting of . . . , The, 188
Healing. *See also* H: Heal Your Heart
   aids for
      helping others, 40, 41
      hope, 131

mistakes, 71
nature, 202
poetry, 213–14
writing, 29–30, 32, 212–13
from emotional wounds, 52–53
emotions as guideposts in, 24–32
from trauma, 28–32, 111–12
Healing Back Pain, 215
Helping others
   as part of healing, 40, 41
   as spirit elevator, 204–5
Hero's journey, stages of, 93, <u>94–95</u>
Hero with a Thousand Faces, The, 93
H: Heal Your Heart, 46–47
   components of
      courage to be afraid, 54–59
      forgiveness, 60–68
      overcoming guilt, 74–76
      positive self-talk, 84–85
      self-compassion, 78–82
      self-forgiveness, 69–73
      wisdom of the wound, 52–53
   exercises, 59, 66–67, 76–77, 81–82
   need for, 48–51
Higher order, belief in, 134
Hope
   healing from, 131
   ideas for building, 132–35
   loss of, 127
   power of, 127, 129, 131–32
   return of, 128–30
   Vito and Deborah's story, 125–27
   wishing vs., 132
Hope in the Age of Anxiety, 131
Horowitz, Alexandra, 201
How Does Your Storm Make You Feel? exercise, 32
How questions, 41
Human durability, 143–44
Humanity, needed for self-compassion, 79–80
Humility key, exercise for tuning, 66–67
Humor, 119, 121–24

I

Identity, leading to wholeness, 36–37
Immunity, from creativity, 200, 201
Imposter syndrome, 159
   as power puller, 151–52
Inaction. *See* Doing nothing

About the Cover Art

Kintsugi (Japanese: *golden joinery*) or *kintsukuroi*
(Japanese: *golden repair*) is a centuries-old Japanese
philosophy of repairing broken pottery with lacquer
dusted or mixed with powdered gold, silver, or
platinum. It is a method that emanates a sense of
wabi-sabi, a Japanese concept of seeking beauty in
imperfection and avoiding disguising the flawed
history of an object.[1]

The word *healing* comes from the Anglo-Saxon
word *haelen*, which means to make whole.

---

[1] Erin Marie McDonald, "Darien Arikoski-Johnson," *Ceramics:
Art and Perception* 100 (June 2015).